KEEPER
OF THE
FLAME

(((HOW TO INSPIRE OTHERS ON THE CUSP OF CHANGE)))

KEEPER OF THE FLAME

Someone who goes first; someone with a heightened awareness of her impact on others; someone who is her own best coach; someone in total sync with her environment; someone embedded with the authority of both competence and character; someone who inspires others to be their Personal Best; someone who lives each day as though it were both her first and her last; someone who listens, learns and lets go; someone who lives in wonder; someone who is forever fresh so the people around her never grow stale.

Someone like you. Someone like the person you will become. Or someone like the person you need to rediscover.

Unifying Idea:
There is no such thing as
Ordinary.

Just beneath the surface, the magic is percolating. Everything, everyone, every day is exceptional. Every thing has distinction. Everyone is gestating a hero within them. We're all a giant to someone else. Every day is an opportunity to break through. The smallest actions can have the biggest impact. God is in the details, the subtleties, the nuances, and the hints all around us. Fascination is the only lens through which life should be observed. A look, a thought, a gesture, a smile can make history. One act can make all the difference. One person with courage can change his world. Small is the Real Big. The Miracle is the Here and Now.

This book is a celebration of Mr. and Ms Everyman. The stories you'll read about are the stories of the people all around you. Each one is compelling. Each one is valuable. Each one, in part, is your story. We're all angels with one wing. We can only fly while embracing each other.

Design and Function

The only thing that matters is that you get what you need to become a Keeper of The Flame. I want you to get the good stuff fast. I want you to have a great time getting it. And I want you to use what you've learnt immediately.

So every page is an invitation to action. Write down your commitment to act, and then follow through, over and over again. Repetition is the mother of learning.

In Part 1 ■ I'll get you warmed up so you know what you're getting into...

In Part 2 ■ I'll help you get ready for the call when it comes...

In Part 3 ■ You'll learn the Six Nuclear Dimensions to become a Keeper of The Flame.

Thank you for making it to the start.

I look forward to being with you at the finish.

Let's get going...

Contents

Part One

Warm-Up Time: Helping You Understand What You're Getting Into

Welcome. You're just in time.

Look around you. You're being watched.

People are following you.

Where are you leading them?

ET'S GET STRAIGHT TO THE TRUTH: SOMEONE IS WATCHING YOU.
They're watching the way you talk. They're watching what you do. They're watching you because they're not sure what to do.

You may be a CEO or you may be a PA. You may be a salesperson or you may be a nurse. You may be in government or you may be a one-man band. But someone is being guided by your actions. He may be your colleague or he may be your child. He may be your customer or he may be your fellow citizen. Whether you know it or not, your behavior is affecting the behavior of others.

Imagine there's a cosmic webcam tracking your every move. It's broadcasting your life to a viewing audience of millions. What would they see? Would it be a show that inspired them to be more, give more, love more, laugh more, grow more, try more? Or would it be a cautionary tale of wasted moments, wasted feelings, wasted opportunities, wasted adventures?

Life is theater with consequences. All the world's a stage. Every day is a new drama. Every interaction with every person is a scene you act out with your fellow cast members. What kind of play are you creating?

Here's what I'm asking you to do in this book: Step outside yourself, but be yourself. Be conscious of yourself, but don't be self-conscious. Be in the moment, but watch the moment with the eyes of others.

Each of us has to navigate the duality of the private and the public persona. We need to be true to ourselves while living the perception we want others to have of us. We need to be the best we can be while helping others become the best they can be. We need to be authentic while we are being social.

After studying thousands of people all over the world, I believe there's a powerful synergy between the inner and the outer self. The one develops in sync

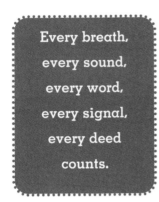

Every breath,
every sound,
every word,
every signal,
every deed
counts.

with the other. In trying to make others better, we become better. To quote Nelson Mandela, "As you let your own light shine, you unconsciously give others permission to do the same. As you liberate yourself from your own fear, your presence automatically liberates others."

I like to watch—it's how I make a living. I'm always just outside the box, studying what's going on inside it. My company, Environics/Lipkin, is the motivation company within the Environics Research Group, one of Canada's most sophisticated research houses. Every year we poll thousands of people across the United States and Canada. I personally conduct over thirty focus groups a year with people all over the world. That means every two weeks I sit down with groups of people all over the world to talk about one thing: their perception of how their lives are changing, how they feel about it and what they're doing to manage change on both a personal and professional level.

I have my finger on the pulse of social change. I can tell you that it's beating faster and it's beating more erratically. We're all hovering between anxiety and excitement, and very little time is being spent in the neutral zone. Think about your life. Think about your social or professional circle. How many times over the past year have you kicked back and thought, "Well, not much happening here. Things are pretty much as they've always been. Not much likelihood of anything changing any time soon . . ."? Yeah, right.

It's like living in a permanent crisis. In fact, a major client of mine has the philosophy "If it's not a crisis, why bother?" But here's what happens in a crisis, and this is the theme that underpins every line in this book: People become hypersensitive. Every pore is opened, nerves are exposed, actions are amplified. That's why Webster's Dictionary defines a crisis as a turning point, a defining moment. Elephants have got nothing on humans—it's humans who never forget.

That's why I wrote these words, and that's why you're reading them. From now until forever, you matter a whole lot to so many people. In the tiniest way you can be the difference between somebody making it or losing it. A throwaway line to you may be a lifeline to another. Remember, inspire comes from the Latin word *inspiro*. It means, literally, "to give breath." Every breath, every sound, every word, every signal, every deed counts.

Our Social Values data tell us that almost 70 percent of people underestimate their "individualism." That means they lack the confidence and conviction to back themselves against their environment. They are afraid to challenge the world. They're scared of pushing back. Even when they have a good idea or a valid point, they hang back. Fear of rejection or failure haunts them. Their music goes unplayed. Their ideas are stifled. They live their lives in quiet desperation.

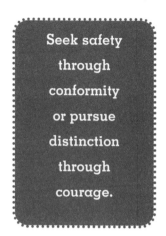

Seek safety through conformity or pursue distinction through courage.

But that's not you, right? That's why you're with me. You understand that you have a choice: Seek safety through conformity or pursue distinction through courage. That's the choice that will either plunge you into despair or produce a lifetime of fulfillment. That's the choice you have to make consciously if you want to become a Keeper of The Flame.

Right up front, I'll share with you what I've found out about the great ones, those that lead the way: They're not smarter than everyone else. And they're not better educated. They are simply invested in their own ability to make a difference. They understand that they have to do what they have to do—and they do it. Not just sometimes, but every time.

Hmm, how about you? Are you stoking your inner flame with every action? Are you helping others to burn brightly? Remember, you can curse the darkness or you can light a fire. It's your call. And I want to help you make the right call; that's why I've designed this book as a dialogue between the two of us. I'm writing to you the way I would speak to you—directly, simply, respectfully, affectionately, gratefully. You'll enjoy what you're about to read. You'll also find it very easy going. One thing, though: You have to do a little writing yourself—that's the only way you'll truly integrate what you're reading. I'm also inviting you to respond to me whenever you want to. My coordinates are sprinkled throughout the book. Agreed? Then let's move on . . .

Beware the Eighth Deadly Sin: Regret.

It's more lethal than the other seven put together.
Keepers of The Flame lead and learn
by doing, not delaying.
Remember: every saint has a past
and every sinner has a future.
So up front, here's your call to action: at the bottom
of every page, write down what you're going to do
as a result of what you've just read. And then
do it, as soon as you can and as often as you can.
Repeated action is the most direct route
to personal mastery.
It's all about a single daily basis point –
one tenth of one percent every day.

REED, ENVY, PRIDE, SLOTH, GLUTTONY, LUST, ANGER. I DON'T
know about you, but I'm guilty of almost all those sins every day. What's more, everyone I know is guilty of the same sins to a greater or lesser degree. There's a name for this condition—it's called being human.

And yet I'm happy. I'm fulfilled. I'm helping people. I have lots of friends. I'm doing what I'm passionate about. I give back to my community. And so do many of the people I hang with. I call that success. You can be flawed and ful-filled at the same time. In fact, the seven deadly sins can become your allies if you use them to build mental, emotional and spiritual muscle.

It's the Eighth Deadly Sin that terrifies me. That's the stuff my nightmares are made of. It's the pain of what might have been. It's the guilt of "I could have, but I didn't." It's the loss of what was there but now is gone. It's the immortal

My personal call to action: I _____

18

lament of Marlon Brando in his role as the washed-up boxer Terry Molloy in *On the Waterfront*: "I coulda had class. I coulda been a contender. I coulda been somebody, instead of a bum."

I have worked with over a million people in twenty-eight countries, and I can tell you this without a shadow of a doubt: Regret is the real enemy of happiness. Regret is the disease that eats away at your attention and energy. Regret is untreatable, because nothing can be done about it. On planet Earth you cannot go back.

So what's the antidote to regret? Action. Do what you know you have to do when you have to do it. The pain of rejection, embarrassment or failure is nothing compared to the pain of regret. Rejection, embarrassment and failure are just figments of your imagination anyway.

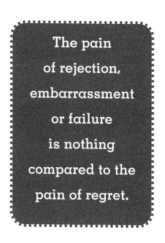

The pain of rejection, embarrassment or failure is nothing compared to the pain of regret.

What happens if you take the wrong action? Yes, you may encounter negative consequences. But know this: 99 percent of the things we regret are the things we didn't do, not the things we did. Think about it. Unless one of your actions injured another person, what's to regret anyway?

Keepers of The Flame are people of action. They're not rash or reckless; they don't act just for the sake of acting. They act when they know they must act. They say what they know they must say. They burn their excuses. They fight the good fight. The more they do, the more they learn; the better they become, the greater their power to influence others. And the virtuous cycle continues.

Every day, you and I meet people who can talk the good talk. Throughout the U.S. and Canada I meet so many intellectually gifted people. They're sophisticated, learned and oh-so-clever. But when the rubber meets the road, they falter. They're scared of trying something new and failing. So they do very little. They don't embarrass themselves, they don't fall on their faces, they don't break down. And they don't break through, either. They don't self-actualize. They don't fulfill their hopes and dreams. They live on the sidelines, always judging the efforts of others, never savoring the fruits of their own.

An ounce of action is worth a ton of theory. In fact, every act is a cause set in motion. Do something extraordinary today and you ignite a process that never ends. Just thinking about something today, however, yields zero results until you apply your thoughts. Remember, it's easier to act yourself into a way

My personal call to action: I _____

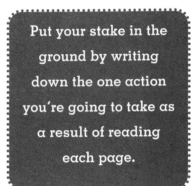

Put your stake in the ground by writing down the one action you're going to take as a result of reading each page.

of thinking than it is to think yourself into a way of acting. So act like a person of thought and think like a person of action.

In case you haven't figured it out yet, this is not a book on abstract thinking or ethereal theories. It's not a trip to the mountaintop where revelations and epiphanies await you. Rather, it describes the things we have to do on our way to becoming a Keeper of The Flame. It's a distillation of the experience and wisdom of thousands of people who've been there already. They blazed the trail this book is following. Your challenge is to blaze a trail for others to follow. You begin where this book ends. Your mission is to take it a little farther before you pass the torch on to others.

So put your stake in the ground by writing down the one action you're going to take as a result of reading each page. Then do it. At the end of the book you'll have taken about 200 actions, each one of which may have the potential to open up a whole new channel of opportunities for you. One small step may be one giant leap in disguise.

Have you ever read something that instantly rearranged the way you look at your world? That moment happened for me when I read the following story from *The Globe and Mail* (June 18, 2005):

When the Human Genome project was completed in 2000, its most touted result was that it showed no genetic basis for race. In fact, some scientists went so far as to dub race a "biological fiction."

The project was a 13-year international drive to map all of the three billion chemical bits, or nucleotides, that make up human DNA. Particular nucleotide sequences combine to form the estimated 25,000 genes whose proteins help to produce human traits, from the way your heart beats to the wave in your hair.

My personal call to action: I _____

> *The map indicated that humans as a species are 99.9 percent genetically identical—that, in fact, there are greater differences between any two frogs in a pond than between any two people who find themselves waiting for a bus.*
>
> *A teeny 0.1 percent, a mere genetic sliver, helps to account for all the profound diversity within the human race, with its freckles, dimples, afros and crimson tresses, its shy and bombastic types, its Donald Trumps and Dalai Lamas, Madonnas and Mr. Dressups, Bill Gates, Billie Holidays, George W. Bushes and Osama bin Ladens.*
>
> *Hardly a hair of code separates us. According to Alan Bernstein, the president of the Canadian Institute of Health Research, 0.1 percent is actually far from an insignificant difference in the genome's chemical sequence. In fact, he said, the genetic distance between humans and gorillas is not much greater.**

If one-tenth of one percent makes such a huge difference to the entire human race, how much difference could it make to your life? Seriously, what would be the impact on your growth if you simply enhanced your capacity by one one-thousandth every day?

I've done the math: If you grew by one-tenth of one percent every day, you would grow by over 40 percent a year. That's the power of consistent growth. And, by the way, it doesn't require a superior intellect. It simply requires an awareness of the need to grow through conscious thoughts and action. So, for example, I know that every one of these paragraphs I'm writing is a deposit on my one-thousandth expansion every day.

I also know that those who would be Keepers of The Flame cannot afford the indulgence of mindlessness. The price that you and I pay for the privilege of inspiring others is constant alertness to the implications of everything going on, both inside and outside of ourselves. This is not a burden, it's a conditioned way of living.

I often joke that I'm so motivated because I attend all my own seminars. It's true. I'm always writing and talking about being a Keeper of The Flame. Extracting the most meaningful lessons from every experience has now become instinctive for me. It's the most important reason why I'm on fire most of the

* Reprinted with permission from *The Globe and Mail*

My personal call to action: I _____

time. Every time I learn, I celebrate. So every day I'm engaging in hourly mental micro-parties. Win or lose, I expand my capacity to succeed in the future. In my world there are no defeats, only temporarily delayed triumphs.

Yup, I may sound like I'm living on the edge of delusion, but it's a great way to stay up. I'm also in good company. Frank Lloyd Wright, the great architect, said, "If an idea does not appear to be absurd at first, it has no chance in the future." Any time you introduce a new thought, someone is going to try to shoot it down. Protect it. As soon as it begins to fly, it will find lots of champions.

My personal call to action: I _____

Thriving on the Cusp

I know what you want. It's what we all want.
To thrive – on the Cusp.
That's what this book is about: thriving on
the Cusp, with a passion that helps others
do the same.

SO, WHAT IS THE CUSP?
It's the border between when-it-all-hangs-together
    and when-it-all-falls-apart.
It's the edge of your competence.
It's the limit of your capacity.
It's the moment just before change happens.
It's the space between what is and what could be.
It's the outer layer of your self-confidence.
It's the mental state line between panic and excitement.
It's the decision to be bold and dare or to be timid and dare not.
It's an invitation to your future or a retreat into your past.
It's the threshold you have to cross to become what you have to be.

In the last twelve months I've surveyed, interviewed or motivated over 100,000 people throughout the United States and Canada. Here's the most powerful message I've heard:

> *The new normal is pushing me to the edge. I'm being squeezed up against my limits—socially, professionally, mentally, emotionally, financially, spiritually, physically.*

I can see you nod your head in agreement. What I can't see is what you're feeling.

....

My personal call to action: I _____

....

If you're instinctively excited about thriving on the Cusp, you're a natural Keeper of The Flame. This book will give you insights and strategies to burn even brighter for the people around you.

If you're instinctively threatened by the thought of thriving on the Cusp, you're holding back. You're not using all of your gifts. Too much of you is being held in reserve. You're part of the 70 percent of the population who are afraid of risk, complexity and the unknown. Your flame is still unlit. This book will help you ignite and help others catch fire as well.

No matter what you do, life will keep driving you to the Cusp.

If you want to thrive, here is the fact we all have to confront: There is no middle ground. You're either on the Cusp or you're bringing up the rear. Seeking the safety of the comfort zone is giving in to an illusion. If all you do is keep your nose to the grindstone, you'll end up with a very short nose. If you keep your head down and just do your work, you won't see very much. The middle of the pack is no place to be. In the human jungle, being invisible means that no one notices you when you're gone.

Anyway, I'm telling you that you don't have a choice. No matter what you do, life will keep driving you to the Cusp. Every day, in ways both large and small, you will be offered opportunities to cross the threshold to become your best self. Take them, even if you're not sure how. The path will become clear when you begin it.

It's not meant to be easy. It's not meant to be hard. It's simply meant to be. Whether you find your path is a function of your willingness to keep searching for it. And remember an ancient Zen truth: As you seek your higher self, your higher self will be seeking you. We're all living in the space between who we are and what we can become. Intention is a powerful magnet. If you want it, if you pursue it, if you honor it, it will come.

On the Cusp, nothing is fixed. Everything is shifting. That's why we can go from living in our fortress to being a nomad overnight. Today's wisdom is tomorrow's roadkill. Every day our existing models are being invalidated—our assumptions are being torn down, the world is being flattened, external barriers are being obliterated. We're all being exposed to the gale force winds of change. It's brutal out there. If you don't know where you're going, you could get so lost that no one will ever find you.

My personal call to action: I _____

I've been witnessing a new social phenomenon: People who have no reason to worry about their physiological, shelter, security or social needs are worried about them all the time. Their mindset is not linked to their reality. Even though they appear to have sufficient, they're scared it could all be taken away. They're scared because they see it happening all around them.

In these conditions it's impossible to be comfortable.

At Environics we call this trend "apocalyptic anxiety." It's a sense that the world is heading toward major upheavals, and it anticipates these changes with dread. In an all-or-nothing world, the distance between the two is getting smaller and smaller.

The paradox of the Cusp is that the Keeper of The Flame feels more anxiety than those she inspires, because she is more exposed. She sees more, she tries more, she helps more, she is trusted more. And the more she does, the more she wants to do, the more pressure she applies to herself—and the more anxiety she feels.

If you're the sentinel, you cannot doze off on your watch. That's the curse of the blessing. Self-appointed responsibility for changing the world one person at a time carries a price: You're judged by a different set of standards than Mr. and Ms Everyman. For you the bar's been raised, sometimes to unrealistic levels. But people want to believe in someone. If they've chosen to believe in you, it's your call how you choose to handle them.

In these conditions it's impossible to be comfortable. It's impossible to experience peace of mind for longer than a few moments. It's impossible not to worry about the one thing that could blow your enterprise away at any moment. On the Cusp, everything is magnified, and so much doesn't make sense. Only the paranoid survive. And only the hyper-vigilant thrive.

So what am I saying? That you can never have serenity if you're a Keeper of The Flame? Uh-uh. You can—but it has to be earned. It's being comfortable when you're uncomfortable. It's learning how to turn worry into your own personal security system. It's understanding the signals that are being sent to you. It's sharpening your vision so you miss nothing. It's raising your metabolism so you live more rapidly. It's consistently evolving to a higher state of performance.

It's about being conscious of your personal evolution. If you know that you're doing all you can to become all you can be, you can hand the rest over to your higher power—whoever and whatever that may be. If you know that

My personal call to action: I _____

you're playing full out at whatever you're doing, you can relax. You can free up your energy to go where it will generate the highest return.

So I'm feeling serene as I write these words. I believe I'm doing what I'm supposed to be doing. And I'm doing it to the best of my ability. I'm also feeling an "expected anxiety," an emotional hybrid that gives me both edge and balance. On the Cusp, opposites do attract. Serenity and anxiety go hand in hand. There is no such place as an anxiety-free zone. It's what we do with anxiety that counts.

> Who dares may not always win. But the doubters will always fail.

Here are the two most important words in the Keeper of The Flame's vocabulary: "as if." Keepers of The Flame act *as if* they are confident, serene, secure, happy, centered, even when they may not be feeling any of those emotions. They know that emotion comes from motion. The more they act a certain way, the more they think a certain way. They condition themselves to play their personal best by acting as if they are the person they're aspiring to become.

Keepers of The Flame know that, on the Cusp, hesitancy will hang you out to dry. Who dares may not always win, but the doubters will always fail. If there's one core lesson I want you to take away from this book, it's this: Make the call. Then act with conviction, even if you're scared half to death. Fear has a wonderful way of dissolving in the face of determined action.

Most important, on the Cusp of change, behavior is contagious. The people around you will catch your courage or your fear, depending on what they see you do. They're judging what's going on inside you by what they see happening on the outside. Remember, on the Cusp of change we're all looking for examples of what's possible. If one person can, then another person can. You and I need to be that person who can. The rest will follow.

My personal call to action: I _____

Go First.

**On the Cusp of Change,
everyone is stepping into the unknown.
No-one truly knows what's going on.
Only you know what's right for you.
So don't wait for someone to tell you what to do.
Go First.**

F YOU WANT TO MAKE GOD LAUGH, SHOW HIM YOUR PLANS. OR, TO QUOTE John Lennon, life is what happens to you while you're busy making other plans. Remember, in the new normal, plan is a verb, not a noun.

Think about your world. Think about the people with whom you live and work—your leaders, your colleagues, your clients, your partners, your suppliers, your friends, your relatives. What's their win/loss record? How often have they called it wrong? How often has their advice not worked out for you? How often have they appeared to slip, slide and stumble around? How often have you asked yourself, "Do these people know what they're doing or what?"

And here's the classic question of all time: "What were they thinking!?"

I'll tell you what they were thinking: "Based on what I know, what I see, what I feel, what other people tell me, what the report says, what my colleagues think—I think this is right. I hope it's right. At least, I hope it's not too wrong. But I don't know. I've never been here before."

We're all aliens in our own country. Tomorrow is a strange land. Get used to it. Predictability and stability don't live here anymore, and they're never coming back. They've been replaced by surprise, shock and stun. It's not the medium that's the message anymore, it's the mess. We're living in the mess-age.

Since January 2001 I have worked with leadership teams from over two hundred of North America's leading companies. The best of them own one outstanding quality: enlightened boldness.

My personal call to action: I _____

27

Yes, they do their homework, they're well resourced, they have the processes and systems to execute their plans. Yes, they have the right people in the right seats. But, above all, they're decisive, they're imaginative, they fuse the information with their intuition. And they galvanize their people. They understand that there is no certain guarantee of success, but there is a certain guarantee of failure: THT—timidity, hesitation and tentativeness.

So here's your first "Lipkinism"—a truth that cannot be denied:

> **In the fog of change, even the best leadership teams are making judgment calls based on imperfect data and gut feel. Yesterday's guru is tomorrow's neophyte. So don't invest anyone with the power of knowing what will happen next. Even the titans are trembling.**

Hmm, I can hear you thinking, if even the titans are trembling, what chance have I got? Should I be even more afraid than I was before I read these words?

That's my point: You know as much as the titans about your world. You're closer to the action. You're there, you're immersed in the day-to-day facts. There's a Japanese word for where you are; it's called the *gemba*—the front line, where the action really is, where the truths lie.

The questions are: Can you handle the truths? Can you translate the truths into actions? Can you see the truths? Are you even thinking about the truths? As an old Mexican proverb states, "Some men can walk through a forest and not see any firewood." And remember, there is always more than one truth to every situation. Truths can even be contradictory. Truths themselves may not set you free. It's what you do with them that counts.

That's the core *raison d'être* of this book: to help you see, handle and act on the truths so that you do what's right for you, live the life that's right for you, get the results that are right for you, and help others find their path as well. You and I are partners. This book is a joint venture. I need you to achieve your personal success so I can pay it forward. Your triumphs become my credentials. That's the truth—my future success as a motivator and coach is a direct function of how useful you find this book. Without your word of mouth and enthusiasm for my work, I'm going nowhere.

So if you like what you're reading, let me know. If you apply any of my insights successfully, let me know. If I help you achieve even a small victory, let me know. If I help you help someone who needs help, let me know. Feedback is the diet of champions. I live for it. I live on it. Call me at 416-969-2811 or e-mail me at mike.lipkin@environics.ca.

My personal call to action: I _____

Trust Yourself, Trust Others, Trust Your World.

Before we go any further. I'm going to ask you to trust. Trust yourself. Trust others. Trust that your world has been designed to help you get exactly you need (and maybe not what you want).

You can't always get what you want.
But if you try sometimes, well you might find
You get what you need.
— The Rolling Stones

LTIMATELY, THERE ARE ONLY TWO KINDS OF PEOPLE: THOSE WHO TRUST and those who don't. Those who trust have found an empowering answer to life's most important question: Am I living in a friendly or a hostile world?

Friendly means that you believe your world is designed to help you get what you need. It means that you believe you're designed to get what you need, even when you don't. It means that you believe others are motivated to give you what you need, even when they don't. It means that you begin every day believing it will go your way, even when it doesn't. It means that you begin every task knowing you will succeed, even when you don't. It means that you begin every relationship believing it will work, even when it doesn't.

Friendly means that when you don't get what you want, you know you've just received what you need. Yup, let me repeat that:

My personal call to action: I _____

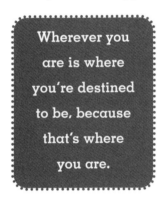

" When you don't get what you want, you know you've just received what you need.

That could be the most important Lipkinism of the entire book. It means that you know nothing ever happens that wasn't supposed to happen. It means that you know there's a powerful lesson in every experience. It means that you accept the rightness of what just happened. And it means that you accept responsibility for what happens next.

> Wherever you are is where you're destined to be, because that's where you are.

If you don't trust that your life is evolving just the way it should, part of you will always be holding back or pushing back. Resistance and resentment will become part of your DNA. You won't be able to throw yourself fully into any endeavor. Part of you will always be asking the fatal question, "Should I really be doing this?"

Of all the challenges I'll throw out to you over the next few pages, this one may be the most thought-provoking: How much do you trust yourself and the resources around you to come through for you when you find yourself in dreadful circumstances? Think about this challenge, because you know it's going to happen, just as it's happened so many times in the past. Al Siebert, ex-paratrooper and author of the book *The Survivor Personality*, has studied hundreds of stories of survival. He has found that in many cases the answer may lie in a handful of specific behavioral traits.

"Survivors rapidly read reality," says Siebert. "When something horrible happens, they immediately accept the situation for what it is and consciously decide that they will do everything in their power to get through it." That is, they have the ability to accept dreadful circumstances rationally without becoming angry or passive, two common responses to extreme stress. "Getting angry is just a waste of precious energy," continues Siebert, "and playing the victim dramatically increases your chance of dying."

Remember, wherever you are is where you're destined to be, because that's where you are. So be there and be there fully. If you're engaged in an action, engage fully or disengage fully. Don't kind-of or sort-of-engage. Ambivalent execution is the hallmark of mediocrity. It's also the norm. You know why? Because it's easier to doubt than it is to trust. It's easier to focus on the perils of what could go wrong than it is on the possibilities of doing it right.

My personal call to action: I _____

Think of the people around you who epitomize success. What are their signature attributes? A willingness to trust? A bias to action? Enthusiasm for their cause? And are they not the kind of people who constantly evoke criticism from the people around them? That's right—the more successful you become, the more negative chatter you generate around you. People who are crazy enough to believe that it can be done will always encounter ridicule from those who don't.

Now, don't get me wrong. I'm not advocating Pollyanna-ism. I'm not suggesting that you march naively where angels fear to tread. I'm simply requesting you, even if it's just for the course of this book, to assume that life is always catering to your needs—whether you understand it at the time or not.

Think about it: How would it affect your psyche if you always saw everything that happens to you as a way of getting what you need? What would happen if you always looked for the reason *why* you've received just what you need, whether you've just been through a pleasurable or a painful experience? How much would you learn? How much would you grow? How much more happiness would you experience? How much more would you be able to help others?

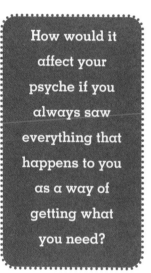

How would it affect your psyche if you always saw everything that happens to you as a way of getting what you need?

What's the opposite of seeing everything that happens to you as a way of getting what you need? It's extreme vulnerability to anxiety, fear, depression and despair. It's not having a mental filter to screen out the pessimism, trauma, disasters and perversions that we are exposed to every day. It's the lack of a personal philosophy that neutralizes negativity. It's not having a lifeline to hold on to when the storm breaks.

Pain is inevitable, but suffering is optional. Life hurts. Love hurts. Losing hurts. Leaving hurts. Pain is real—that's the point. Until the pain is big enough, we don't heed it. What's more, no matter how impeccably you lead your life, there's more pain on the way. The greater the pain, the greater the lesson. We can choose to become better or we can allow ourselves to become bitter. Trust in the lesson makes pain our teacher, not our tormentor.

Think about the last time lightning struck. Think about your most recent profound crisis. Here's some very personal questions: What got you through it? Who got you through it? Are you proud of yourself today because of how you acted then?

My personal call to action: I _____

Inspiring others on the Cusp of change means that you're at your best when things are at their worst. It means that when everyone is waiting to see what will happen next, you're making things happen. It means that while others are standing frozen, you're fired up. It means you understand that life is one test after another—tests not just of character and skill, but also of understanding how you've just been given what you need.

So trust me, trust yourself and trust the hundreds of people who made this book possible. In the next 200 pages you will learn insights that will transform your life and the life of all those you serve. In the next few days you will learn insights that will transform your life and the life of all those you serve. In the next few months you will learn insights that will transform your life and the life of all those you serve. It's a good feeling, isn't it? Nurture it.

Life can only be lived forward, but it can only be understood backward. Have you noticed how hindsight clarifies everything? Even the most bizarre experiences leave a benign legacy if you review them through the correct lens. Right now, write down the three most traumatic experiences you've been through. Next to each one write down the most powerful benefit that each of your "Big Three Crises" has delivered to you. Here are mine:

Event	Lessons Learned
Death of my father when I was sixteen: *1975*	Be self-reliant. Act with urgency. Make every day count. Be grateful. Live in the now. Love people. Everyone's time is limited, so help them make the most of it. It's not the years I add to my life, it's the life I add to my years.
Episode of clinical depression: *1990–91*	Be vigilant. Focus on the magic, not the tragic. Put first things first. Honor myself. Live my true values. Help others succeed. Apply the most empowering meaning to whatever happens to me. I am in control of my own thoughts and attitudes. Be brutally optimistic.

My personal call to action: I _____

Spinal fusion to repair a broken back: *2001*	We're all mortal, but we're all surprisingly tough. The body is extremely resilient. Modern science is miraculous. Keep my body strong to support my damaged infrastructure. I can come back from anything. My attitude is as healing as the surgeon. Someone up there is looking out for me.

I now know that each of the above three experiences was instrumental in making me who I am today. In fact, I couldn't write this book and or deliver my talks without the perspective of my "Big Three Crises." That's why I look back in wonder, not at what might have been. And that's why I'm still on fire, not burned out. How about you? How could you look at your "Big Three" differently, so that they fire you up, not burn you down?

Trust is the glue that holds our worlds together.

Here's one final insight on trust before we move on: Do you drive a car? If your answer is yes, every day you put your life and the lives of your passengers in the hands of strangers. Think about it: Every time you drive on a two-lane road, you trust the driver coming toward you to stay on his side of the road. You trust him not to fall asleep or lose concentration as he talks on his cell phone or argues with his spouse. You trust him even though you know how easy it would be for him to veer just a few feet to the left or the right. You know that if this were to occur, it could mean pain, mutilation and death for you and whoever is with you. You trust him not because you want to, but because you have to. So if you're prepared to trust a stranger with your life, why would you not trust yourself? Why would you not trust the world around you? Why would you not trust people who have already proven they're worthy of your trust? Makes you think, doesn't it?

Trust is the glue that holds our worlds together. Without it, everything falls apart. Think about someone or something you don't trust. Think about all the negativity, doubt and worry that accompany your thoughts around these people or things. Think about how scared you are to commit your time, effort or resources to them. Now think about the things you trust implicitly. Think about the people you trust implicitly. Focus on those things, those people. Become

My personal call to action: I _____

one of them. That's my mantra: I will act in such a way that others always trust me to come through for them.

What do you trust? Whom do you trust? Have you ever thought about trustworthiness? Try it. The very act of listing the things and people you trust will strengthen your trust. Here is a list of my top ten, trustworthy things and people:

1. I trust the fairness of Canada—its people, systems and government.

2. I trust the superiority of the American free-enterprise system.

3. I trust myself to do the right thing in a crisis.

4. I trust my body to respond to the care and conditioning I provide it.

5. I trust my family to love me unconditionally: my wife, Hilary; my three children, Anthony, Carla and Dani; and my two dogs, Toby and Jasmine.

6. I trust my partners at Environics to continue to support, inspire and coach me.

7. I trust everyone with whom I work to treat me the way they want me to treat them.

8. I trust that the good guys always win in the end.

9. I trust my higher power to keep astounding me with new truths, lessons and wisdom.

10. I trust life to keep introducing me to people who will befriend me and empower me to be all that I can and choose to be.

Plus one:

• Any time that anything happens to test my trust, I trust my ability to absorb the lesson, adapt to the new reality, shift my thinking and rise to the next level.

E-mail me your top ten list: mike.lipkin@environics.ca.

My personal call to action: I _____

The Five Themes of The Keepers of The Flame

We all have our own path. Most are unaware of their path, so they do not seek it. Some are aware of their path but they do not take it. A few are aware of their path and they take it all the way.

They are The Keepers of The Flame. And there are Five Themes to their story.

F YOU ASPIRE TO BEING A KEEPER OF THE FLAME, I KNOW YOUR STORY. It's my story too. It's the story of someone in search of more—more insight, more contribution, more juice, more understanding, more resources, more pleasure, more of the good stuff.

It's the story of someone who is restless. He's kinetic. He needs to flow, he needs to grow, he needs the challenge. He needs to find out how far he can go.

It's the story of someone who is courageous. He knows that luck favors the brave, so he takes his chances. He knows he cannot win unless he's prepared to fail.

It's the story of someone in love with life. He remembers the magic in every moment. He knows that tomorrow isn't promised to anyone, so he lives fully in the now.

It's the story of someone who has to help others. He knows he's only as good as the company he keeps. So he makes his company great.

It's the story of someone who keeps replenishing and reinventing himself. He's forever young. As the earth revolves around the sun, he revolves around life.

My personal call to action: I _____

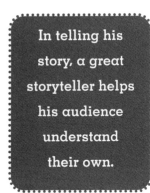

In telling his story, a great storyteller helps his audience understand their own.

What's my point here? Simply this: At a certain level the stories are universal; it's only the names and nuances that change. What do I mean? Well, tell me if you've heard this story before:

Once upon a time, in a land far away, there lived a young man who was gifted in so many ways: He was smart. He was charismatic. He was gifted with an array of social skills that attracted others to him like a magnet. His friends, family, clients and colleagues all adored him. He had the Midas touch. It seemed as though the gods smiled upon him permanently.

The years passed, and this young man turned thirty-one. His string of unbroken successes had made him arrogant and narcissistic. He measured his self-worth in recognition and in cash. He was addicted to adulation and the rush of achievement. He took his family, his health and his gifts for granted.

Then he messed up big time. He put all his eggs in one basket and then dropped the basket. He lost his money, he lost his status, he lost his recognition and, worst of all, he lost his confidence. He became tentative. His gifts deserted him. His shaky foundation collapsed. He descended into clinical depression.

For three years he languished in self-pity and despair, losing the support of his friends and his credibility among his peers. Only his wife refused to give up on him.

Then he met an extraordinary human being: a seventy-eight-year-old Zen master, a Buddhist psychiatrist with an intuitive understanding of how to stop the young man's negative spiral. After just three months' treatment, the young man regained his vitality and optimism. He lost his arrogance and narcissism. He even shaved his head because his psychiatrist had told him that a shaved head symbolized enlightenment in one of the Buddhist traditions. It made him feel lighter, as though he had shed another layer of his past in search of his future.

With his newfound humility and gratitude, he became even more compelling than before his fall from grace. People were now attracted to him because of his authenticity and his caring. And he sustained his success, because he never forgot the lessons of his breakdown.

Today he shares his lessons with people all over the world. He's continually reinventing himself with new insights. He has surrounded himself with people who both nurture and challenge him. And he's not so young any more—he's me.

My personal call to action: I _____

That's my story. But it's also the story of every Keeper of The Flame in one way or another. As a mentor of mine once told me, in telling his story, a great storyteller helps his audience understand their own.

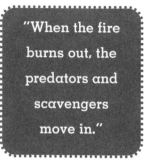

"When the fire burns out, the predators and scavengers move in."

Here's the truth we all face on the Cusp: There is so little time to go within, to pause, to reflect, to meditate, to interpret, to discuss, to consciously sculpt a life philosophy, to bounce ideas and concepts off others, to emote without fear or embarrassment.

There is so little time. But we must find what time we can. I call it "stoke time" because that's when I get to refuel my fire. And here's what I know: If I don't consciously and consistently stoke my spirit, it will go dark. I will go back to where I was fourteen years ago—in a state of depression and despair.

I'll tell you a fascinating story: In June 2001 I delivered a motivational workshop to a leadership team around a campfire in a game park in South Africa. Imagine the scene: fifteen of us around a crackling fire, each clutching a glass of vintage South African shiraz; a full moon and a galaxy of stars shining so brightly that the trees and shrubs cast shadows on the ground. It was a magical moment of camaraderie and fellowship, with people in free flow sharing their insights, hopes, fears and goals.

Every now and then the local staff would throw another log on the fire. After a few minutes it would ignite and the flames would shoot higher. The glow and crackle of the fire, the aromatic smell of the burning wood, the openness and the wine cast their spell on us. In the distance we could hear the laugh of a hyena, the yap of the jackals and the occasional flap of wings as bats left their trees in search of prey. If I've ever experienced a moment of total contentment, it was that night. I was doing what I loved, with people I loved, in a place that I loved. That's called nirvana.

Eventually the hour became late and we headed back toward our tents a few yards away. "Make sure to tie the flaps of your tent securely," the game rangers advised us. "When the fire burns out, the predators and scavengers move in."

I've never forgotten that advice. "When the fire burns out, the predators and scavengers move in." As I write these words, on a snowy January morning in Toronto, Canada, I know that if I let my mental, emotional, physical or spiritual fires burn out, scary things will move in. So burnout is not an option. Not for me—and not for you.

My personal call to action: I _____

What's more, as a Keeper of The Flame you have to burn even more brightly for others. Your fire demands more fuel. I want to help you create it.

We're about to explore the five themes of the Keeper of The Flame's story. But before we do, I want you to explore your own. Just as I did earlier on, please write your life story in about three hundred words or less. How's that for a challenge this early in the book? Why am I asking you to do this? Because here's your next Lipkinism:

> **If I tell you, you'll forget. If I teach you, you'll remember. If I involve you, you will learn. If I enroll you, you will act. If I help you tell your story, you'll burn brightly for everyone to see.**

Jean Shinoda Bolen, MD, is clinical professor of psychiatry at the University of California at San Francisco and a distinguished life fellow of the American Psychiatric Association. She uses the example of *The Little Engine That Could* to demonstrate the power of stories:

> *The Little Engine That Could* is a healing story. In this children's book, the little engine pulled a load that was bigger than he had ever attempted over a mountain, by saying to himself, "I think I can, I think I can, I think I can," and then, as he gained momentum and confidence, "I know I can, I know I can, I know I can," until he was over the hump, and coming down the other side, with "I thought I could, I thought I could, I thought I could" to the cheers of children.
>
> In *The Little Engine That Could*, we have a story with an emotional message, pictures to go with the story, and a positive statement that the engine (and the child) says over and over again. Each one of these three elements has something in common with ways people have of mobilizing healing through drawing on physical and psychological resources. Identifying with the story happens emotionally. Without knowing the word "metaphor," the child uses the story of the little engine as a metaphor: which means she knows that she is not an engine and she knows that it is her story. The child makes a connection between the engine's successful effort to make it over the mountain and the particular difficulty she has to overcome.

Here's my promise to you: You have a primary metaphoric story within you that could shift both you and the people around you from where you are to where you want to be. Here's another Lipkinism:

My personal call to action: I _____

"" It doesn't take people years to change. People can change in a heartbeat if they experience the right story.

Over the past fourteen years I have witnessed instant, enduring shifts in people who have related to a story that I've shared with them. Often I wasn't even aware of the significance of my story; I was told about the impact of my message after the event. But, every time, I'm amazed at the power of the imagination to rearrange the mind to perceive the outside world so differently, so quickly. To quote Bruce Springsteen, "You can't start a fire without a spark." But sometimes that's all it takes—one mind-spark to set someone on fire.

Bolen continues with a commentary on the physical impact that great stories have on us:

> The inspirational stories we hear and believe and apply to ourselves get into the marrow of our bones to influence healing and recovery. The cells of the body respond through peptide receptor sites to true stories of remarkable recoveries and stories that are metaphors for what the body is capable of doing, when we have a positive emotional response to these stories. They are transmitted in ways that we are just learning of as energy or biochemical reactions to activate or inspire the healing response.
>
> Visualization is a mind/body technique that a child instinctively does when applying *The Little Engine That Could* to some difficulty in her life. As a technique to heal, to reduce pain, or to mobilize their immune system, you can learn to create pictures in your mind that are as simple as the illustrations in children's books. When you visualize a metaphor, the physiology of the body responds. Just as the child sees the illustrations of the train when she identifies with the story, so do patients see the story they are telling their bodies through visualization. The ability to activate the archetype of the child, to suspend logic (and skepticism) and enter the magical world of the inner child for whom metaphor is real makes visualization work for adults.

So act now. To quote Jerry Maguire, "Help me help you." Write your story. Send it to me at mike.lipkin@environics.ca. Only I will see it. Exploring the five themes will be so much more valuable to you if you relate them to your own path. After talking to over a million people in twenty-eight different countries, I know that your story is an inspiring one. So describe your drama. It may surprise even you.

My personal call to action: I _____

However, to make sure you carry on, it's okay if you're not ready to write your story just yet. By simply reading these words you're already demonstrating a superior commitment to your path. I also want you to commit to visualizing at a bone-marrow level each story I tell you. Thrust yourself into it so that you become part of the story and the story becomes part of you. Deal? Then let's review the five themes.

theme 1. The Unlit Flame – Being Unaware

The unexamined life, said Socrates, is not worth living. Maybe, but that's the life the vast majority of us lead. Ignorance may not be bliss, but it doesn't require the conscious effort of constant discovery. The pursuit of comfort is as powerful a motivator as the pursuit of happiness. For many, it's the same pursuit—of freedom from FUD: fear, uncertainty and doubt.

Being a Keeper of The Flame is within everyone's grasp. In some small but significant way everyone can influence somebody else to be more than they otherwise would have been. But 90 percent of people don't break out of their unawareness because it's simply not on their mental radar to do so. They're unaware of what's going on, inside and outside of them.

So they envelop themselves in their personal bubbles and go about their business, hoping that life will leave them alone. You and I both know, though, that life doesn't work like that. Something will happen that we can either deny or realize fully . . .

theme 2. Trial-By-Fire – Shattering The Status Quo

If you've ever tripped or slipped and fallen, you know the horrible feeling of shock, then pain, when you hit the ground. It's the same feeling we have when something shatters the status quo we've been taking for granted.

It's the personal quake that convulses our world. It's the job we lose, the partner who leaves, the child who gets into trouble, the sickness that invades, the environment that changes, the bully who threatens—or it's simply an awakening that alters everything.

Usually our immediate response is to protect ourselves by raising our defenses. Then we make a choice. We answer the call and graduate to the next

My personal call to action: I _____

theme. We have the guts to cross the threshold into the unknown. Or we're overcome with timidity and go back. We come to terms with our disappointment, we become cynical, we lower our hopes. We become part of the walking wounded. Over time we become bitter, not better.

theme **3**■ Reaching For The Torch

For the vital few who cross the threshold, it's a whole different life on the other side. It's about living on your own terms. It's about embracing the lessons with grace and gusto. It's about resolution, discipline, education and personal transformation. It's about "fighting the good fight, keeping the faith and staying the course."

The vital few who reach for the torch train themselves to excel at a higher level. They consciously achieve mastery along the Six Nuclear Dimensions: Focus, Strategy, Learning, Emotional-Power, Action and Social-Kudos.

There comes a time when the master must accept the responsibility of passing on the torch to illuminate others. Not to do so means getting stuck in *Me*. It means suffocating your gifts. That's when narcissism and arrogance snuff out the flame. And that's when we get pushed back across the threshold to the unlit flame, to begin again. Whatever you don't share willingly, you lose involuntarily.

theme **4**■ Keeper of The Flame

You've awakened from your slumber. Your flame has been lit. You've made your realizations. You've been through your trial by fire. You stepped up. You answered the call with courage and commitment. You reached for the torch with discipline and resolve. You developed yourself along the Six Nuclear Dimensions. You achieved mastery. You've accepted responsibility for passing on the torch.

Now you've become an example of what can be done. You become the reason why people try harder, fly higher, move faster. You become the source of other people's breakthroughs. You become the go-to advisor in the crunch moments. Through your words and actions you motivate others to reach for the torch.

The more you give, the more you are asked to give. You never want to say

My personal call to action: I _____

no. You feel fatigue dimming your flame but still you carry on. You begin to feel stale. You begin to lose your passion for lighting others up. You flash back to what it was like when your flame was unlit. You know it's time for renewal . . .

theme 5∎ A Fresh Mind

No fire burns forever. Without constant refueling, the flame dims. So the true Keeper of The Flame opens himself to new possibilities, new philosophies, new influences, new environments, new people. He gives himself frequent sabbaticals that may last a year—or a weekend.

He begins every day with a fresh mind. He is not afraid to play the apprentice role. His past doesn't determine his future. He lives every day on the Cusp of a breakthrough. He expects to succeed massively. But he understands that victory and defeat are in the hands of the gods, so he celebrates the struggle.

The fresh mind always sees new things, even in familiar situations. You *can* go home again—and discover things that you never saw before. But you have to be willing to go back across the threshold, where you will become a beginner all over again. Only when the student is ready does the teacher appear.

The 5 Themes Always Run Concurrently
We're all Actors in Multiple Roles

Life is one long lesson in pride and humility. For every triumph there is a setback to balance our ego. We can be a Keeper of The Flame in one role and still remain unlit in another. It's the ability to distinguish our status in our respective roles that determines our success in whatever roles we are called upon to play. I don't know about you, but some of my most challenging moments come when I confuse my status in one area with my lack of status in another.

I may be a global Keeper of The Flame in the motivation business, but at home I'm just another Boomer struggling to understand his "twenty-somethings." I may be a coach to hundreds in the workplace, but in my personal space I'm just another spouse learning how to sustain romance in a lifetime connection. I may be a lead partner on a number of highly successful teams, but

My personal call to action: I _____

42

in my community I'm just another volunteer offering up his time to make even the smallest difference. Whenever I forget my role I receive a sharp AAK—an attitude-adjustment-knock —from above.

All of us are actors in multiple roles. Sometimes we're accomplished masters and sometimes we're rank amateurs. Think about it: At any point in time we're individuals, parents, spouses, children, colleagues, customers, volunteers, partners, team-players, winners, losers, athletes, coaches, players, friends, opponents, competitors, patients, caregivers, experts, beginners, listeners, talkers, tourists, residents, veterans, rookies, drivers, passengers.

▶ Relish your role. If you're the leader, lead. If you're the follower, follow. If you're in the wrong role, get out of it. Do what you do with passion and understanding or don't do it at all. That's what this book is all about.

My personal call to action: I _____

Live Brilliantly.

Remember, there is no small stuff. Everything is significant. Be proud of how far you've come. Have faith in how far you will go.

Live Brilliantly. And take it to a whole new level every day.

OUR LIFE IS A CONTEMPORARY SAGA. YOU ARE A WALKING DRAMA. YOUR story is as compelling as anything Hollywood ever produced. So, see your challenges in mythic dimensions. See your crises as rites of passage taking you to the next level. And give yourself credit for the hero you've already become.

I make a living interviewing people and telling their stories. I also make a living sharing my experiences with others. Wherever I go I collect anecdotes that I can use to illustrate key principles in my books or seminars. I know that my audience may forget a rational point, but they'll always remember a moving story.

And guess what? The most moving stories are those of everyday people who step themselves up through their attitudes and actions—especially when other people need them most. I've found that people are tired of being offered examples from the immortals. It's hard for someone who's doing all she can just to get through her day-to-day challenges to relate to a giant who appears to have changed the world. What people want are examples of peers being confronted by the same challenges they face.

Often, the most powerful part of my seminars comes at the end, when I ask people to share their key takeaways from the program. Person after person stands up and shares their personal "aha"—the one thing they believe will make a difference to their life. Sometimes they are passionately exuberant. And sometimes they are still a little shy as they quietly share their thoughts. But, every time, the audience is spellbound by the messages. Every word resonates

My personal call to action: I _____

44

with the group as a whole. Every person empathizes with every other person. There is so much more binding us together than there is pulling us apart.

From this moment on I want you to see all the experiences of your life from a new perspective. I want you to use magnifying lenses. There is no small stuff, so make every experience bigger. Every experience carries magic within it. Think about your last twenty-four hours. How much magic have you taken for granted? I'm writing these words around 5:35 p.m. on a sunny spring Saturday afternoon. Here is a list of some of the magic-filled experiences I've had in the past twenty-four hours:

- Meeting with two important business partners in a park, where we resolved a major issue getting in the way of our relationship. The talk was frank and open. We spoke honestly and we cleared the air so that the relationship could breathe again.

- Meeting with friends where the beer was cold, the conversation was sparkling and the laughter was loud. I savored every second with these remarkable people and their joie de vivre.

- Without his knowledge, watching my twenty-year-old son at work in his new job as a bank teller. I felt the pride that only a parent can feel as he watches his child perform with diligence and grace.

- Watching the movie *Kinsey* with my wife, Hilary, on our giant-screen TV in the room next to our bedroom—our own private cinema. Liam Neeson was extraordinary. We marveled at his genius and felt richer for it.

- Enjoying my first coffee this morning. Every time I open the bag of Starbucks Espresso Roast, I relish that intoxicating aroma. I think about what it took to get that coffee into my hands. It's always so damn good.

- Writing these words that I know thousands of people will read. It's a gift and it's a privilege. Every thought that is captured on the screen amazes me. Where did it come from? I don't know, but I'm grateful.

- Working out at my local gym while I listen to Pearl Jam on my iPod. After about thirty minutes I feel the flow of endorphins lift me up. After fifty minutes I'm spent. As I stretch on the mat I look at myself in the mirror. At forty-eight years old I'm taking care of my body and my body is taking care of me. Even the slight aches and pains are comforting signs that I'm pushing myself as hard as I need to.

My personal call to action: I _____

- Having a sushi lunch with my wife, my twenty-year-old twins and my niece. We always go to the same place—Takara on Yonge Street, north of St. Clair, in midtown Toronto. Every piece is a work of art. With every delicious mouthful I whisper a silent prayer of thanks to the great sushi chef in the sky.

- Taking my two Staffordshire terrier/Maltese/poodle-mix dogs for a walk along a path near our house. I hear their enthusiasm. I feel their eager pull against their leashes as they sniff everything. The late sun is still bright; the trees are resplendent in their bright new leaves. People are reveling in the warmth. A sense of celebration is in the air. Summer is almost here.

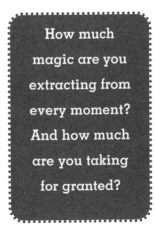

How much magic are you extracting from every moment? And how much are you taking for granted?

So let me ask you: How different is my life from yours? How many similar experiences have you had today? How much magic are you extracting from every moment? And how much are you taking for granted?

One of the biggest themes permeating my research is that everything is becoming more intense. I call it emotional inflation. People are becoming more sensitive. They're reading more into every action, especially in the workplace. The smallest act can cause the biggest consequences.

As someone who is always mixing with a wide diversity of people, I've learned how much a single word, look or gesture can influence others. I'm continually amazed at how much people are affected by something I may not even have been aware of at the time. I'm always thrilled when it's positive, and I'm always stunned when it's negative.

Excellence, said Aristotle, is a habit. We become what we repeatedly do. The slightest shift eventually has a major impact on our life's trajectory. You never know how much an action can change your life. But what we do know is that everything leads to everything. Good deeds done well yield equivalent results. Bad deeds or negligent actions yield the same. Every action is a future asset or a future liability. What we do today echoes throughout our tomorrows.

So don't underestimate your experiences. Don't underestimate your influence on others. Don't underestimate your life and don't underestimate yourself.

My personal call to action: I _____

If you're going to err, err on the side of overestimating yourself. People who overestimate their ability achieve more than those who don't. They live large. They risk more, they go farther, they dream bigger. And they reap the results. I often joke with my seminar audiences that I'm living proof of the power of overestimating one's ability. And I'm serious. If the outcome is compelling enough and if I think I can even remotely achieve it, I'll sign up for it. I know that if I go to the edge and jump, I'll sprout wings on the way. I've been living this philosophy for the past fourteen years, since my renaissance from depression in 1992. It works.

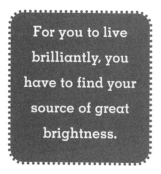

For you to live brilliantly, you have to find your source of great brightness.

Raul Julia, the actor and activist, beautifully expressed the ethos of being extraordinary: "We have to stop the idea that you have to be perfect in order to make a contribution. You don't have to. You can be full of flaws. You can be an ordinary person and make a difference. There's no such thing as an extraordinary person, only extraordinary deeds, because they made the commitment, in spite of their flaws."

We're all on a journey to our own Middle Kingdom. Our own personal brass ring awaits us. But there are peaks and valleys ahead, friends and foes, pleasure and pain, certainty and doubt, love and hate, health and disease. Above all, there is the great adventure. There are the dragons to be slain, captives to be rescued and riches to be discovered.

Live brilliantly. What does that mean? According to *Webster's Unabridged Dictionary of the English Language*, brilliance is "great brightness; having or showing great intelligence, talent or quality; conspicuous mental ability."

For you to live brilliantly, you have to find your source of great brightness. You have to discover and develop your great intelligence, talent or qualities that will help you become a Keeper of The Flame. You have to apply your conspicuous mental ability in a way that's uniquely you. That's the mission you're signing up for by continuing further.

I must warn you that living brilliantly comes with a price. It means never settling. It means stepping up. It means assuming responsibility for making things better. It means living in anticipation of the next wake-up call. It means being willing to cross the threshold into unexplored territory. It means burning your excuses so you can travel light.

My personal call to action: I _____

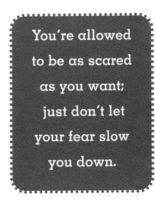

You're allowed to be as scared as you want; just don't let your fear slow you down.

Steve Balmer, CEO of Microsoft, describes it this way: "We have to be a place that can, with great energy and passion that's baked into the place, do amazing things on a regular basis. We have to be able to predictably do the amazing" (*USA Today*, January 1, 2005). That's the "brilliance standard"—can others rely on you to predictably do the amazing? You need to decide what "amazing" means to you. For me it means consistently being able to exhilarate my audiences with my energy and insights, so that they mobilize themselves to take the action they otherwise would not have taken to achieve their desired results. What is it for you?

Even if you meet the brilliance standard, here's the scary truth: You've only qualified to raise your game even higher tomorrow. What do I mean? It's called the "performance paradox." As reported in the April 2005 issue of *Fast Company* magazine, the performance paradox means that if you deliver, you only qualify to deliver more. Greatness lasts only as long as someone fails to imagine something better. Inevitably the exceptional becomes the expected. Great people have always endured this treadmill of expectations, but these days the brewing forces of technology, productivity and transparency have accelerated the cycle to breakneck speed. "The root behind the paradox is unrealistic, unconstrained expectations," says Michael Weissman, coauthor of *The Paradox of Excellence*. "They tend to chase ahead of your ability to perform."

So what does that mean for you? You have to be up for the challenge of rapid personal change. You're allowed to be as scared as you want; just don't let your fear slow you down. There is no alternative: You have to evolve your performance at a rate that exceeds the industry benchmark. That means embracing a tempo of development that outstrips your competition. Second, while you're changing, you need to constantly manage the expectations of your stakeholders by letting them know the magnitude of both your results and your efforts. Successful change and communication go together, especially when there is no precedent for what you're doing and where you're going. Don't just whistle while you work—talk, talk, talk.

However, living brilliantly also means forgiving yourself when you don't meet your own standards. Keepers of The Flame are masters of relativism. What do I mean? They know that criteria or judgments vary with individuals and their

My personal call to action: I _____

environments. You're not a machine. No matter how awesome you are, there will be people who don't buy into you. There will be environments that are not favorable to you. You're a fallible, vulnerable part of a much larger ecosystem. You will stumble, you will slide backwards, you will slack off—it's inevitable. Give yourself a break. There's a time to be strong and there's a time to be weak. Don't try to be one when it's time to be the other. Knowing when to be what is key to being a Keeper of The Flame.

> Successful change
> and communication
> go together, especially when
> there is no precedent for
> what you're doing and
> where you're going.
> Don't just whistle while you
> work—talk, talk, talk.

My personal call to action: I _____

Part Two

Be Ready:
You're About to Receive
a Wake-Up Call

Those who are unaware are unaware that they're unaware.

You don't know what you don't know.
But what you don't know can hurt you.

What are you looking for?

Do you see a blur?

Or do you see a pattern?

Are you drowning in information?

Or are you infused with insight?

Are you getting the big picture?

Or are the minutiae obscuring your vision?

What are the trends?

And how are they shaping your world?

You can look back in anger.

You can look forward in fear.

Or you can look around you in awareness.

I get hit by a BUS every week.

That's a Big Unexpected Surprise. Sometimes it's the kind of surprise I like. And sometimes it's the kind of surprise that sends me into a tailspin. Usually it's a surprise that appears out of nowhere like an out-of-control runaway vehicle.

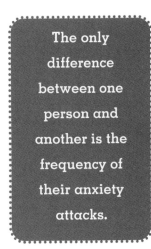

The only difference between one person and another is the frequency of their anxiety attacks.

When it's bad, I think about the unfairness of it. I think about how unpredictable life is. I think about how unreasonable my fellow human beings are. I question my survival skills. I question my ability to navigate my way through a world gone mad.

"What was that all about?" "Why didn't I see it coming?" "I should have known." These are the doubt seeds I sow in my mind. They usually grow into episodes of self-pity, a sense of victimhood and powerlessness. I know you know the feeling. The only difference between one person and another is the frequency of their anxiety attacks. For me, it's weekly. Even so, I'm still stunned and winded every time it happens.

But it's not the BUS that's really the issue—an infinite supply of big unexpected surprises is waiting for you over the course of your lifetime—it's how you respond. It's how quickly you recover. It's how readily you accept what has happened. It's how tuned in you are to the new normal. Then it's about how you ride the BUS to where you have to go.

Because I'm "Mr. Motivator" I have to recover quickly. I have to embrace the lesson. Five times a week I'm in front of people who are buying my energy and optimism. Anything less than an outstanding, hit-the-ball-out-the-park performance is unacceptable—both to my clients and to me. I have to play at my personal best or I starve. When you position yourself as a professional source of insights and inspiration, you have to burn your excuses and step into the moment.

Some people do things for a living. They build things, design things, make things. I make things up. I talk. Almost every day I try to give people better ways to achieve the results they want. And every time I teach, I learn. I learn from the members of my audience or focus group. I learn from the words and actions that work and from the words and actions that don't work. I learn what to stop, what to start and what to change. Once again, I have no choice—either I get it right or I disappear. There is no middle path for me; I'm hot or I'm not. And once my clients decide I'm not, it's over, baby!

My personal call to action: I _____

Recently I delivered a half-day program in Ottawa to group of leaders in the automotive industry. As I was waiting for my session to be announced, one of the delegates approached me with a question: "How many of these do you do a year?"

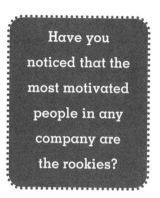

Have you noticed that the most motivated people in any company are the rookies?

"About a hundred and fifty," I responded.

"You must be pretty tired of doing them by now, right?" he asked

"Actually, I've never been more turned on" I replied. "Every time is my first time. You've never heard me before. Because it's your first time, it's mine as well. I'm as thrilled and as nervous as I was the first time. What's more, I think myself into this state before every talk."

At the bar after the session, he raised his beer to me with a toast: "To the first time!" He got it.

What I was really referring to is another Lipkinism called the *Rookie Paradox*. What do I mean? Well, have you noticed that the most motivated people in any company are the rookies? They're on fire. Anything is possible for them. They join a company because they believe it's the best place for them to build a successful career. Then, as they encounter one disillusionment after another, they become cynical. They lose their enthusiasm. Their experience becomes their biggest liability. The longer they spend in the job, the less effective they become. But that's not you, right? You and I are the perennial rookies!

Now think about this: How much of your work involves talking or communicating with others? If you're in a service environment, between 70 and 80 percent of your time will be committed to communication via the written and spoken word. So what's the difference between you and me? Not a heck of a lot. We're both transferors of knowledge and beacons of possibility.

So how aware are you? Are you alert, informed and knowledgeable about your world? How developed are your personal antennae? Are you plugged into the Zeitgeist, the spirit of the times? Do you understand the signals? What are the signs, warnings, lights, commands, events that point to the next change or BUS?

Here's a claim that will blow you away: According to *The National Post* (March 26, 2005), Medcan is considered to be Canada's largest executive health care provider. It has a roster of 15,000 patients, which includes managers from every major bank, law office and consulting firm in Toronto. *Medcan claims to uncover*

My personal call to action: I _____

undiagnosed diseases in 48 percent of its patients! This statistic suggests another reason for the growing popularity of executive health services. Every year the clinics offer more tests that can predict disease.

My message to you is twofold. First, make sure that you get a comprehensive annual checkup to alert yourself to the signals within you. And second, live your life with a heightened awareness of the undiagnosed signals around you: people signals, media signals, social signals, mind/body signals, and emotional signals.

People Signals: You're Becoming the Company You Keep

What kind of people am I winning? What kind of people am I losing? What kind of messages am I getting from the people I'm currently serving? What do they want? What am I giving them? Remember, when all is said and done, we become the company we keep. Your ability to attract magical people will be the main reason why you eventually become a Keeper of The Flame or not. People signals are the most powerful signals because they are the most real and the most relevant. If you get your people signals wrong, you're heading for one train crash after another.

There is an ancient Zulu saying, *Umuntu ungumuntu ngabantu*—a person is a person because of other people. I am because you are. We are all connected. We all define each other. We all have a responsibility for lifting each other up, even when we're down.

So what kind of people signals are you getting? What kind of people signals are you sending? Are the people around you raising your game? Are you raising theirs?

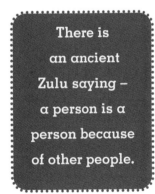

There is an ancient Zulu saying – a person is a person because of other people.

What I'm talking about here is the quality of the energy you're transmitting and receiving from the people around you. Magical people infuse others with a transformational energy. They lift them up through their optimism, insight and sheer caring for others' well-being. You always know when you've been with a magical person. You feel lighter and stronger when you leave her presence. In ways both big and small, you're better able to face the day ahead.

On the other hand, there are people I call the wear-you-downs. Wear-you-downs tire you out. They are the

My personal call to action: I _____

bearers of bad news, bad feelings, bad omens. Sometimes they're malicious. They get a perverse pleasure from inflicting pain or discomfort on others. At other times wear-you-downs are oblivious to the damage they may be doing to others. They're "interpersonal illiterates," unable or unwilling to understand their adverse impact on you.

There are no in-betweeners, just variations in intensity, the way a heater or an oven operates. Someone is either a magical person in your life or a wear-you-down. And, by the way, you don't have to be charismatic to be either. Some of the most magical people in my life are quiet, reticent, keep-to-them-selves kinds of people. And some of the most tiresome wear-you-downs are extroverted, forceful folk. It's all about the impact they have on you, and vice versa.

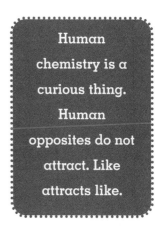

Human chemistry is a curious thing. Human opposites do not attract. Like attracts like.

Human chemistry is a curious thing. Human opposites do not attract. Like attracts like. And whatever you have within you is what you draw toward you or push away from you. So whenever I sense that I'm not being the people magnet I need to be, I immediately go within for the cause. Inevitably I discover that I'm out of alignment. Once I'm back on track, others come along for the ride.

Media Signals: You Are What You Read, Watch and Hear

What are you reading, watching and listening to? Your conversational ability is a direct function of the media you consume. More and more, your role is to provide perspective to others in confusing times. But you can't give what you don't have. So miss a meal, but don't miss your media. Maybe it's your local paper, in hard copy or online. Maybe it's your favorite websites. Maybe it's your new satellite radio station. Maybe it's the latest issue of a magazine. Maybe it's a trade journal or industry report. Maybe it's a best-selling piece of non-fiction or a novel. Consume a wide range of media and be alert to the common themes expressed across them. Know something about everything and everything about something.

The vast majority of people are undernourished when it comes to media. They simply do not have a clear point of view on so many of the key issues. And because they don't have a clear point of view, they cannot communicate with authority and conviction. So they become prisoners of the status quo rather than

My personal call to action: I _____

agents for change. How about you? Are you a provider of new possibilities? Or are you same old same old? Best-in-class people help others see the world through different eyes. That's often the real reason for their success—they bring something extra to every engagement.

I confess I'm a media freak. I'm fascinated by Google. I'm spellbound by newspapers. I enjoy my nightly engagements with CNN, ROB-TV, FOX and CNBC. I love the gloss and pace of my favorite magazines. I'm lost without my iPod. I listen to as many books as I read. That's why I can offer you the perspective of this book. So choose your preferred medium and commit to consuming it every day.

Social Signals: You're Only as Strong as the Diversity of Your Network

What key themes permeate your conversations with the people around you? What's on their minds? What's keeping them up at night? What are they looking for?

How diverse is your range of contacts? Are you stuck in a homogeneous cluster of friends, colleagues and family? Or are you consciously seeking the strength of weak ties? The more widespread your social circle, the more likely you are to see the patterns swirling around you.

As someone who engages with over fifty different companies a year, I get around. I can tell you that my most valuable insights always come from the people who are farthest outside my inner social circle. They are travelers in a space to which I have no access, so it's their points of view that help me see a whole new world.

Here's a marvelous example: In Georgetown, a small town about twenty miles northwest of Toronto, there is an association of women graduates who network on a regular basis to stay in touch and raise funds for their community. In March 2004, I was asked to deliver an after-dinner speech in aid of a local charity. It was a delightful crowd and the evening was a great success.

After the talk, as I sat signing books for audience members, I was approached by a Hindu woman who appeared to be in her seventies. This is what she said to me: "Michael, you know, we Hindus believe in reincarnation. My family believes that if you were extremely good in your previous life, you get to come back as a Canadian."

Every time I share this story in Canada, the audience breaks into a spontaneous round of appreciative laughter. No one but this extraordinary woman,

My personal call to action: I _____

from a culture so different from mine, could have provided us with such a different but relevant observation on the merits of living in Canada.

I'm gregarious. That means I'm fond of the company of others. I like to be around as many people who are different from me as I can. At the same time, though, I can be shy. I can be self-conscious. But my thrill at learning and sharing far outweighs any initial awkwardness or self-consciousness. Get over your shyness. Reach out. You'll discover that the people to whom you reach out will reach out back to you.

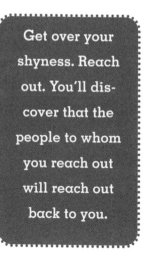

Get over your shyness. Reach out. You'll discover that the people to whom you reach out will reach out back to you.

As an economic nomad I'm always the outsider at my clients' events. At the opening cocktail party or dinner, before the group knows who I am, I stand at the periphery of the crowd and watch its dynamics. Then I walk around the room, introducing myself and absorbing information that I'll use in my session that evening or the following day.

I have no choice. I *have* to engage people so I can customize my presentations specifically to their challenges and interests. The difference between a knock-your-socks-off great session and merely an excellent one is the personal anecdotes I can share with my audiences that I've learnt from their peers. That's what makes my sessions real.

After fourteen years as a professional motivator, I can tell you that it still feels awkward to introduce myself to groups of strangers. I still feel the self-consciousness that comes with intruding on a clique of people engaged in their own conversation. I have to justify my intrusion by giving them a reason to want to talk to me. So I tell them who I am, what I've been hired to do for them and why they will enjoy my session. Then I immediately get them to talk about themselves. Very quickly, a dialogue develops and connections are made that I'll leverage in my programs.

Here's the first interesting insight: I always have to take the initiative. I'm almost never approached by others at these corporate events. Maybe I don't look interesting or attractive enough, or people are not curious enough, or they just don't think it's worth it, or they're simply wary of someone they don't know. My point is that people are inherently conditioned not to talk to strangers. So they not only don't take the first step, they're nervous about someone who does.

Here's the second interesting insight: If the cocktail party or dinner is after my

My personal call to action: I _____

session, almost everyone approaches me. They shake my hand, pat me on the back, offer to get me a drink, compliment me on my talk and invite me to join their table. In sixty to ninety minutes I go from being an anonymous outsider to a desirable dinner companion. There is a double lesson learned here. First, engage everyone as though they are full of truths that will amaze and delight you. Second, when faced with wariness or skepticism from strangers, keep talking. Very quickly your presence will connect with them and they'll invite you into the fold. Ultimately, you have no choice anyway. Just as I need the information to tailor my talks to my audience, you need the information to tailor your communication to your stakeholders.

Remember, there are no strangers, just friends we haven't met yet. We can never have enough friends, so we should never squander an opportunity to make new ones.

The following story from CNN.com (June 22, 2005) dramatizes how deeply imprinted our fear of strangers can be—from a very early age:

Fearing Kidnapping, Brennan Hawkins, Lost for Four Days in the Utah Mountains, Hid from Searchers.

BOUNTIFUL, Utah – The 11-year-old boy lost for four days in the Utah mountains had deliberately hid from searchers, thinking they were strangers who might kidnap him, his mother said Wednesday.

"His biggest fear, he told me, was that someone would steal him," Jody Hawkins said of her son Brennan, who was rescued Tuesday afternoon by a searcher who came across the boy before he could hide.

He had two things on his mind, she added, "stay on the trail and don't talk to strangers," she added at a press conference outside their home in Bountiful, Utah. As a result, she said, he would walk along a trail but then hide when someone approached.

His father, Toby, said they had never talked with Brennan about how that stranger rule shouldn't apply if he got lost. "This may have come to a faster conclusion had we discussed that," he said.

Forrest Nunley, the man who found Brennan, echoed that version of

My personal call to action: I _____

events, telling NBC's "Today" show earlier that Brennan "had been hiding" in some trees from other searchers on horseback and that, when offered water, "he was a little bit worried about whether he could have the water or not."

Bob Hawkins, Brennan's uncle, told "Today" that he had been taught the idea of "stranger danger" and that "all of that kind of kicked in. . . . he was just going on that instinct."

Brennan vanished last Friday evening after playing at a climbing wall at a Boy Scout camp where he had been camping with a friend and his friend's family.

Sheriff Dave Edmunds told "Today" that Brennan apparently "was taught not to talk to strangers" and must have been hiding during the search since "so many people" had been in the area looking for him.

I like the story of Brennan Hawkins because many people significantly older than Brennan suffer from fear of "stranger danger." How many opportunities are you missing because you're reluctant to reach out and connect with someone new? Remember, the other person wants you to take the first step and make it easy for them to connect with you. Do it. You'll be amazed at how quickly people will respond to you after the initial contact.

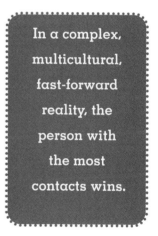

In a complex, multicultural, fast-forward reality, the person with the most contacts wins.

Everyone around you is a potential gift. So why would you not open it up? Obviously it's easier if you're outgoing or an extrovert. However, one fact is beyond dispute: In a complex, multicultural, fast-forward reality, the person with the most contacts wins. So it doesn't matter whether you find it easy or hard to approach others—you have no choice. Make the connection or get left behind. If you aspire to being a Keeper of The Flame, you have to do the things that other, more timid souls are afraid to do.

My personal call to action: I _____

Mind/Body Signals: Your Body Is Talking to You – Are You Listening?

Just before I wrote these words I went to the bathroom. Everything happened just the way it should. There was no pain, no spillage, no mess. This may be more information than you need. So why am I sharing this incident of intimate personal hygiene with you? Simple—I'm telling you because I'm forty-eight years old, and I take nothing for granted any more. Just the opposite. I thrill every time my physical machine obeys my instructions. I thrill to the fact that I have a resting heart rate of fifty beats per minute. I'm grateful that I can swim for over an hour without feeling fatigued. I revel in my constant feeling of vitality and joie de vivre.

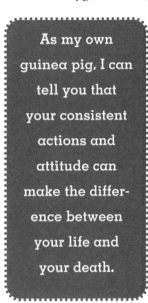

As my own guinea pig, I can tell you that your consistent actions and attitude can make the difference between your life and your death.

As someone whose father died at the age of forty-two, I now regard every healthy day as a bonus. Every day is proof that miracles are real. Every day is also proof that one's genetics need not be one's future. Determination, action, attitude, discipline, diet, science, friendships, love, connection, faith *can* come together to build health, longevity and happiness.

I'll share some fascinating news with you: Because of the genetic factors that render me susceptible to coronary disease, I have my blood checked three times a year. In 1991, during my period of clinical depression, my cholesterol level was 9.5—that's more than double the desired limit of 4.0. I was truly an accident waiting to happen. Today, with a stringent mental, emotional, physical and spiritual regimen in place, combined with the magic of modern-day science, my cholesterol level is 3.6. It's gone down 40 percent in the past three years alone as my family and I have adapted to our new environment. As my own guinea pig, I can tell you that your consistent actions and attitude can make the difference between your life and your death.

Dr. Richard Perrin, professor of neurological surgery at the University of Toronto, told me that the word *pain* comes from the Latin word for penalty: *poena*. So when you feel pain, you're probably paying a penalty for something that happened in your past. Think about your physical ailments. How many of them are due to actions you've taken? About 70 to 80 percent of the things that ail us have nothing to do with genetics; they're a function of lifestyle and past behavior.

My personal call to action: I _____

So don't curse the signals that your body is sending you—heed them. The older we get, the more attuned we should be to our physical machine. Love your body, flaws and all. Think about the magic and the mystery of the thousands of functions it performs every day. Most of us walk around without celebrating the multiple activities going on just beneath our skin—until they cease. Then we'll do anything to restart them.

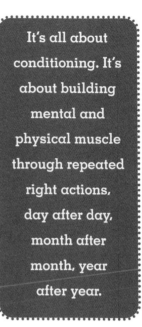

It's all about conditioning. It's about building mental and physical muscle through repeated right actions, day after day, month after month, year after year.

So here I sit with a titanium rod holding my lower vertebrae together. My right knee is almost worn out from too much jogging. My upper right and left gums are populated by a series of tooth implants. My cholesterol is moderated by daily doses of Lipitor. My thyroid is regulated by Synthroid. My contact lens prescription grows stronger by the year. I'm on a permanent diet of high-fiber bran to sustain my regularity. And I feel that I'm in the best shape of my life. I welcome all these clues to my mortality because they help me maximize my physical performance.

To quote Tim McGraw, "Live like you were dying." Every day all of us are getting closer to our final day. For some it may come around your seventy-eighth birthday, the life expectancy of the average person in the U.S. and Canada. For others it may come a heck of a lot sooner. My point is that tomorrow isn't promised to anyone. Your body is not an automatic system that functions irrespective of abuse or neglect. The older you become, the higher the *poena* you pay.

Government surveys indicate that only a quarter of adults pursue a regular exercise program. Based on our polls, I would put that figure even lower—around 20 percent. Most of us, therefore, are being hit by a triple whammy: our stress is increasing exponentially, we're aging and we're not conditioning our bodies to rise to their escalating challenges.

It seems we're not prepared to sweat it out, both literally and figuratively. According to *Maclean's* magazine (June 20, 2005), we've entered the age of "cosmetic neurology"—the use of drugs among otherwise healthy people to manipulate mood, memory, concentration, libido, capacity to learn and general ability to cope. A person could take Prozac to alleviate down days, or Paxil, another top-selling antidepressant, to combat social awkwardness. An architect may take Ritalin to boost his ability to memorize spatial layouts. And a classical musician might pop

My personal call to action: I _____

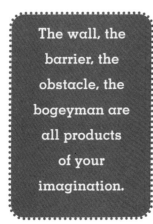

The wall, the barrier, the obstacle, the bogeyman are all products of your imagination.

a beta blocker like Propanol, a heart medication, to prevent stage fright from spoiling her performance.

In 2004 Canadians filled over forty-five million prescriptions for psychotropic medications, a 40 percent increase over 2000. Dr. Norman Hoffman, director of McGill University's Mental Health Service in Montreal, estimates that 20 to 25 percent of Canadians are on some kind of mood-enhancing drug. "Probably only a fifth to a quarter of those should be," he says.

I believe there are no shortcuts. There is no pharmaceutical panacea. In the heat of the many crunch moments we all have to endure, no outside agent can help us toughen up. It's all about conditioning. It's about building mental and physical muscle through repeated right actions, day after day, month after month, year after year. It's about the stamina and resilience that sustains you when all around you are giving up. That's the hallmark of the true-blue champions with whom I work. They turn on their power when others fade away. They access their accumulated reservoirs of mojo to make the final extra effort that wins them the game.

We're all faced with a stark choice: Make the tough decisions and take the tough actions today or pay the price tomorrow. I believe that mood enhancers may even heighten your risk, because they weaken your mental muscles. I speak from experience. In 1990 and 1991, when I went through my depressive episode, I was on a steady diet of Prozac and other mood enhancers. They helped me get through each day, but they eroded my ability to manufacture my own levels of optimism.

One of the biggest roadblocks in the way of my convalescence was the temptation to revert to mood enhancers every time I came face to face with a crisis. But I resisted. Since February 22, 1992, I have not taken any kind of psychotropic drug. Instead, my narcotic is exercise. I'm fanatical—seven days a week for an hour a day. One day I swim, the next day I cycle. Every day I keep my abdominals strong through stomach crunches. I believe Nike when they tell me, "If you have a body, you're an athlete." We're all athletes in the game of life. The fittest don't just survive, they thrive. If I don't look like I walk my talk, I lose all authenticity. For me, therefore, it's not about just physical and mental health, it's about my professional health as well.

My personal call to action: I _____

Don't get me wrong: If you're sick, you need help. But I know that if you've got this far, you're far from sick. So don't be an early settler. Don't be someone who is intimidated by the size of the challenge. The wall, the barrier, the obstacle, the bogeyman are all products of your imagination. You conjured them up. You can obliterate them as well.

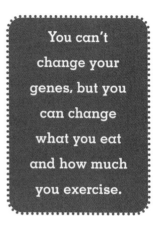

You can't change your genes, but you can change what you eat and how much you exercise.

Once again, I'm here to tell you it ain't easy. But then, "easy" is your wake-up call. If you find things too easy, you're not expanding your capacity. You're not building muscle. Someone or something is about to shake you up. So celebrate the struggle. Take yourself to your personal Cusp. Savor the stretch. Bring on the burn. Give it all you have, and you'll have it all.

The Mike Collins story sums up everything I'm talking about: Any way you cut it, Mike Collins is a success. In 2004 he was the leading new business developer for Rogers Media, one of Canada's biggest media companies. He has many close friends, a great marriage and two happy, healthy kids. He's also extremely fit, having recently completed his first marathon in just over four hours. He weighs 158 pounds—the perfect weight for him. But it wasn't always like that. Just two years ago he weighed a massive 280 pounds—on a frame of just five foot seven. He was digging his grave with a knife and fork.

Then two life-changing events hit Mike like a personal tornado: his thirty-eight-year-old friend and neighbor died, and his son was born. He made the decision to stop killing himself and get busy living. He sought professional help. He began a regular exercise schedule. He says, "Looking back, every time I had lost weight in the past I had gone back to my old eating habits and eventually regained the weight. I am now vigilant about what I eat every day. I'm vigilant about what I do. I'm vigilant about how I think. I can never eat the way I used to. I'm never going back. Never." If Mike can do it, you can do it. If you want Mike's point of view, contact him directly at Mike.Collins@680news.rogers.com.

According to *Time* magazine (August 30, 2004), only about 20 to 30 percent of our lifespan is genetically determined. The dominant factor is lifestyle. "You could have Mercedes-Benz genes," says Dr. Bradley Willcox of the Pacific Health Institute in Honolulu, "but if you never change the oil, you're not going to last as long as a Ford Escort that you take good care of." The bottom line, as both Mike

My personal call to action: I _____

Collins and Mike Lipkin found out a long time ago, is that you can't change your genes, but you can change what you eat and how much you exercise.

Dr. Thomas Perls, a geriatrician at Boston University and leader of a major study under way at the National Institute on Aging, says, "I strongly believe that with some changes in health-related behavior, each of us can earn the right to have at least 25 years beyond the age of 60—years of healthy life at good function. The disappointing news is that it requires work and willpower." But remember, my fellow Seeker of The Flame, you're not just doing this for yourself. You're doing it so you can set an example to all the people around you who need proof that it can be done. When you do the right thing, you make it possible for others to do the same.

Emotional Signals: What You Feel Is Real

How are you feeling right now? What emotions do you experience most often? What are the emotions you'd like to experience more? Which emotions would you like to experience less? What really, really makes you happy? Why?

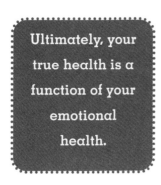

Ultimately, your true health is a function of your emotional health.

Everything you and I do, we do in the pursuit of happiness. Happiness is the state in which your most dominant desire is being met. So I'm writing this book because Mike Lipkin's happiness is a function of exciting as many people as possible into living at their personal best. Mike Lipkin really, really wants the feelings of contribution, fulfillment and connection that come with exciting as many people as possible into living at their personal best. Thank God, after almost half a century on the planet, I've discovered what makes me happy. I've discovered how to achieve my happiness. And I've discovered I'm willing to endure whatever it takes to get to my happy state.

How about you? What's your most dominant desire that needs to be met? What's the best way for you to achieve your most dominant desire? What are the benefits to others and to yourself if you meet this desire? Is it empowering or destructive?

I know that my dominant desire is the right one because so many people benefit from it. Think about it: Life doesn't get better than consistently being your personal best. So I'm thrilled to help people become their personal best. They are thrilled by it as well. I want what they want. They want what I want. And

My personal call to action: I _____

so I'm building alliances with everyone around me in pursuit of my personal happiness. It's a beautiful thing.

Ultimately, your true health is a function of your emotional health. Even if you're physically well, if you're not in a state of "emotional homeostasis", you'll feel miserable. Emotional homeostasis is when you've achieved the right balance of feelings to create internal stability. It's when you feel that all is right with your world. That's how I feel right now. Like you, I have many unresolved issues in my life. I have people who are against me. I have crises swirling around me. I have competitors out to steal my lunch. I have angst and self-doubts. But all of that simply fuels my happiness because it helps me achieve the state of personal best for myself and the people I serve.

> I know that sometimes I'll find myself in a difficult place, and I know that sometimes in a difficult place I'll find myself. That's called life.

Of all the things I'll share with you in this book, this is the truest for me: My sanity depends directly on my emotional homeostasis. If I lose my emotional balance, I lose my internal stability—then I come apart. It's happened before, and I never want it to happen again. That's why I'm constantly conscious of the range of emotions I'm experiencing. Without the right balance of up and down feelings, my emotional homeostasis cannot hold.

I need to experience the up feelings at least 80 percent of the time. I want to live my life with a spirit of zest and celebration. That's who I am: a merchant of positivity and passion. I cannot sell what I do not practice. I have to live my message in order to be authentic, so up feelings are my real narcotic. I'm addicted to the positive emotions I'm about to outline for you. I don't need to ingest anything to get high. I just need to be able to manufacture the right moods to stay at the right altitude.

I accept that three to four hours of my day may be spent in a negative state. A world without negative states is called Disneyworld—it's not real. So I know that sometimes I'll find myself in a difficult place, and I know that sometimes in a difficult place I'll find myself. That's called life. Sometimes it's even desirable. Just as the resistance on my cross-trainer builds physical muscle, down times build emotional muscle. "Tall trees do not grow with ease; the stronger the wind, the stronger the trees."

However, I also know that if I'm spending more than three or four hours a day in a down mood, I'm losing my mojo. That's my signal to take action to turn myself

My personal call to action: I _____

around before my down state becomes chronic. As someone who spent over a year in clinical depression, I know how easy it is to go into an emotional nosedive. What's more, once you go into that nosedive, it gets progressively harder to pull out of it.

I now see my down states as shadows to my up states. I know that I cannot have one without the other—one defines the other. So just as you can't have a vacation without having work, you can't savor the sweet without the bitter. The challenge is to continually heed the signals that down states send.

Here is the range of emotional signals I experience on any given day in pursuit of happiness, together with the messages they send me. As you'll see, not all of them are pleasurable, but that's called life. Think about your range.

Excitement	A sharp, highly pleasurable anticipation of events that will thrill me. It means I'm turned on and at my best.
Gratitude	A deep appreciation for the life I'm living. It means I truly value my gifts.
Engagement	A conviction that I'm playing full out at a game I'm born to play. It means I'm focused on being my Personal Best.
Love	A passion for what I do and who I'm doing it with. It means I'm receiving and radiating a powerful energy.
Connection	A state of interdependence with the hundreds of people who are part of my network and beyond. It means I'm fulfilling my mission as an agent of excitement.
Fascination	Being spellbound by the world and the people around me. It means I'm being what I'm telling others to be: hyper-sensitive to the wonders of life.
Curiosity	A desire to find out more about so many things that interest me every day. It means I'm sustaining my inquisitiveness and hunger for knowledge.
Vitality	A highly conditioned state of health and fitness that helps me live at my Personal Best. It means I'm operating at maximum capacity—on the Cusp of change, where I want to be as often as I can.
Pride	A delight in what I've achieved and the people I've impacted. It means I'm celebrating what I've done, who I am and how far I've come.

My personal call to action: I _____

Power	A belief that I can move mountains, part seas and change my world—one person at a time. It means I'm just crazy enough to stand in front of five thousand people at a time and motivate them to move mountains, part seas and change their worlds.
Growth	A sense that every day I'm expanding my capacity to inspire and motivate others. It means that every day, in some small way, I'm getting better and better.
Admiration	Awe and respect for people at all levels who have become models of what's possible through their innovation and inspiration. It means I'm finding multiple mentors to show me the way forward.
Adventure	A constant adrenaline rush that comes from doing something for the first time—over and over again. It means I'm living every day like it's my entire life in miniature.
Restlessness	An uneasy feeling that I could be doing more to be worthy of my gifts. It means that I need to shift gears and kick it up a notch.
Anxiety	A fear that somebody or something somewhere will disrupt my success and happiness. It means that I need to be aware of the dangers ahead while focusing on why I'll continue to grow and prosper. It also means I'm normal.
Anger	Dissatisfaction with my performance or the performance of others. It means I need to either raise my own game and help others do the same. Or I need to change the way I'm perceiving the situation to find a positive message.
Overwhelm	A fatigue brought on by trying to do too much too often. It means I need to give myself time-out to recharge and recover. It also means I may need to focus on fewer things.
Disappointment	The sting of being let down by others or losing an assignment. It means that I still care deeply about so many things. It also means that I trust others to always deliver. Of all my "down" emotions, this is the one I value the most. It means the fire is still burning bright. It means I'm not cynical or pessimistic. I always expect the best, even when things are at their worst.
Nervousness	A state of uncertainty that sometimes afflicts me before a presentation or meeting. It's a flash of self-doubt that vaccinates me against complacency. It means that I either have to improve my preparation or I have to improve my perception of the situation. Sometimes, just changing the way I view a challenge changes the challenge.

My personal call to action: I _____

Surprise	The shock, both good and bad, associated with events that are unexpected. It means that life has an infinite ability to shake, rattle and roll my beliefs around. It also means that I'm always being opened up to new possibilities.
Confusion	The inability to understand what led to a negative or unsatisfactory result, combined with having no idea what to do next. It means I'm about to have a breakthrough. I've learned what doesn't work but I don't yet know what does. I know the solution will present itself when it's ready—it always does.
Isolation	A feeling of aloneness in my work, as though it's me versus the rest of the world. It means I need to call, talk or meet with another human being. It's called perspective.
Self-Pity	Being miserable because I think I've been treated unfairly. It means I need to change the way I'm viewing my experience so I can find the lessons learnt. Losing means learning.
Rejection	A feeling of being inferior because I've failed to win the approval of others. It means that I have to maintain my own self-esteem by understanding that others are not rejecting me personally. They're simply not accepting my message or the service I've offered them. It means I have to change the way I engage them or I have to change the people with whom I'm engaging. Rejection is simply an invitation to try again with something else or someone else.
Embarrassment	A feeling of looking stupid in the eyes of others. It means that I'm probably "catastrophizing" by seeing things as far worse than others saw it. I've discovered that people are far more understanding than we think they are. I've learned that every now and then, a little screw-up is a good thing. It's called staying humble.

I know that as you read through the range of emotions you recognized that you experience many of them as well. It's true—you do. In my seminars, when I ask delegates to share their range of emotions with each other, the above twenty-five emotions almost always come up. So be aware of them. Understand what they mean to you. And train yourself to spend at least 80 percent of your time in an up-state.

▶ Remember, the state you're in communicates more than any words you can say. Feelings have frequencies. Make sure yours are humming at the highest levels.

My personal call to action: I _____

Love Change or Change What You Love.

If you're alive, you have to change. But the only way to truly change is to love change or to change what you love. It's always personal.

Change: to make the form, nature or content of something different from what it is or from what it would be if left alone; to transform or convert; to become altered or modified; variety or novelty; the passing from one place, state, form or phase to another; fresh set of clothing.

~ Webster's Dictionary

T'S TIME TO REVISIT THE RAISON D'ÊTRE OF THIS BOOK: TO HELP YOU become a Keeper of The Flame who inspires others to consistently play at their personal best. In other words, my mission is to help you thrive on change in such a way that you make it easier for the people around you to do the same.

That means I have to help you not just to understand but also to internalize the change around you. Climatically, socially, economically, technologically, culturally, professionally—we're constantly passing from one place, state, form or phase into another. Whether we're conscious of it or not, we're all being altered and modified every single day.

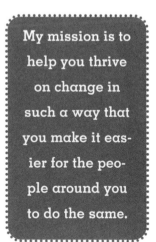

My mission is to help you thrive on change in such a way that you make it easier for the people around you to do the same.

There is a chasm of difference between being conscious versus being unconscious of change. If you're conscious of the change around you, you tend to see things that others don't see. You discern distinctions that elude others. You're more likely to succeed because you're not flying blind. You know what's going on around you, so you can adjust your actions accordingly.

My personal call to action: I _____

71

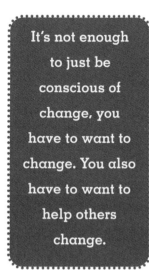

It's not enough to just be conscious of change, you have to want to change. You also have to want to help others change.

The vast majority of people with whom I work are not conscious of the change around them. They're too entrenched in their own problems. They're so busy doing that they're not watching. They look at opportunities and see only problems. Or they look at the problems but don't see them until the problems blindside them. They choose not to look at what they don't want to see. No one can awaken a man who is pretending to sleep.

But it's not enough to just be conscious of change, you have to want to change. You also have to want to help others change. We all have to become change agents, whether we find it easy or not. It's not about what's easy, it's about doing what has to be done when it has to be done.

I work with many smart people who are conscious of change. They see the future coming, but they don't take action. Either they don't think they'll be rewarded enough or they think it's too much effort, or they're immobilized by fear, or they simply believe it's not their job. So they just watch, waiting for someone else to do something. And you know what? Someone always does.

Have you noticed that when the crisis becomes severe enough, the right person always comes along to save the day? That day may be postponed and it may be more painful than it needed to be, but the story of humankind is that a hero always emerges in response to a need that is great enough. So who are you, the watcher or the doer? Are you standing on the sidelines, quarterbacking on Monday morning? Or are you in the arena, daring to make an impact?

All around me, I see people struggling with the deluge of information that descends on us every day. They scramble from one unwelcome surprise to another. "Why me?" has become their constant lament and blame is their constant refuge. They feel that control has been ripped away from them, and been replaced with confusion and chaos. Their sense of being overwhelmed has become chronic. And it's made worse by the unease they sense in others.

Change can be an affliction if you look it with the wrong attitude. The author of *The Irritable Male Syndrome*, psychotherapist Jed Diamond, studied data from more than six thousand men. He found that an alarming 46 percent said they were often or almost always stressed, 40 percent were often or almost always irritable, and 45 percent were often or almost always frustrated.

My personal call to action: I _____

How much time do you feel stressed, irritated or frustrated? Anything over 20 percent of the time means that you're struggling with change. What's more, it's only going to get worse. Stress, irritation and frustration are all emotions manufactured from within, because people misinterpret the meaning of what's going on around them. They see promises as perils, friends as foes and gaps as traps.

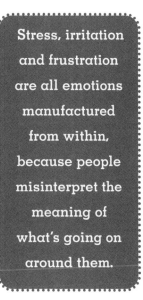

Stress, irritation and frustration are all emotions manufactured from within, because people misinterpret the meaning of what's going on around them.

If your life is anything like mine, change is accelerating and magnifying daily. If you let it, change can make your life a lot more uncomfortable. But if you pursue the path of Keeper of The Flame, it can enrich your life beyond imagination. Very few people understand this simple point. I call them the one-percenters, because that's the percentage of people I research who are true change masters. They understand that change always happens for the better. Yes, always. I say that because nothing is anything but thinking that makes it so. Once change has transformed something, it ain't going back to the way it used to be. So train yourself to see why the new way is the better way, then see how you can make it even better. This skill alone will help you become a Keeper of The Flame.

Although we're recovering from the post-9/11 low, only 23 percent of Canadians tell us that they're attracted to uncertainty and complexity. Thirty-nine percent are stuck in neutral, hanging on to the status quo. A whopping 38 percent tell us that they're averse to uncertainty and complexity. They go about their business with extreme caution. Risk and novelty are hazards to be avoided. They don't venture out of their DWA—designated walking area.

Only 32 percent of Canadians tell us that they're committed to idealism and individualism. This means that less than a third feel strongly about major issues, want to make a difference and have the confidence to take action. Forty percent are on the fence, waiting for someone else to effect change. Twenty-eight percent feel excluded from the promises of life; they seek safety in conformity and anonymity.

Where are you on the change-mastery spectrum? On a scale of 1 to 10, if 1 is a stubborn change resister and 10 is the go-to-change champion, what's your score? If you're not at least a 9, you cannot be a Keeper of The Flame. Unless change is a highly desirable state for you, some part of you will always resist it. In these uncompromising, brutally competitive, blink-and-you'll-miss-it times, it's

My personal call to action: I _____

Fear isn't the great motivator – love and excitement are.

an all-or-nothing deal: Love change or die. Not "accept change." Not "tolerate change." Not "adapt to change." *Love change*. Head and heart will always beat head alone.

So, love change or die. What if you were given that choice—for real? What if it wasn't merely a corporate cliché? What if you knew your life would end very soon—for real? Could you love change? *Fast Company* magazine (May 2005) offers scientifically studied odds on people's ability to change: nine to one. *That's nine to one against you.*

For any human being, a heart attack has to be the ultimate wake-up call. It's a cataclysmic physical signal that a vital part of the body is very, very sick. For people who survive a heart attack and undergo bypass surgery to repair the diseased organ, you would imagine that the message would be even more devastating. You might also imagine that the patient would do whatever it takes to change his lifestyle to prevent similar attacks in the future. Not so. According to Dr. Edward Miller, dean of the medical school and CEO of the hospital at Johns Hopkins University, "If you look at people after coronary-artery bypass grafting two years later, 90 percent of them have not changed their lifestyle. Even though they know they have a very bad disease and they know they should change their lifestyle, for whatever reason, they can't." Makes you think, doesn't it?

Even in the face of such an undeniable call for change, people's fear of change overwhelms their instinct for self-preservation. In fact, such crises may drive people into even deeper change-resistance because their new, highly negative reality compels them to seek the familiarity of what they know—even if what they know will kill them. So what's the moral of the story? Change before you're forced to change. Change before most people even think you need to change. Change by consciously assigning an empowering meaning to change that overwhelms the stress attached to it. Fear isn't the great motivator—love and excitement are.

Fast Company quotes John Kotter, a Harvard Business School professor who has studied dozens of organizations in the midst of upheaval: "The central issue is never strategy, structure, culture or systems. The core of the matter is always about changing the behavior of people. Behavior change happens mostly by speaking to people's feelings. In highly successful change efforts, people find ways to help others see the problems or solutions in ways that influence emotions, not just thought."

My personal call to action: I _____

Kotter believes in the importance of "short-term wins" for companies, meaning "victories that nourish faith in the change effort, emotionally reward the hard workers, keep the critics at bay, and build momentum. Without sufficient wins that are visible, timely, unambiguous, and meaningful to others, change efforts invariably run into serious problems."

Feelings come first; change follows.

That's why, as you may have noticed, this entire book is written in a way that provides you with an emotional lift. Over the past fifteen years I've witnessed the impact of powerful emotions on people's motivation to change. Feelings come first; change follows. Dr. Michael Merzenich, a professor at the University of California at San Francisco, says that the brain's ability to change—its "plasticity"—is lifelong. So we can continue to learn new things throughout our lives, provided we're emotionally turned on.

I'll share an extraordinary story of emotional transformation with you. At the beginning of 2004 I was asked to coach a management team from one of the world's largest pharmaceutical companies. This was a new team, assembled to launch a new drug that had just been cleared by federal regulators. While most of the team was hugely excited about the launch, one of its central members—a woman who was the acknowledged authority on and co-developer of the drug— was continually dismissive of the team's efforts to craft a business plan that would turn the drug into a blockbuster. No option appeared acceptable to her. Furthermore, she made it awkward for any of the team members to work with her. It seemed that she was highly effective in the more low-key environment of the laboratory, working with other white-coated technicians, but in the rah-rah world of marketing and sales she was clearly uncomfortable.

During my one-on-one session with her (a key component of my coaching program) I asked her gently why she appeared to be negatively disposed toward the team's efforts. After some probing she revealed that she had grown up in a communist Eastern European country. There, she told me, any kind of emotional display was discouraged. She added that in an environment where children were encouraged to spy on their parents, trust was a commodity that was also in scarce supply. Even though she had lived in America for over a decade, she still found it difficult to embrace its open, extrovert culture.

At the same time, this woman was profoundly committed to her work. A brilliant young scientist, she was massively grateful for the opportunity to make a life-

My personal call to action: I _____

changing difference to the lives of thousands of people. Tears came to her eyes when she described her work over the previous four years.

First, I applied a mild mental shock by pointing out that her current hard-to-deal-with attitude was putting the entire future of the drug at risk. I overlaid that insight with the impact that such a failure would have on the entire team. I highlighted how much the rest of the team needed and respected her. I sensitized her to the fact that after ten years it was time to let go of the mindset and baggage that were weighing her down. I boosted her self-esteem by reminding her of her presence, her intellect and her humble dignity. I also reminded her that she was now an American living in America—with all the rights and expectations that came with her new nationality. I asked her to change because of the enormous energy such a change would unleash. I told her that she had to change, because the alternative would be to submit to an outdated paradigm from an obsolete place and a long, long time ago. I left her with a simple message: "It's your call, but you'd better make it soon. You should have made it a long time ago and you're running out of time."

The result was riveting. It didn't take her a year to change; it didn't take her a month or even a week. It took her two hours, the time between our conversation and her next team meeting. She got it. And while she didn't become an instant cheerleader for the team, she collaborated with warmth and openness from that moment on. Today she's considered a star within the company. She has also just got married. I've seen her twice since our chat. We smile, we embrace, we move on. She can do it. You can do it. Together, we all can do it.

Aydin Olcum is a master tailor from Turkey who emigrated to Knoxville, Tennessee, to work for high-end custom suit-maker John H. Daniel. He sums up the mandate for change as follows: "It's hard to leave home. But now the world has changed. You're not supposed to live where you're born. You're supposed to live where you can feed your family" (*Wall Street Journal*, April 12, 2005). Olcum may have been talking about a physical move, but his insights also apply to the journey we all must make to the psychological domain where we can feed our families very well.

My personal call to action: I _____

The Nine Life-Transforming Trends

The nine Life-Transforming Trends on the Cusp of change are the forces that have an impact on every molecule of your success – in the workplace, at home, and beyond.

SINCE 1985 ENVIRONICS HAS POLLED HUNDREDS OF THOUSANDS OF AMERICANS and Canadians. Since 1993 I have personally spoken to more than half a million people in the U.S. and Canada. Every year I conduct more than thirty focus groups across North America and deliver more than 150 motivational talks and seminars. In writing this book we read over a thousand newspapers and two hundred magazines and spent countless hours Googling social evolution in 2005 and beyond. All in search of the trends shaping the ways we live, work and play.

In his book *The Alchemist*, Paulo Coelho talks about the importance of recognizing "omens." These are the signs and events around us that signify a future development that could strongly affect our lives and the lives of our communities. People who are alert to the omens take action before others do. They enjoy the rewards that others don't. They also have a capacity to make the world better for others, if they're driven by the right motivation. How about you? Are you a reader and recognizer of omens? What's your track record on anticipating the future? Are you usually a heartbeat ahead or a heartbreak too late?

The omens are all around you. They're looking at you, touching you, talking to you, inviting you to take action. That's why I'm writing this book. All the omens that Environics and I are reading point to a greater appetite for researched motivation and inspiration. There is a growing desire for the tools and techniques required to construct a compelling future in the face of massive challenges. More and more people are acknowledging their need for coaching and guidance in the art of "successful living." You're living proof of this omen. What's more, there's a

My personal call to action: I _____

fifty-fifty chance that this is the first book of this nature that you've read. This thrills me: half of my readers buy this book because they've heard me speak and they want to find out more about my message. They're not readers—until they open my books. Then they embrace the learning like a long-lost family member.

I make a living reading the omens. I'm a twenty-first-century reader of the bones. But you have the skill too. It's called intuition—that little voice that tells you what to do before you have proof or evidence that it is the right thing to do. Learn to listen to your intuition. Grow it. Act on it. In fact, think right now of some trends that are transforming your world and write down at least five. In my workshops, when I ask people to do this exercise, they struggle. They can identify a couple of the obvious vectors, but they haven't thought beyond the obvious. Here's a Lipkinism:

 Just thinking about the omens will help you see them. Thinking about something sensitizes you to it. Thinking about something changes your personal frequency, so you pick up more messages. Thinking about something also attracts it to you. That's why successful people are, first and foremost, success thinkers.

Here's what we've seen as a result of our thinking: Nine Life-Transforming Trends will have a massive impact on your "success-ability" over the next two years. These are the forces you need to harness to your cause if you aspire to being a Keeper of The Flame. Like gravity, they're working on us all. Irrespective of your calling, you'll recognize these trends as major influences on your well-being and progress. You'll also notice that they're all interrelated—sometimes obviously and sometimes weirdly. Specifically they are:

1. **The Intensification of Everything**
2. **The Activity Frenzy**
3. **Winner Takes All**
4. **Autonomy Rules**
5. **Truth and Transparency**
6. **The New Uncertainty**
7. **The Return of Faith and Optimism**
8. **Global Citizenship**
9. **Engage or Get Lost**

Let's explore them one by one.

My personal call to action: I _____

The Intensification of Everything: Burn, Baby, Burn!

Intense: existing or occurring in a high or extreme degree; acute,
strong or vehement as sensations or feelings; very great, keen, severe.
Intensity: concentration of activity or thought.
~ Webster's Dictionary

If you're standing in the middle of the road, you'll get run over. Bland, ordinary, mild, average, plain, standard, acceptable, expected, conventional, usual and common just don't cut it any more. "Same old same old" will kill you.

We're numb. We're fatigued. We're overwhelmed. We're cynical. We're hardened. We're frustrated. We're attention challenged. We're anxious. We're blasé. We've heard it all before. So pass the wasabi, hand me the chilies, bring on the curry powder, sprinkle the coriander—spice it up! If you want me to hear, crank up the volume. Give me some shock, dazzle and awe.

Extra-strength is the new regular. It's the triple shot latte, Dentyne Fire, guarana-laced beer, caffeine-charged Red Bull, the 340-horsepower 5.7-liter V-8 Hemi engine, the 60GB iPod, eight-hour Tylenol, the eat-the-roadkill *Fear Factor*, *Lords of Dogtown*, *The L Word*, the extreme makeover, the all-you-can-see safari. It's anything-you-want-to-know-in-0.00001-seconds from Google. It's any-computer-you-want-made-in-forty-eight-hours from Dell. It's the breathtaking ease and convenience of iTunes. It's the iconoclastic artistry of Cirque du Soleil. It's the superhuman stamina of Lance Armstrong. It's the feel-it-in-the-solar-plexus punch of *Million Dollar Baby*. It's the scenes of carnage from Iraq. It's the Sex Bomb from Lush. It's the phenomenon of Harry Potter. It's the steaminess of *Desperate Housewives*. It's the how-did-they-do-that? of *The Incredibles*. It's the you-can-play-god genius of *SimCity 4*. It's the how-do-they-always-make-it-taste-so-good? glazed cinnamon roll at Tim Hortons. It's perfectly white teeth in just two weeks from Crest.

Extra-strength is the new regular.

In the vocabulary of Canada's Wonderland, welcome to the age of the Sledge Hammer, the Psyclone, the Shockwave, the Vortex, the Dragon Fire, the Thunder Run, the Jet Scream and the Xtreme Skyflyer. The intensity quotient of every life experience has been ramped up to the next level. So either you grab my attention and my affection with maximum flair and firepower or you'll remain an interruption. Supersize your impact—not just once but over and over again.

My personal call to action: I _____

79

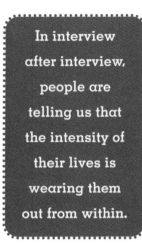

> In interview after interview, people are telling us that the intensity of their lives is wearing them out from within.

Even Hollywood is being penalized by the intensification trend. The 2005 summer box office takings were down 11 percent compared to 2004, according to *The Globe and Mail* (August 25, 2005). Marc Shmuger, vice-chairman of Universal Pictures, states, "People [in Hollywood] are just beginning to wake up to the fact that what used to pass as summer excitement isn't that exciting or that entertaining any more. This is vividly clear in terms of the other choices that consumers have." Yup, even Hollywood is struggling to get through the thick skin of apathy brought on by just about everything else. When the real world becomes more intense than the celluloid one, life can be either a dramatic adventure or a demoralizing grind.

In interview after interview, people are telling us that the intensity of their lives is wearing them out from within. It's the infinite need for speed, the penalties for failure, the constant demand for added value, the off-shoring specter of China and India, the threat of the next merger, the Wal-Mart factor, the blood-soaked insanity of al-Qaeda, the obsession with growth in a mature market, the bruised psyches of our customers and colleagues, the ever-present threat of personal obsolescence. It's our aging bodies in a brave new world, our wounded souls in the-fight-for-every-dollar commercial reality, our sleep-deprived minds in a 24/7 existence, the escalating angst caused by our lives of not-so-quiet desperation.

In such intense conditions, cruise control is not an option. Inertia is not a place where any of us can spend time. Complacency is a luxury no one can afford. Every encounter is make or break. Feelings are running high all the time. You don't know what the person in front of you has just been through. What you do know is that she's been through a lot. "We are middle-aged and we are tired" is the lament of the North American worker. So kick it up a notch! Find a way to break through without burning out.

Here's another Lipkinism:

 " Your clients and colleagues may forgive you for an honest mistake, but they won't forgive you for lack of intensity. Your future commercial success will be a direct function of your ability to sustain a visibly intense commitment to your stakeholders' success.

My personal call to action: I _____

Think about what irks you most about your problem stakeholders in the workplace or at home. Is it not a suspicion that they're not fully committed to your well-being? Is it not a sense that they may be cruising on your dime or complacent about what they've already done for you?

So ask yourself how you can most forcefully channel your intensity. Ask yourself how you can most colorfully merchandise your intensity to the people around you. Ask yourself how your personal intensity compares with your competitors'. And, by the way, style is less important than intensity. Some of the most intense people I know are also the most understated. But they're the people that other people never have to worry about. They're always concentrating on adding value to everyone around them.

Intensity is not always a guarantee of success, but lack of intensity is always a guarantee of failure. As John Schwartz writes in *The New York Times* (December 26, 2004): "Increasingly America is the attention-deficit nation, moving to ever sharper sound bites and smaller quanta of meaning. Citizens live in a blizzard of information without wisdom, content without context, and are being pulled a million ways by tech toys and a zillion cable channels and the multitudinous blogs. A white noise of data is the ambient soundtrack to our lives." Schwartz goes on to quote David Shenk, the author of *Data Smog: Surviving the Information Glut*: "I'm afraid that the increasing distraction virtually guarantees that the culture of shock will prevail." And shock leads to exhaustion, which can lead to numbness and tuning out. That is why, as we go forward, one of the most valuable commodities in a changing world will be the opposite of distraction—attention.

Schwartz and Shenk call it shock: the magic laser that cuts through the thicket of stimuli competing for our attention at any moment. I call it intensity. I hope you've felt some of my intensity in this book. Specifically, I hope you've felt my intense commitment to your success. I want you to succeed not just because I'm striving to be a Keeper of The Flame but also because I need your success story to validate my work. If you don't succeed, I don't succeed.

I want to give the last word on this trend to Jerry Seinfeld. As reported in *The Wall Street Journal* (May 19, 2004), Seinfeld states, "There is no such thing as an attention span. There is only the quality of what you're viewing. This whole idea of an attention span is, I think, a misnomer. People have infinite attention if you're entertaining them." By the same token, I believe that if you're delivering an intense performance in any discipline, people have infinite attention. People recognize it, they reward it and they want more of it—especially since it's so rare.

My personal call to action: I _____

81

Intensity and boredom are mutually exclusive. Bring on the intensity—and watch other people's interest in you soar.

The Activity Frenzy: I Need to Do So Much More with So Much Less

I am woman. I am invincible. I am tired.
~ mantra of the supermom

Imagine you're in front of a buffet of the most delicious food. You're starving, but you have only a few minutes to partake of your feast. You have to make your choice and eat your food before your time's up. Just as you start loading your plate, the time is shortened. So you pile on the food as fast as you can and wolf it down without even stopping to sit down. The whistle goes just as you take your last swallow. You made it, you've finished. But you feel the beginnings of the indigestion and heartburn that come with eating like an animal. You feel the tension that comes with having just barely beaten the bell. You're full, but you're not satisfied. What's more, despite the quality of the food, you're not looking forward to your next meal.

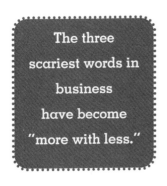

The three scariest words in business have become "more with less."

That's the new reality. So many opportunities, so little time. So many windows opening and shutting so quickly. So many competitors who could eat our lunch so quickly. So many bosses, colleagues, customers, friends and relatives who want so much from us so much of the time. So many races we have to win, people we have to please, tools we have to use, places we have to go. So many dangers that could get to us, so many risks that could trip us up, so many mistakes that could be made—so many failures that could happen. So many potential disappointments. So many shocks ahead. So much noise, so much distraction, so many interruptions. Where are we running? Why are we running? We don't know—we're too busy trying to keep up with everyone else. We just pick up the pace, we put the pedal to the metal and hope that we don't hit the wall.

The three scariest words in business have become "more with less." In every company, in every category, people are being ordered to raise their productivity. Good enough isn't good enough any more. In fact, to quote business guru Jim

My personal call to action: I _____

Collins, "Good is the enemy of great." Instead we're continually being asked to ratchet up our performance to the next level—whatever that is.

We're all being swept away by the "hurry-cane." Faster, faster. Better, better. Higher, higher. Now, now. And we're being asked to enhance our personal ROS—return on salary—with fewer and fewer resources. In the name of streamlining, right-sizing, rationalizing, economizing and reorganizing, fewer and fewer people are doing more and more. Every day the pressure level rises while the support level drops.

In 2004 Americans worked 200 hours a year more than in 1973—that's five work-weeks. That means less time for personal activities that yield satisfaction and well-being, and all this work appears to be diverting our minds from higher, more spiritual issues. In 1992 the proportion of Americans saying that it was becoming more important to them "to have a more intense and more spiritual inner life" was 52 percent. By 2004 that proportion had dropped 14 points to 38 percent. Diminishing interest in what we might call mindfulness and introspection is a growing and dangerous trend. Why?

Because in addition to all this activity we're also being asked to bring our own perspective to every challenge. It's not enough just to follow orders. It's not enough just to know the facts. It's not enough just to comply with performance requirements. In the face of instant change and unprecedented crises, employees at all levels are being challenged to offer their own solutions to problems that no one else has even anticipated. Customers and clients are demanding on-the-spot, individualized responses to their issues.

All of us have to become trusted advisers to the stakeholders around us. We're all becoming sources of empowerment for others. Like it or not, the people in both your professional and social circles are increasingly dependent on your contribution, just as you are on theirs. It's a new, higher interdependence. If you contribute your share, you build your personal value to others. If you don't, you slip into isolation and irrelevance.

Environics Social Values research indicates that 21 percent of Canadians were located in the "personal development" quadrant at the end of 2001. These are the people who focus on personal growth. They seek fulfillment through a lifestyle that combines learning, experimentation and personal health. By the end of 2004, 28 percent of Canadians found themselves in this quadrant—an increase of over 33 percent.

My personal call to action: I _____

Your job is to make working with you the next best thing to play.

It's clear that the people who make it happen have grasped the new reality: In a more-with-less world you have to become more, through self-growth and personal enhancement at every level. You have to become more so that you can help others become more. You cannot give what you do not have. If you are not in personal-growth mode, you cannot help others grow. A stalled engine cannot move anything.

There's also a powerful collective yearning for a simpler, less harried way of life. More and more Canadians are telling us that they are prepared to "reprioritize money" in order to change their lifestyle—they want to make money less important. People who feel very strongly on this issue aspire to a life centered more on emotion, intuition and meaningful communication with others. They also want work to have less priority in their lives.

"Reprioritizing money" has recorded the single biggest growth of the 105 social trends tracked by Environics: 39 percent from 2001 to 2004. The harder we have to work and the more we have to do, the more we want to re-engineer our lives so we don't have to. So remember, the majority of people with whom you work would rather be doing something else. They're working because they have to, not because they want to. Your job is to make working with you the next best thing to play.

And guess what? The social trend with the second-biggest growth over 2001–2004 is "neo-romanticism," which is defined as "wanting to escape the daily routine through imagination and dreams, mystery and romanticism." The rational takes second place to intuition, discovery and amazement. This trend has grown by 38 percent over the 2001–2004 period. Walter Mitty is alive and well and living in all of us. So celebrate the dream within you. Acknowledge the dream within others, and help them live it. Keepers of The Flame are also dream catchers.

The pressure is relentless. As organizations flatten we're all being asked to assume wider responsibility. The job description changes by the day, along with the customers and the markets we serve. We're all suffering from role overload. We're being asked to perform so many functions that our personal identity is unraveling.

To quote *The Wall Street Journal* (August 10, 2005), "Never have there been more slow-burn mental torments, all of which do a number on your head. The

My personal call to action: I _____

line between work and play has become so blurred that work isn't just work, it's the anticipation of work while you play. According to a survey conducted in the fall of 2004 by the Families and Work Institute, 42 percent of Americans do some form of work while on vacation, while only 14 percent of Americans take a vacation of two weeks or more. It seems the more you work, the less secure you feel about it."

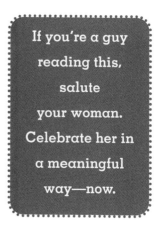

If you're a guy reading this, salute your woman. Celebrate her in a meaningful way—now.

And here's my message to the men reading these words: You have a far lighter load to carry than women. In almost all the focus groups I conduct, even the SNAGs ("sensitive new-age guys") acknowledge that their wife or female partner carries a far heavier domestic load than they do. It's usually the woman who has primary responsibility for the well-being of the children and the home. If you're a woman managing a job, a home and a family, I salute you. Take a bow—you're amazing. Never underestimate the significance of how far you've come to get where you are.

If you're a guy reading this, salute your woman. Celebrate her in a meaningful way—now. The Environics research says that she is feeling more overwhelmed and anxious than ever before. She's looking for relief, she's looking for an escape, she's looking for a solution. Help her find one by being there for her. Without her, you wouldn't function. All our research says that men who lose their partners are far more susceptible to mental and emotional breakdown than their female counterparts. While the data tell us that women are twice as likely to feel depressed than men, it also tells us that men are twice as likely to abuse alcohol or other drugs than women. Women acknowledge their angst; men hide from it.

Another area in which women are diverging from men is in their embrace of values associated with inwardness, reflection and self-expression. Despite their activity-packed lives, American women are expressing a growing desire to exercise creativity in their lives. They also say that they would like to better understand the "mysterious forces" in their lives and act upon them. Both these trends indicate a personal search for meaning and fulfillment among women that is not tied to any particular spiritual or social practice. American men show none of this introspective impulse. Maybe that's why women are increasingly demonstrating superiority in dealing with ambiguous situations where a direction or solution is not immediately apparent.

My personal call to action: I _____

"Help me prioritize my workload" is the single most frequent request I get.

How many times have you been with someone who seems to mistake motion for progress? They always appear to be so busy and yet seem to achieve so little. They're in "everything is a priority" mode. And when everything is a priority, nothing is a priority. In both my focus groups and motivational sessions, "Help me prioritize my workload" is the single most frequent request I get. And it's about more than just time management. It's about understanding what's truly important—and then understanding how to resolve it in the most effective way.

The bottom line is that you and I need to become prioritizers for the people around us. In the activity frenzy, people major in minor things. They lose sight of the forest for the trees. They don't know when to say no and when to agree. What they desperately want is someone to help them streamline their focus and their energy. What they want is someone who can help them stave off their feeling of being overwhelmed. What they want is someone who can help them feel in control in an out-of-control world. Look around you. I guarantee you that the most successful people in your professional circle are the people who understand that "the main thing is to keep the main thing the main thing." Do you?

When I am being briefed or when I'm consulting with a client, I always ask questions like these: What is the most important outcome we want to achieve? What are the key challenges facing your people? What is their biggest fear? What do they want most? What are the strengths that characterize your best-in-class people? What are the skills that are most likely to help them rise to the challenge of change?

Initially my clients usually struggle with their responses. They're not used to pinpointing the "main things" with clarity and specificity. But very quickly, with the help of a few well-directed prompts, they identify the "game-changers"—the issues that really have an impact on their current reality and future success. Then we can begin the real work on the real issues to get real results.

A.G. Lafley, CEO of Procter & Gamble, the world's largest packaged goods manufacturer, understands the power of simple clarity. As reported in *The Wall Street Journal* (June 1, 2005), he referred to his key operating principles in selling laundry detergent as follows: "The simple principle in life is to find out what she wants and give it to her. It's worked in my marriage for 35 years and it works in laundry. We discovered that women don't care about our technolo-

My personal call to action: I _____

86

gy and they couldn't care less what machine a product is made on. They want to hear that we understand them." That's why Procter & Gamble executives are spending a lot more time these days visiting and talking with their actual customers. Do you pass the "simple clarity" test? Are you directing your colleagues to focus their stretched resources where they're going to get the highest return? Or, like most people, are you being distracted by the swarm of small things bugging you for attention?

Winner Takes All! Darwin Survives

> *Winning is everything. The only ones who remember you*
> *when you come second are your wife and your dog.*
> ~ Damon Hill, 1996 world Formula One champion

Winner's Mindset: *the thrill of competing against the best in the world; a need to be recognized as the best; a love of victory matched by a hatred of defeat; a faith in your ability to outplay anyone, especially when it counts; an understanding that life is a long game in which superior character and conditioning ultimately prevail; a willingness to do whatever it takes to achieve victory; a desire to build a team in which all the members achieve their own win.*

From Toronto to Milwaukee to Dallas to Seattle, Darwinism is getting stronger. Competition is becoming more brutal. Change is cataclysmic. China and India can do it faster and cheaper. Failure can happen in the blink of an eye. The choices are abundant; the differences are tiny. You're either recognized as the best or you're history. If you're not out in front, you'll be trampled into oblivion. Mediocrity is a death sentence—if you don't look like a winner, your prospects will choose someone else who does.

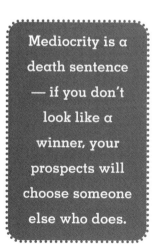

Mediocrity is a death sentence — if you don't look like a winner, your prospects will choose someone else who does.

Winning, like risk and apple pie, has always been part of America. Even greed could be seen as a virtue. In the nineties it seemed that there was so much to go around, anyone could win. Excess ruled. Efficiency was held hostage by fantasy. Money grew on virtual trees. I did well,

My personal call to action: I _____

Learn to love the thrill of competition so you can thrive on it.

and I hope you did too. The rising tide lifted all the ships, as long as their leaks weren't too big.

In 2006 it's a whole new, meaner game, and it's called hardball. Every point counts. Every penny counts. Your most recent win/loss record is the only résumé that means anything. The margin for error is razor-thin—it's all or nothing. Life is reality television, and the chosen apprentice or survivor gets all the spoils. In the amazing race there is one winner—and then there is everyone else.

Here's a key insight: In a marketplace characterized by fierce competition, the odds against success are bigger than in a market populated by fewer rivals. In order to win, you have to either love competition or back yourself strongly against the odds. If you don't have a Winner's Mindset, the odds are gonna get you.

Throughout the United States and Canada, more and more of us do seem to be adopting a winner's mindset. At Environics we track a trend called "penchant for risk," meaning a desire to take risks for the pleasure and emotional thrill of it. It also indicates a willingness to take risks in order to get what you want out of life. In the U.S., the percentage of people who say, "In order to get what I want, I would be prepared to take great risks in life," has risen from 26 percent in 1992 to 40 percent in 2004.

We also offered Americans another statement in this regard: "From time to time, I like to do things that are dangerous or forbidden just for the sake of the risk and the sensation." In 1992, 18 percent of Americans answered in the affirmative. By 2004 that number had risen to 32 percent. Clearly, Americans' appetite for risk is healthy and growing, a sign of symbiosis between social values trends and business trends.

Canadians are a little farther behind. Risk has never been an entrenched feature of the national character, but even that fact is changing steadily. In 2004, 23 percent of Canadians told us that they are strongly attracted to uncertainty and complexity, up from 20 percent in 2001. However, in 2004 there was also a 10 percent decline in the trends "aversion to complexity in life" and a 9 percent decline in "risk aversion."

In the United States, the penchant for risk on a social level reinforces the imperative for risk on a business level. In Canada the business imperative for risk outstrips the social affinity for risk. In focus group after focus group, respondents tell me that the drive for results is a huge source of stress. The top 20 percent,

My personal call to action: I _____

though, understand that this is the new reality—deliver or die. They understand that whatever cannot be avoided must be embraced. If there is one truth you have to take from this book, it's this: Learn to love the thrill of competition so you can thrive on it. All my winning clients have at their core a passion for victory in the face of intense competition.

As an aside, in Canada over 80 percent of what we produce is exported to the U.S. In other words, from an economic standpoint we are joined at the hip. We have to walk in step with our biggest customers and suppliers, and I believe those are the right steps to take.

All the winning clients with whom I work are also great places to work. They get the most out of their people and their people get the most out of themselves. Resources are fully utilized. Potentials are fully realized. Personal growth is the order of the day.

Two iconic companies epitomize this spirit. The first is Procter & Gamble, the largest consumer packaged goods company in the world, with brands like Tide, Crest, Pampers and Gillette. They define one of their core values as follows:

> **Passion for Winning**
> We are determined to be the best at doing what matters most.
> We have a healthy dissatisfaction with the status quo.
> We have a compelling desire to improve and win in the marketplace.

I participated in a recent seminar with leaders from both the Canadian and American operations of Procter & Gamble. This fierce commitment to win, combined with a hatred of losing (their words), was a theme that permeated every presentation. By the end of the presentations I could feel the collective will to win growing in the room. At Procter & Gamble, losing is not an option.

The other iconic company that epitomizes the winning spirit is the Kellogg Company. One of their core "K-Values" is:

> **We Love Success**
> Achieve results and celebrate when we do.
> Help people to be their best by providing coaching and feedback.
> Work with others as a team to accomplish results and win.
> Have a "can-do" attitude and drive to get the job done.
> Make people feel valued and appreciated.
> Make the tough calls.

My personal call to action: I _____

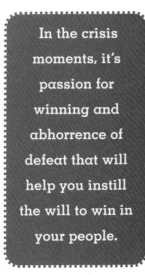

In the crisis moments, it's passion for winning and abhorrence of defeat that will help you instill the will to win in your people.

Having worked with the Kellogg Company, I can tell you that they walk their talk, combining respect for the individual with an obsessive quest for market leadership. Winning doesn't mean surrendering more humane values. In fact, the two synergize with each other. It's a heck of a lot easier to laugh, grow, share, reward and appreciate each other when you're winning.

So where are you on Darwin's scale? What's your personal penchant for risk? Do your customers see you as a winner? How much of a competitor are you? How much do you love to win? How much do you hate to lose? If these questions do not resonate with you at the deepest level, you may not be cut out to be a Keeper of The Flame. In the crisis moments it's passion for winning and abhorrence of defeat that will help you instill the will to win in your people. The will, said Muhammad Ali, is stronger than the skill.

In *The Globe and Mail* (August 11, 2005) Stephen Brunt brutally summed up this trend as follows: "That's human nature, to break the story down to its baseline, to blur the fine points and to divide the planet into winners and losers." Which side of the divide do you stand on? Do you have the mindset of a winner? Do you have the heart of a winner? Are you defining your world in terms that make you a winner? Are you at your personal best when it really counts?

The tougher the game becomes, the more your Winner's Mindset will be tested. Pass the tests, because the rewards are increasing exponentially. Being a loser, feeling like a loser, acting like a loser—sucks. No one can win every time, but the best never allow defeat to make them feel like losers. It's not the result that makes you a loser; it's your interpretation of the result. There are no setbacks, just delayed victories and trials of stamina. Keepers of The Flame never allow their fire to go out.

Autonomy Rules: I'm in Control of My Own Destiny, Y'Hear?

If you haven't the strength to impose your own terms upon life,
you must accept the terms it offers you.
— *T.S. Eliot*

My personal call to action: I _____

Two of the strongest trends we've tracked over the past three years are the need for autonomy and the desire to control one's own destiny. We define "need for autonomy" as the desire to exert as much control as possible over all aspects of daily life. We define "control of destiny" as the desire to escape from the domination of society over daily life, to control all aspects of one's life, even those determined by forces over which we seem to have little control. It's also a tendency to believe that not everything is predetermined, that one can influence the course of events. In Canada, since 2001, both trends have grown by almost 25 percent, a highly significant number in social trend terms.

How about you? I know that need for autonomy and control of destiny are important to you, otherwise you wouldn't have bought this book, never mind got this far. Think about the following five questions:

- How great is your desire to control as much as possible in your life?
- How much control do you believe you have?
- Do you believe that you can influence the course of events that shape your life?
- How are you feeding your need for autonomy?
- How are you asserting your control of destiny?

Your answers to these five questions will be the strongest indicators of your future success or lack of it. So pause here for a minute before you continue. Reread these five questions. Write down your answers, and revisit them at the end of this section.

Here's a fascinating insight: In 1996, 64 percent of Canadians told us that they were living lives of personal development, autonomy and well-being. It was clearly an extraordinary year, with almost two-thirds of Canadians feeling that they were both growing and in control. Near the end of 2001—immediately after 9/11—that figure had dropped to 46 percent, a decline of almost a third. By the end of 2004 it had recovered to 54 percent, up from 2001 but still significantly below the 1996 level. That means almost half of all Canadians currently feel that they're not in charge of their own destiny.

Here's another powerful insight: Americans with high incomes are different from those with lower incomes primarily in their desire to exercise personal control in all aspects of their lives. Americans with lower incomes are more afraid of complexity and they're weaker on personal control. It's not a lack of work ethic

My personal call to action: I _____

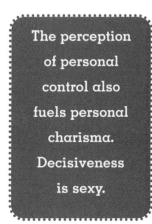

The perception of personal control also fuels personal charisma. Decisiveness is sexy.

or industriousness, but rather a lack of flexibility and aversion to exercising personal autonomy that most differentiate low earners from high earners. Read that sentence again. Based on my qualitative research, it's the same in Canada. More than anything else, it's your belief in yourself and your ability to thrive in the new reality that will determine your success in the workplace.

Americans earning over $80,000 per year are almost 50 percent more likely to believe in their personal control than those earning $20,000 to $40,000. Evidently, self-confidence pays well. From my work with senior leadership and successful entrepreneurs, I can tell you it's not about IQ. It's about the perception of one's ability to prevail in the face of crises and challenges. When it comes to personal success, there is no clearer proof that perception is reality.

The perception of personal control also fuels personal charisma. Decisiveness is sexy. It radiates an aura of certainty. It conveys the impression of knowing where you are going and knowing how to get there. Perception of personal control is usually accompanied by action, when no one else is taking any. So remember this truth: The best thing to do is the right thing to do. The next best thing to do is the wrong thing to do. The worst thing to do is nothing. On the Cusp of change, who knows what's right or wrong anyway?

The year 2005 also brought us the "ubersexual." According to *The National Post* (August 15, 2005) ubersexuals are "the most attractive (not just physically), most dynamic and most compelling men of their generation. They are supremely confident (without being obnoxious), masculine, stylish and committed to uncompromising quality in all areas of life." Ubersexuals have a "masculinity that combines the best of traditional manliness (strength, honour, character) with positive traits traditionally associated with females (nurturing, communicativeness, co-operation)." Yup, gentlemen, the bar for what makes a "real man" has just been raised considerably higher. So you either step up and take control of your masculine destiny or watch all the pleasure accrue to a man who can. "Ouch," I can hear my male readers thinking. I'm sorry, but that's my role—to provide you with the heads-up and the wake-up calls to help you live at your highest level and inspire others to do the same.

Any psychiatrist will tell you that perception of control is a precursor to both

My personal call to action: I _____

mental and physical health. People who feel as if they're influencing events, rather than the other way round, live longer, happier lives. But here's a key Lipkinism, maybe the most important point of the entire book:

> **So many unprecedented events are happening so quickly, with such unpredictability, that all perception of personal control of outside elements is an illusion. You cannot control anything or anyone except yourself. As far as "yourself" is concerned, you are very close to being a supreme commander. Act like it. Control yourself, and the rest of your world will follow.**

Unilever, the company that markets the Dove brand of skincare products, understands the trend toward autonomy. Their iconic "Dove girls" campaign features full-bodied women dressed only in their underwear, with the headline "Real women have real curves." The Dove website welcomes visitors with these words: "For too long, beauty has been defined by narrow, stifling stereotypes. You told us it's time to change all of that. We agree. Because we believe real beauty comes in many shapes, sizes and ages. It is why we started the Campaign for Real Beauty. And why we hope you'll take part." The *New York Times Magazine* (September 5, 2005) describes the success of the campaign:

> Perhaps there is something here that's a backlash against not just the waif-ing of American media culture but also the self-improvement imperative: enough counting carbs, enough lectures from Dr. Phil, enough pressure to learn how to dress well enough for the "Queer Eye" crew and achieve Martha-like aesthetic perfection in bathroom décor. The flip side of "Don't you care enough to do better?" could be "Stop telling me how to live."

From real people to virtual assistants, what's your attitude toward technology? Are you a "digital ignorant" who needs others to print out your e-mail? Are you a digital immigrant who has migrated to the new digital reality and is learning your way in the new world? Or are you a digital native, so comfortable with the new technology that you feel as if you belong there?

We define technological anxiety as "anxiety about the encroachment of technology. Tendency to believe that technology is progressing at the expense of our autonomy and privacy. A concern that new technologies cause more problems than they solve."

My personal call to action: I _____

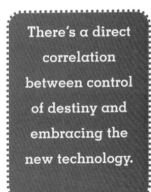

There's a direct correlation between control of destiny and embracing the new technology.

In the U.S., higher-income earners suffer from less than half the technological anxiety that afflicts their less affluent compatriots. From my qualitative research with Canadians at all levels, I see this trend mirrored in Canada.

A little technological anxiety is normal. It's caused by the "technological paradox": Technology's chief aim is to save us time, yet the more technological help we receive, the less time we have. It's a function of time expectations. In the age of Google, even a New York minute is an eternity. This is called time compression—we're packing more and more activities into less and less time.

Get used to it, get over it and take charge of it. There's a direct correlation between control of destiny and embracing the new technology. Being connected, efficient and organized are increasingly important components of personal control. Since 2001 Canadians' approach to the new technology has become increasingly pragmatic. Cell phones, Blackberries, laptops, iPods and the Internet are both accelerators and enhancers of our daily lives.

My Blackberry is my umbilical cord to the world. I love it, need it, sleep with it. My laptop is my digital canvas. It's an ally that's helped me write the four books that drive my entire business. My iPod, together with iTunes, is my constant source of inspiration and recreation. To me as a writer, Google is the ultimate gift, showering me with instant information like manna from a cyber-god. My website, with its video, audio and written content, is my personal manifesto to the world. The ability to talk to thousands of people live and free via webcam has amplified my impact beyond my wildest imaginings.

I'm in love with technology, but I'm not a digital native. However, my assistant, Erica Cerny, is. She's a digital scout helping me navigate my way through the technological forest. If, like me, you're not a digital native, find a scout of your own, or you're going to get lost.

It's not just a digital world you have to learn how to master; it's also a flattened one. It's a faster one, a fluid one. It's a world where hierarchy is a recipe for disaster and heterarchy rules. Yup, you read it right—heterarchy. That's a uniquely Environics term that describes the archetypical shape of a successful enterprise in the new reality.

Heterarchy is a belief that leadership in organizations should be flexible and fluid, that the "leader" shouldn't take control of everything, and that initiatives

My personal call to action: I _____

and leadership should emerge from different individuals as a function of their strengths. It's a belief that teamwork is more effective than autocracy and that the leadership role should be earned. It's also a conviction that everyone bears responsibility for the performance of their business. Everyone is the CEO of their own function, which can evolve daily. Titles are obsolete, job descriptions are just broad guidelines, career paths are pipe dreams. There is no *they*, only *I* and *we*. Mistakes are the currency of learning. Adaptation needs to be instant. The roadmap is an illusion, and so is upward mobility. Growth equals enhanced personal capacity, and promotion is something that you achieve for yourself. But the compass must be true: The end zone must be meaningful and motivational.

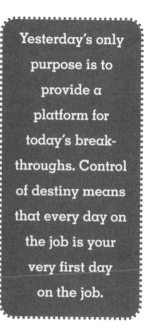

Yesterday's only purpose is to provide a platform for today's breakthroughs. Control of destiny means that every day on the job is your very first day on the job.

Unless you're a sorter on an assembly line, there is no routine any more. Every activity can be upgraded. But it's the person doing the job who needs to figure out "The Better Way." Adaptive leaders offer their people as many opportunities as possible to grow professionally, gain new experiences and express creativity in their work. This means granting more freedom and trust to your colleagues and associates. It also means that you come to work every day with a mindset of fresh possibility. Yesterday's only purpose was to provide a platform for today's breakthroughs. Control of destiny means that every day on the job is your very first day on the job.

Best Buy, the giant Minneapolis-based electronics retailer, is helping its people control their own destiny by rethinking the very concept of work. Under their ROWE (results-oriented work environment) employees can work when and where they like, as long as they get the work done. As reported in *Time* magazine (May 25, 2005), it was expected that by July 2005 half the 3,500 employees at Best Buy's headquarters would already be part of the effort. The freedom, employees say, is changing their lives. They don't know if they work fewer hours, but they are measurably more productive. Says Darrel Owen, a fourteen-year Best Buy veteran, "It takes away everything that you thought was normal." I think that just about sums up the kind of change we should all be going through.

Toronto-based Carlson Wagonlit Travel Canada has also introduced an employee flexibility program that I believe is brilliant: Employees can donate their unused

My personal call to action: I _____

vacation days to colleagues whom they believe might need it more. As *The Globe and Mail* (December 28, 2004) reported, one employee gave a week to a colleague who had a seriously ill child. It's all about choice and delegation of decision making to individuals in a way that fosters teamwork, connectivity and commitment.

One of the strongest social trends tracked by Environics since 2001 is "flexibility of gender identity." This describes a feeling that you have both masculine and feminine sides to your personality. It's also the desire to actively explore and express these different facets of your personality, feeling more feminine at certain times and more masculine at others. This tendency is much stronger among women than men, and the trend rose a whopping 21 percent from 2001 to 2004. Clearly this increase reflects the new reality in which so many women are either living by themselves or performing the role of single parent—for example, it's estimated that over 40 percent of all women in Toronto are single. But it's also a reflection of people's growing desire to live life on their own terms, leaving no possibilities unexplored.

Truth and Transparency: It's About Character – If You Want to Be Trusted, Be True

Transparent: open, frank, candid; easily seen through, recognized or detected; shining through, as light.

Character: the aggregate of features and traits that form the apparent individual nature of some person or thing; moral or ethical quality; qualities of honesty, courage or the like; a significant visual mark or symbol.

Trust: reliance on the integrity, strength, ability of a person or thing; confident expectation of something.

True: the actual state or condition; real, genuine, authentic; reflecting the essential character of something; consistent with a standard; of the right kind, such as it should be; unfailing and sure; honest, honorable, upright.

~ Webster's Dictionary

My personal call to action: I _____

The emperor has no clothes. In fact, the emperor has no empire. The emperor is an ordinary, fallible human who is struggling to come to terms with having to bare it all every day. The emperor is you and me.

I know you've screwed up. Maybe it was a big one, maybe it was a lesser misdemeanor. Maybe you've got over it, or maybe it still rattles you every time you think about it. Maybe the people around you know about it and maybe they don't. But here's my message: If the people around you are going to be affected by your misstep, let them know *now*. Confess your sin, or any other lapse of judgment. *Mea culpa* may be the only Latin words you need to know. The six most important words in the English language are "I admit I made a mistake."

Whether it's an individual or a company, the standards against which we're being compared are darn near impeccable.

In the age of the cell-phone camera, the webcam, Google, highly mobile populations and sophisticated background checks, there is nowhere to hide. E-mail leaves a very traceable digital trail. No matter how many times you press the Delete button, your message will remain on somebody's hard drive somewhere. You may be able to fool some of the people for a very short time, but the truth will come out sooner rather than later. The truth will not set you free if you aren't the source of it. A cover-up will turn into a body bag.

What's more, trust is a one-time deal. People may give it to us at the start of a relationship, but if we lose it, like a pebble thrown into the ocean, it's gone forever. In 2006, integrity is no longer an assumed attribute; it's the first quality that people probe for. In the hiring process or the buying process, the first questions that have to be answered are these: Can this person be trusted? Is this person the real deal? Is she what she professes to be? Will he hold together under fire? Is there true character underneath the skin that will stand the test of time?

Whether it's an individual or a company, the standards against which we're being compared are darn near impeccable. Even a small breach of character or conduct can mean the loss of trust or authority. As a professional speaker I live this reality every time I'm on stage. People listen for consistency, respect, openness, sensitivity and authenticity. One ill-considered phrase

My personal call to action: I _____

can mean the implosion of my entire message. So every time I talk, I play by three cardinal rules:

- Through my words and actions I must enhance the reputation of the person who hired me. During my time on stage I am the custodian of that person's credibility. I have to be an ambassador for that person's character and discretion.

- I am positioned as a role model for my audience. I have to consciously play that role. Everything I do and say is a signal that reinforces or invalidates my status.

- I have to demonstrate how much respect and passion I have for the people in front of me. I can be true to the people I serve only by valuing them as equal partners in the search for a better way.

What's the difference between you and me? What happens if you don't play by the three cardinal rules? I'll tell you what happens—you'll always come up short. You'll always be someone who is regarded with a degree of doubt and concern. You may be admired for your expertise and your intelligence, but the accolade of Keeper of The Flame will elude you.

Character is the theme of this decade.

As nations, both Americans and Canadians are aging. Almost 50 percent of North American workers are over the age of forty. By 2013 it will be closer to 55 percent. But emotionally I think we're getting younger all the time. In fact, the average emotional age of the people to whom I speak is about five years old. What do I mean? People's psyches are fragile. When so many people filter their experiences through layers of fear and angst, even the smallest demonstration of disrespect is perceived as a major affront. People's skins are thin, and they're getting thinner.

A new etiquette is governing our behavior in the workplace. It's an unwritten code of civility that demands we engage everyone around us the way we would like them to engage a member of our family. You and I might be prepared to take some flak, but we would react violently to someone who treated our family members poorly. Remember, everyone you and I encounter is a member of someone else's family. So be firm, be strong, be forthright—but never, ever indulge your mood, whim or temper.

In the light of all this angst, there's a heroic irony—it's easier than ever to be a hero to others. Pay attention to their moods. Understand their whims. Be

My personal call to action: I _____

unfailingly polite. Excel in the everyday interactions and you'll become a hero in their eyes. I like the following quote from George Lucas, creator of the *Star Wars* franchise:

> Heroes come in all shapes and sizes, and you don't have to become a giant hero. You can be a very small hero. It's just as important to understand that accepting self-responsibility for the things you do, having good manners, caring about other people—these are heroic acts. Everybody has the choice of being a hero or not being a hero every day of their lives. You don't have to get into a giant laser-sword fight and blow up three spaceships to become a hero.

Character is the theme of this decade. If the eighties were about "Greed is good" and the nineties were about "Indulge yourself because you deserve it," the second half of the first decade of the 2000s is about "Always do the right thing in the right way." In the past, people might have forgiven you for lack of character if you were brilliant, creative or the ultimate new business developer. No more. The penalties for misconduct are too great. As the New England Patriots team motto says, "If you're going to play like a champion, act like a champion." Character is an all-the-time thing. It's also much easier to play like a champion if acting like a champion has become a habit. First we make our habits, then our habits make us.

From 2001 to 2004, one of the most powerful social trends in Canada was the surge in "ethical consumerism," which grew by 21 percent over the three-year period. This is defined as consumers' willingness to base their buying decisions on the perceived ethics of the company making the products or supplying the services. It's also consumers' desire to see companies be good corporate citizens in terms of these new social concerns. And while the trend refers primarily to well-established companies serving Canadians, the principle is entirely transferable to you. What are your perceived ethics? Are you being a good citizen? What are you doing to let others know what you're doing? This isn't about bragging; it's espousing your cause, serving as a beacon to the people around you, letting others know what's important to you, ensuring that they know your values and how you're living them.

"Ecological consumption" is also up sharply, increasing by 16 percent from 2001 to 2004. This means that Canadians are giving a high priority to integrating ecological concerns with purchasing criteria. Clearly, more and more of us understand that every action has consequences for our world. Even the smallest gestures make a difference. Money talks—and the smart people listen.

My personal call to action: I _____

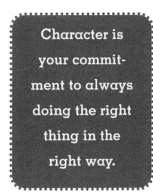

Character is your commitment to always doing the right thing in the right way.

From ecological consumption to ethical investing: According to *The Wall Street Journal* (August 3, 2005), the value of "socially responsible" mutual funds is up 137 percent since 2000, compared with 24 percent asset growth for all stock and bond funds. What's more, shareholders move money in and out of socially responsible funds at a significantly slower pace than investors in other funds. This suggests that investors in these funds are not focused on short-term performance. Professor Mark Cohen of Vanderbilt University says, "When people buy a socially responsible fund, they want to make money but they also want to feel good." More and more people, it seems, want to feel good by doing good. In the second half of the 2000s, greed is bad. Good is good.

Despite recent high-profile cases of unethical behavior, the strength of the North American workplace is that the vast majority of people in it are honest. Corruption is far less common than in many other parts of the world. People play by the rules, and as a rule they don't lie, steal or cheat. But that's not character. That's the minimum moral requirements for coexisting with others.

Character is your commitment to always doing the right thing in the right way—when it may not even be expected of you, when no one knows that you're doing it, or when it means putting yourself at personal risk. I'm talking about extra courtesy or care with a customer, the refusal to settle for good when you know that great is nearby, the willingness to confront the tough issues when no one else will, to challenge yourself by not taking the path of least resistance. In short, I'm talking about being willing to pay the price that is being asked of you in the defining moments. I'm talking about having the courage and the conscience to do whatever has to be done when it has to be done.

William Shakespeare got it right over five hundred years ago when he said, "This above all: to thine own self be true / And it must follow, as the night the day, / Thou canst not then be false to any man" (or woman, as the case may be). So honor yourself. Honor the people around you. Always do the right thing in the right way. And you'll find your way, irrespective of whatever happens around you. People of character always land on their feet. They have an inner compass that guides them, they have friends and allies who help them and they have a higher strength that sustains them.

My personal call to action: I _____

The New Uncertainty: It Could All Blow at Any Minute or It Could Come Together in Ways You Would Never Have Imagined

"This is our moment," said Sebastian Coe, leader of London's bid for the 2012 Olympic Games. "It's massive. It's huge. This is the biggest prize in sports" (*The Globe and Mail*, July 7, 2005). That was Wednesday, July 6, 2005. The whole of England celebrated.

"The mood of a city has never swung so sharply. On Wednesday, there was no better place on earth. After the victory of the Olympic decision, Londoners were celebrating the prospect of an explosion of new energy and creativity. But terror's war on us opened another front yesterday morning," wrote celebrated British author Ian McEwan. "The mood on the streets was of numb acceptance, or strange calm. It is unlikely that London will claim to have been transformed in an instant, to have lost its innocence in a course of a morning. But once we have counted up our dead, and the numbness turns to anger and grief, we will see that our lives here will be difficult. We have been savagely woken from a pleasant dream" (*The Globe and Mail*, July 8, 2005). That was Thursday, July 7, 2005. And the whole of England mourned.

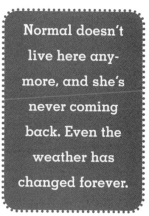

Normal doesn't live here anymore, and she's never coming back. Even the weather has changed forever.

"Markets around the globe—particularly London's FT-SE—nosedived on news of yesterday's transit bombing only to rebound later in the day, reflecting what one trader called 'adapting to a new reality'" (*The Globe and Mail*, July 8, 2005).

"More than half the workers in America could not meet their financial obligations if their paychecks were delayed for just one week" (2004 "Getting Paid in America" survey).

It could be the attack on the twin towers, the bombings in London and Madrid, the earthquake in Taiwan, the hurricane in New Orleans or the virus in Toronto. It could be the loss of your job, your spouse or your best friend. It could be the disease that suddenly appears—or the truck that collides with you—out of nowhere. It could be a new competitor, product or service that renders you instantly obsolete. It could be the bankruptcy of a client or supplier that threatens your own solvency. It could be the lawsuit that threatens to exhaust you, both

My personal call to action: I _____

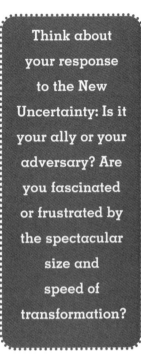

Think about your response to the New Uncertainty: Is it your ally or your adversary? Are you fascinated or frustrated by the spectacular size and speed of transformation?

financially and mentally. It could a merger or acquisition that reshapes your industry. It could be a new technology that revolutionizes the way you go to market. It could be any one of a thousand things that introduces you to the New Uncertainty.

There is one thing I can tell you with certainty: Normal doesn't live here anymore, and she's never coming back. Even the weather has changed forever. According to Environment Canada there's no such thing as normal weather any more. David Phillips, senior climatologist for Environment Canada, says the idea of typical weather is disappearing. "There's nothing normal anymore. Statistically, you should get more normal weather than extreme weather. It's almost as if what nature's giving us is the ends of the spectrum. We've literally clobbered records, smashed them" (*The Globe and Mail*, July 12, 2005).

Extreme volatility is the new normal. The swing factor is dramatic and it's happening at every level. No one escapes unscathed. In the New Uncertainty, change isn't subtle. The message comes at you loud and strong, for better or for worse. It's as if some superpower had magnified life a hundredfold. And that's good news— you can't miss it. But it's not what happens to you, or around you, that counts, it's how you respond to it. We're living in the age of "anything is truly possible." We're also living in the age of "it's all different in a heart beat." That's why many of us suffer from "collapse anxiety"—a fear that all our prosperity and security could vanish overnight. Hurricane Katrina is somewhere out there and she could blow our houses down at any moment. At the same time, those winds of change are bringing in unprecedented opportunities for the brave and the imaginative.

It's the Christopher Reeve story—from B-list actor to iconic activist. It's the Martha Stewart story—from unchallenged sovereign of domesticity to jailed felon to talk-show host/bestselling author/comeback heroine queen. It's the Sergey Brin and Larry Page story—from students at Stanford in 1998 to multi-billionaire creators of Google in seven short years. It's the iPod story—invented in 2001, it has sold tens of millions of units over the past four years. In fact, Apple sold 1.18 million iPods in the three months ending June 25, 2005, alone. The iPod was the

My personal call to action: I _____

reason why Apple shares rose 300 percent in 2004 and continued to rise strongly in 2005. As important, in the first half of 2005 users downloaded 158 million songs from iTunes and other sites as compared to 55 million in the first half of 2004. At the same time, sales of CDs in the U.S. fell 7 percent. How's that for a seismic shift in music distribution? To quote Steve Jobs, CEO of Apple Computer, "With iPod, Apple has invented a whole new category of digital music player that lets you put your entire music collection in your pocket and listen to it wherever you go."

I've taken my own journey into my personal stratosphere. In 2001 I did five talks in Canada. In 2005 I did 152. In 2001 I was a nobody in North America. By 2005 I had sold over 50,000 books and been acknowledged by the professional meeting industry's leading magazines as the most admired speaker in America. I tell you this not to impress you, but to impress upon you that all of us can leverage the New Uncertainty to our advantage, and to the advantage of the people we serve. In the New Uncertainty the mountain can be scaled in a blur—and the descent can be even more rapid. Think about your response to the New Uncertainty. Is it your ally or your adversary? Are you fascinated or frustrated by the spectacular size and speed of transformation?

The people who are thriving on the New Uncertainty are the people Environics calls **Adaptive Navigators**. They have the flexibility to adapt to unforeseen events. They have the imagination to see things that never were. They have the ingenuity to find the people and the resources they need to get the win/win. They're all around you—in your company and in your community. Find them. Talk to them. You'll discover that they're not the super-smart geeks who are gifted with hyper-intelligence. Instead you'll discover that they're ordinary people with extraordinary passion for the possibilities that life offers them. They believe they are where they're meant to be. They're hypersensitive to opportunity, so they hum at a higher frequency. As they seek opportunity, opportunity is seeking them. We attract what we are. If you want to evaluate yourself as an **Adaptive Navigator**, visit www.mikelipkin.com.

"Anything that creates turbulence creates the opportunity for people to get rich," says Christopher S. Jencks, a professor of social policy at Harvard. "But that isn't necessarily a big influence on the 99 percent of people who are not entrepreneurs" (*New York Times*, May 15, 2005). What does turbulence mean to you? I'm no more of a prophet than you are, but I can predict with total certainty that much greater turbulence is ahead. I can also predict that if you don't equate it with opportunity, you're going to deny it or see it as a threat. If you deny it, it will destroy you. If you

My personal call to action: I _____

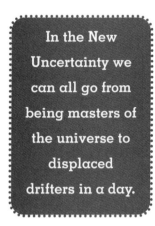

In the New Uncertainty we can all go from being masters of the universe to displaced drifters in a day.

see it as a threat, it will destroy you. Which leaves you only one option: Do whatever it takes to see it as an opportunity. What you see is what you'll get. I'm positive about that truth.

As a motivator, researcher and coach to thousands of people, I've learned how to sustain my own positivity. I've learned how to go quiet, how to focus, how get myself both psyched and hyped on demand. I've learned how to dance my way through turbulence and chaos. But I still suffer the terror of what-if-it-all-falls-apart-because-I screw-it-all-up multiple times a day. Short of becoming the Dalai Lama or going on a permanent diet of Valium, I don't believe that anyone can escape the New Uncertainty angst.

The challenge is to live with it, knowing that it too shall pass very, very quickly before the next thrill of inspiration strikes. Remember Churchill's immortal advice, "If you ever find yourself going through hell, keep going."

Extreme volatility is both an external and an internal environmental factor. In the New Uncertainty we can all go from being masters of the universe to displaced drifters in a day. On a daily basis we can yo-yo between feeling that we're in our personal high-performance zone to feeling as though we're barely hanging on. And every now and then we fall off the cliff.

Here's my favorite story on this trend. It's my favorite because I was personally involved as it unfolded. In January 2005 I was working with the president of Gillette Canada, Pete Manuel, to help instill a high-performance culture within the organization. Like any outstanding leader, Pete was pushing his team to continually take themselves to the next level to sustain their market dominance. We spent almost a month preparing for a gathering of the entire company in Toronto on Tuesday, February 1, 2005.

On the evening of Thursday, January 27, just four days before the meeting, I was in a cab on my way to a hotel in Montreal when I received the following e-mail on my Blackberry from *The Wall Street Journal*:

From: WSJ.com Editors <access@interactive.wsj.com>
To: Mike Lipkin <Mike.Lipkin@environics.ca>
Sent: Thu Jan 27 19:47:43 2005
Subject: NEWS ALERT: P&G Nears Deal to Buy Gillette

NEWS ALERT

My personal call to action: I _____

from The Wall Street Journal
Procter & Gamble is nearing a deal to acquire Gillette in a stock swap that would be valued at about $55 billion, according to people familiar with the matter.

I was puzzled as to why Pete had not shared this information with me, especially as it would mean changing our entire presentation in a dramatically different direction. So I sent Pete this message:

To: pete.manuel@gillette.ca
Subject: Fw: NEWS ALERT: P&G Nears Deal to Buy Gillette

Are you going to talk about this on Monday/Tuesday???

Sent from my BlackBerry Wireless Handheld

Here was his response:

Thanks so much. News to me and I am looking into it.
Best regards,
Pete.

It was the first that Pete Manuel had heard about the impending takeover. As in my case, it came as a complete surprise. It changed *everything*. That weekend we began planning the new presentation from scratch. Pete's first slide said "150 = 0," meaning that 150 slides had been discarded because they meant nothing in the new, dramatically different scenario. Today Pete is running Procter & Gamble's operations in Australia. He and I still smile about that weekend.

The following article from the June 3, 2005, issue of *The Globe and Mail's Report on Business* on developments at CIBC, a leading Canadian bank, illustrates even more dramatically the career volatility of the New Uncertainty.

CIBC Clears Deck at Retail Unit

CEO-in-waiting Gerald McCaughey pulled off another high-level management overhaul at Canadian Imperial Bank of Commerce yesterday, dismissing several senior officers as part of a continuing makeover of its retail banking division.

My personal call to action: I _____

The moves come less than two months after CIBC parted ways with vice-chairwoman Jill Denham and promoted Sonia Baxendale to assume her role as head of the bank's flagship retail unit. Ms. Baxendale, a 13-year veteran of CIBC who previously ran the bank's wealth management operations, wasted little time surrounding herself with a new management team, essentially removing a partial layer of executives that had reported directly to Ms. Denham.

The departures in the retail division yesterday include Gerrard Schmid, executive vice-president and chief operating officer; Stephen Graham, executive vice-president and chief marketing officer; Kenn Lalonde, executive vice-president of branch and small-business banking; and Richard Graham, senior vice-president of strategic development at Amicus, the electronic banking division.

"The management structure has been simplified," said Rob McLeod, a spokesman for the bank. "This is bringing the customer closer to the senior management team."

Mr. McLeod said the moves were part of a larger restructuring CIBC announced in April, in which it transferred parts of its wealth management businesses, including Imperial Service and guaranteed investment certificates, into the retail group. The bank also told investors and analysts last week that it will try to cut $250-million in costs by the end of 2006 to align its expenses more closely with its peers. *

I had worked with all of the dismissed executives. They are outstanding professionals with impressive track records; some had been with the bank for over a decade. Until just before their dismissal, some of them even thought they had a long and lucrative future ahead of them at CIBC. Then a new CEO takes the helm and it's all over—just like that. I have no doubt that the severance packages were fair. I also have no doubt that they'll all land on their feet. But at the time of writing, some very senior, very powerful executives are just another group of professionals touting their résumés in a very tough market. If their hunt for new jobs conforms to the norm, it will take them eight months to find new positions. Career volatility has never been higher, and neither has the need for resilience and reinvention.

*Reprinted with permission from *The Globe and Mail*

My personal call to action: I _____

We're all familiar with a version of the above story. You've been through it and I've been through it. At the time it all seems terribly unjust. In hindsight, though, whatever happened appears utterly predictable. In my case, it happens daily. I'm only as good as my final presentation. I'm not paid to be excellent, I'm paid to be brilliant. That's not hyperbole; it's fact. And you know what? It's the same for you. Excellence is available anywhere, but true brilliance is rare.

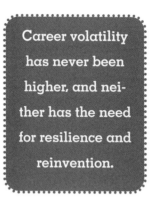

Career volatility has never been higher, and neither has the need for resilience and reinvention.

When I fall short of the mark I know I'll never be hired by that client again. Furthermore, the people who heard me speak will tell others about their underwhelming experience. Negative word of mouth follows and my personal image begins to erode. My career is being built up or dismantled every time I open my mouth. I understand that fact, I embrace that fact and I leverage that fact. I like the New Uncertainty because it keeps reminding me of Rudyard Kipling's immortal wisdom:

> ### IF
>
> *If you can keep your head when all about you*
> *Are losing theirs and blaming it on you;*
> *If you can trust yourself when all men doubt you . . .*
> *If you can dream – and not make dreams your master . . .*
> *If you can meet with triumph and disaster*
> *And treat those two impostors just the same . . .*
> *If you can watch the things you gave your life to, broken,*
> *And stoop and build 'em up with worn-out tools:*
> *If you can talk with crowds and keep your virtue,*
> *Or walk with kings – nor lose the common touch,*
> *If neither foes nor loving friends can hurt you,*
> *If all men count with you, but none too much . . .*
>
> *Yours is the Earth and everything that's in it . . .*

As a final takeaway, remember that the tendency to overestimate the dangers around us is an instinctive human impulse embedded in our psyche. The fear of hurt or pain and the need to avoid them are far stronger urges than the search for enlightenment and opportunity. So establish your own personal override system.

My personal call to action: I _____

When you feel an anxiety attack coming on, condition yourself to focus on why what's happening around you is a good thing. Focus on how you can leverage forthcoming events to your advantage and to the advantage of the people you serve. The New Uncertainty demands that you discipline your psyche to exaggerate the promises—not the threats—around you. That's why the next trend is so important.

The Return of Faith and Optimism: I Have a Dream and It's Going to Be All Mine Soon

Faith: confidence or trust in a person or a thing; belief which is not based on proof; belief in God or in the doctrines or teaching of religion; the obligation of loyalty or fidelity to a person, promise, engagement.

Optimism: a disposition or tendency to anticipate the most favorable result; the belief that good ultimately predominates over evil in the world; the doctrine that the existing world is the best of all possible worlds; the belief that goodness pervades reality.

~Webster's Dictionary

If tomorrow were a stock, I'd buy it. Its value appreciates every day. So many influences are trying to bring it down, but its upward momentum will not be stopped. It's become fashionable to believe in the future. It's in to be positive. We all have permission to dream again. The four musketeers of the new age—Hope, Faith, Optimism and Confidence—are making a comeback.

All around us the signals are positive: low interest rates, low unemployment, healthy economic growth, a buoyant global economy, a reasonably performing stock market, life-changing innovations, great wealth creation, a booming real estate market and increasing longevity.

Cynicism is on its way out. Negativity is so yesterday. Pessimism is the mark of people who are out of sync with emotional fashion. Apathy is the sign of someone stuck in a personal no man's land. Ambivalence will kill you. It's all about passion, baby! It's all about showing what you stand for—and following through. It's about using the new technology and opportunities to let the world know how you're making it better, one word or action at a time.

My personal call to action: I _____

It's not about being Pollyanna, not about Disney make-believe. We're served up too many daily reminders of Armageddon and breakdown not to see what can go wrong. But the return of faith and optimism is a direct response to the destructive forces that strive to bring us down. In company after company we're seeing a resurgence of positive psychology. In community after community, people are telling us they're feeling more confident about the future and their ability to deal with it.

In 2000 over four in ten Americans (81 percent) already agreed with the statement, "I believe in the American dream: It is possible for anyone in this country to have success if they reach for it." The proportion in agreement rose to 85 percent in 2004. But here's the kicker: The proportion agreeing "strongly" rose from 38 percent in 2000 to 48 percent in 2004. That's a massive jump of over 25 percent. It means that nearly half of all Americans believe strongly that Abe Lincoln's climb from log cabin to the White House is still possible in their country—still possible for them, their children or the poorest family in town.

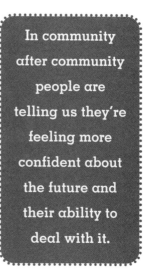

In community after community people are telling us they're feeling more confident about the future and their ability to deal with it.

Mobility is the promise that lies at the heart of the American dream. According to *The New York Times* (May 15, 2005), more Americans than twenty years ago believe it's possible to start out poor, work hard and become rich. They say hard work and a good education are more important to getting ahead than connections or a wealthy background. Most say their standard of living is better than their parents' and imagine that their children will do better still. Even families making less than $30,000 a year subscribe to the American dream; more than half say they have achieved it or will do so.

In Canada the trend toward optimism is also increasing strongly. Canadians are showing greater confidence in their ability to adapt to unforeseen challenges and upheavals. The percentage of Canadians who believe they have what it takes to succeed and to engage life has increased from 20 percent in 2001 to 23 percent in 2004, a significant 15 percent jump. And the number of Canadians who want to withdraw in order to protect themselves declined from 45 percent in 2001 to 37 percent in 2004—a drop of almost 20 percent. The number of Canadians who say they are averse to risk and complexity has also declined to 38 percent in 2004 from 45 percent in 2001.

My personal call to action: I _____

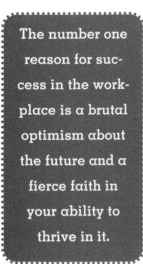

The number one reason for success in the workplace is a brutal optimism about the future and a fierce faith in your ability to thrive in it.

Here's an interesting insight: The number of Canadians who say they are neither attracted nor averse to uncertainty and complexity has increased to 39 percent in 2004 from 35 percent in 2001. What does that mean? It means there are more people in "attitudinal transition." They could go one way or the other, depending on the world around them and the decisions they make about it. Maybe you're one of them. If you are, remember this Lipkinism: Nothing in life has any meaning except the meaning you give it. From now on, whatever happens to you, ask yourself, "What's great about what has just happened? How can I use this event to ensure an even better future for me, my family, my company and my community?"

There can be no better statement about one's faith in the future than a willingness to invest in one's ability to excel in it. Environics measures a trend called "effort for health." It is defined as "the commitment to focus on diet and exercise in order to feel better and have a healthy, wholesome lifestyle; a willingness to transform one's lifestyle through exercise and radical changes to diet." Well, this trend is up 20 percent in 2004 as compared to 2001. Clearly more people are getting the message to exercise and eat properly—or die. Are you?

So where are you on the faith and optimism scale? What are your expectations about the future? Here's what I've learned from the thousands of highly successful people I've personally interviewed over the past five years: The number-one reason for success in the workplace is a brutal optimism about the future and a fierce faith in your ability to thrive in it. You know what else I've learned? A brutal optimism about the future and a fierce faith in your ability to thrive in it create their own reality.

If you're abundantly optimistic you see things that others don't see, because you're looking for things that others aren't. You're focusing on finding proof for your optimism. And what you focus on is what you attract to you. What you focus on is what you become. What you focus on is what you move toward. Focus equals movement—forward or backward. So see optimism as your rudder. It guides your direction, your moods, your motivation and your happiness. Optimism and happiness are Siamese twins—there cannot be one without the

My personal call to action: I _____

other. You'll never find a depressed optimist or an optimistic depressive. I'm not saying that the optimist cannot suffer temporary bouts of despair or that a depressive cannot experience moments of optimism. But, as a Lipkin rule, unless Brutal Optimism is an entrenched mindset, real success and happiness are unattainable and unsustainable.

I've taken Brutal Optimism to a whole new level: I'm a self-confessed "pathological optimist." No matter what the circumstances, I believe in a favorable outcome, even when everyone around me is telling me it could turn out badly. I am simply allergic to pessimism—it makes me ill. I also believe that there is no such thing as false hope. It's thinking that makes things so. However, I'll be frank with you: This mindset serves me beautifully as a motivator and creator of new possibilities, but it sucks as an investment strategy. That's why you don't want me advising you on your portfolio. So remember this Lipkinism:

 "Your biggest strength is always your biggest weakness. But the upside of your strength dwarfs the downside of your weakness.

If Brutal Optimism is your success rudder, then Fierce Faith is your engine. I love the Webster's Dictionary definition of faith: *belief which is not based on proof.* On the Cusp of change you're never going to have enough proof. The past never equals the future. In fact, the disparity between the two has never been greater. It's your belief in your ability to thrive under any circumstances that counts. However, belief alone won't cut it—it may even lead to complacency and under-preparation.

What turns belief into Fierce Faith is action. It's the willingness to do what lesser spirits are afraid to do. It's the willingness to train, to prepare, to risk, to stretch, to fall down, to stand up, to lose, to win, to end it all, to begin it all again. The best thing is winning. The second-best thing is losing, because it means you get a chance to try again. Here is the Lipkinism that defines Mike Lipkin:

"Personal success is the reward you get for the action you took to demonstrate your faith. So personal success may not always result in the glittering prize. It may not bring you the recognition or the big cash that comes with hitting the jackpot. Personal success is the payout you receive in learning, recognition or money that builds your faith in yourself for the next initiative.

My personal call to action: I _____

Think about all the actions you've taken to demonstrate your faith, and think about the results you received. Think about what those results led to in terms of personal development, relationships, finances or health. I can tell you that in every case the action you take to demonstrate your faith will pay out in ways that transcend your dreams. But there's a catch: Once you take action to demonstrate your faith, you are committed to a lifelong course—there's no letting up. Life doesn't come with a rewind button. Brutal Optimism and Fierce Faith must become as much a part of you as your arms and legs.

Here's a weird side effect of the return of faith and optimism: It's burning people out. I'm serious. There are so many opportunities to be pursued, so many tasks to be performed, so many people's expectations to meet, so much profit to be made, so many new things to learn. The more optimistic you are, the more likely you are to take on more than you can handle. Optimists often find it difficult to say no. But say no we must, or the people around us will pay the price. So optimism must be tempered with realism. Discretion is the savior of sanity. I'm seeing more and more people call a time-out before they lose it completely. And the smart leadership teams understand their high performers' need for focus, rest and rejuvenation.

Any psychiatrist will tell you that there's a direct correlation between optimism/faith and resilience. The more faith you have in your ability to prevail, combined with a tendency to anticipate the most favorable result, the more likely you are to keep going when others give up. What's more, you're also far more likely to recover from the setbacks and wrong turns that will derail your less hopeful rivals. That's why, at 1:10 a.m. on a steamy summer's night in Orlando, Florida, I'm still writing these words. I have to have this manuscript finished in two months' time. We're about halfway through the book. It's taken me six months to write what you've already read, but I have to write three times as much in the next sixty days. But I'm brutally optimistic about my chances. You know why? It's summer. It's the low season in terms of speaking engagements. I can devote all my time to completing this mission. What's more, I can write at home or in my hotel, close to my wife and kids. I'm loving it—it's all coming together. You're reading my success. Cheers!

Global Citizenship: It's a Small Planet and I Want to Know More About It

What do all these cities have in common? Kabul. Karachi. Hong Kong. Bangkok. Damascus. Beirut. Bogotá. Johannesburg. Harare. Phuket. Paris. Shanghai.

My personal call to action: I _____

Baghdad. Bangalore. Leeds. Buenos Aires. Madrid. Mexico City. Jerusalem. Moscow. Athens. Sydney. Riyadh. Tokyo. Amsterdam. Helsinki. Nairobi. Caracas. Rio de Janeiro. Rome. Istanbul.

Yes, you're right—none of them is in the United States or Canada. And, yes, you're right again—what happens in every one of those cities influences you in your city. And you're right a third time—you know very little about what happens in most of those cities and very little about the people who live there. But I know you're far more interested than you used to be. You want to know more; you have to know more. The world is a small planet, and it's shrinking daily.

Technology, humanity and the pursuit of prosperity have made the world one big multinational ecosystem. We're all living in symbiosis with one another. A car bomb in Kabul, a video in Baghdad, a gram from Bogotá, a mind in Bangalore, an innovation out of Helsinki, a vote in Rome, a murder in Amsterdam, a trial in Moscow, four young men from Leeds, a monster wave over Phuket, a train explosion in Madrid—all these things affect us in immediate, measurable ways.

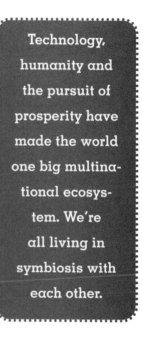

> Technology, humanity and the pursuit of prosperity have made the world one big multinational ecosystem. We're all living in symbiosis with each other.

Who didn't know someone vacationing in the tsunami zone? Who doesn't flinch every time they hear about even a single civilian casualty in a big city? Who didn't feel the chill of shock when the identities of the London suicide bombers were revealed? Who doesn't remember that picture of one young man facing a line of tanks in Beijing? Whose life isn't affected by software developments in Bangalore or cell phone innovations out of Helsinki, home of Nokia? Whose lifestyle isn't influenced by the new big-three auto manufacturers—Toyota, Nissan and Honda—planting roots in the United States and Canada? Who doesn't understand that an AIDS epidemic in Harare, Zimbabwe, leads to pain and suffering wherever you are? Who isn't working with an immigrant from another country far, far away? Who doesn't feel instant wanderlust when they hear about Mombasa, Barcelona, Mumbai, Budapest, Prague, Cape Town, Lisbon or Marrakech? Who doesn't thrill to the sights and sounds of Cirque du Soleil, one of the best examples of corporate global citizenship in action?

My personal call to action: I _____

It will come as no surprise that since 2001 Americans are showing greater interest in the world beyond their state lines. But they are also showing greater empathy for people in other countries. In 2004 three-quarters of Americans said they often or sometimes "feel what other countries are going through when I watch them on television (on international news for example)." This number is a full 10 percent higher than in 2000. Similarly, Americans are registering greater interest in foreign travel. In 2004, 77 percent agreed that "I have an interest in traveling to and learning about other countries and their way of life." This is a 7-point jump over 2000. My personal experience mirrors what our polls tell us. More and more I'm being asked to talk to U.S. companies because of my global citizenship status—born in the U.K., raised in South Africa, now living in Canada.

In Canada the trend toward global citizenship is showing itself in the way people are embracing their "Canadian identity." This is a tendency for people to consider the fact of being Canadian as an important part of their personal identity. From 2001 to 2004 this trend rose by a significant 12 percent. The more angry the world becomes, the more Canadians value the relative calm of their own country. From July to October 2002, the Pew Research Centre conducted a survey of more than 38,000 people in forty-four countries on issues of interest to the entire planet, and two-thirds of Canadians gave their lives the highest rating. This was ahead of all the other countries surveyed in Europe and North America. If you're a Canadian, it seems that living in a globalized world also means being truly cognizant of what you have in your own country.

Here's some more good news if you're Canadian: The world wants more of you. As reported in *The Globe and Mail* (September 5, 2005), international recruiting experts prefer the flexibility and "cultural fit" of Canadian CEOs. "Canadian executives travel well and, as a source of talent, Canada is very important to us," says Damien O'Brien, an Australia-based managing partner of the recruitment firm Egon Zehnder International.

Andrew Ferrier, the Montreal-born CEO of New Zealand dairy giant Fonterra, says, "Canadians are generally a good cultural fit. I think we're a little more flexible, a little more accustomed to finding a way that isn't necessarily about banging people over the head. I think Canadians are particularly good at getting buy-in as they are running businesses."

As well as being a source of international executive talent, Canada has another edge: The country's diverse ethnic makeup has produced a generation of business leaders who mix easily with different cultures, says Caroline Jellinck, a

My personal call to action: I _____

Vancouver-based partner with the international recruiting firm Ray & Berndtson.

In his book *The World Is Flat*, Thomas Friedman states that the flattening of the world started with the fall of the Berlin Wall in 1989. That was the beginning of the world's evolution into a single market driven by one system—capitalism. From there, you've lived what happened next— inexpensive technology, the Internet, e-mails, Web browsers that eliminated geography and governments as an obstacle to international trade, massive global mobility, porous national borders, convergence of cultures, compression of experiences, instantaneity of news, lightning strikes of graphic images, "embedded" sources of information in the events as they happen, cell-phone camera images broadcast on blogs before newspapers or TV even see them.

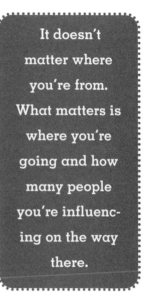

It doesn't matter where you're from. What matters is where you're going and how many people you're influencing on the way there.

Since the dawn of the twenty-first century it seems that global flattening and connectivity are accelerating daily. We're living in a borderless world where people thousands of miles away are as close and as relevant as your next-door neighbor. In fact, I am a lot closer to my colleagues in the U.K., Holland and South Africa than I am to my literal next-door neighbors, with whom I exchange nothing more than a cursory wave a few times a week.

In my adopted city of Toronto, the second most diverse city in North America after Miami, more than 50 percent of residents were not born in Canada. By 2017, Caucasians will be a visible minority in the city. My assistant, Erica Cerny, was born in the Czech Republic. My partner in the seminar business, Salim Khoja, is from Kenya. And my mother, Arca Vigraha Devi Dasi, was a Hare Krishna devotee who lived and died in Vrindaban, India.

Welcome to the age of the global hybrid. It doesn't matter where you're from. What matters is where you're going, and how many people you're influencing on the way there. Never before has a single life had the potential to influence so many people. Never before have we had so many tools to connect with so many people. Never before has a single voice had so much opportunity to be heard. Never before has it been so important for those who support an open society to stand up against those who don't. And the beauty of it all is that you don't have to join a movement, engage in mass protests or put your-

My personal call to action: I _____

self in physical danger. You just have to do what you know you have to do on the Cusp of change—take advantage of the myriad opportunities offered to you every day in such a way that everyone around you is motivated to do the same. If you show that you can, you show others that they can. Pay it forward and you'll be paid very well.

Lisa Bate is a classic example of the new global citizenship in action. She is a Toronto-based architect whose firm, Six Degrees Architecture and Design Inc, is making it big in China. As reported in *The Toronto Star* (July 11, 2004), Bate's firm was a medium-sized operation whose business included designing local bank branches in Toronto. Bate decided to take the leap into China in 2002, when she decided her twelve-person firm needed to raise its profile by going after a new challenge. After doing some research she discovered that 47 percent of architects in Canada are in Ontario, with the majority in Toronto. "China was looking pretty good from that point onward," she says. Bate also leveraged the power of relationships. One of her architects was from China, and she also had a friend who had taught at university there. "That really helped to give us an insight into the culture," she adds. Bate gave herself a year to land a job in China. It took six months, with the help of advice from her friend and her Canadian-Chinese architect, who is now the firm's director of Asian operations. "I think it gave the Chinese a comfort level to see that we were a Canadian firm but we also had roots in China." says Bate.

When Bate cracked China, she cracked it big. In January 2003 her firm won a competition for a 2.2-square-kilometer, $120-million "Eco-City" project in Jiangxi province. Soon after, the firm won a second contract for a bus terminal in Hunan province. And then, in June 2004, it won a project to design a new 4-square-kilometer city housing 28,000 residents. The contract signing was televised on the Chinese national network. Her success in China has also paid dividends at home, where international exposure has attracted local clients. "I think in the end, it came down to whether you were willing to take a risk," Bate says. "I also learned that the overlap of relationships is easier than I thought. It's unbelievable how much you can find in common with other people. We're really not that different. We do want the same things."

From China to South Africa, to Milwaukee, Wisconsin, U.S.A. In April 2005, I received a call from Dennis Groves, a client with whom I'd worked in the late nineties during my time in South Africa. At the time he had been a senior financial manager with South African Breweries, the dominant brewer and distributor

My personal call to action: I _____

of beer in Africa. But now Dennis was calling me from Milwaukee, Wisconsin. South African Breweries had acquired the Miller Brewing Company from Phillip Morris. Together with a few other South Africans, Dennis had relocated to help with the transition. He wanted me to help him empower the 170 people in the Miller Brewing Company's finance division to perform at their highest level.

The engagement was a great success and the people left my session feeling inspired and rejuvenated. But you know what my greatest "aha!" was? When it came to motivation and inspiration, there was no difference between what motivated white-collar workers in Milwaukee, Wisconsin, and what motivated their counterparts in Johannesburg, South Africa. Yes, I changed my references to fit the local culture, but otherwise my message and my delivery were identical to the way I deliver sessions in Sydney, Australia, Amsterdam, the Netherlands, or Vancouver, Canada.

Here's what I believe: There are two kinds of people in the world—those who are part of the global culture and those who are not. *Those who are not* are what I call "insular islanders." They are locked into their local culture, unaware of or resistant to international influences. Their insularity may be motivated by ignorance or by fear, but they are the new cultural illiterates. They are the ones who falter on the Cusp of change, afraid that if they take the next step they'll get lost.

> ▶ Those who are part of a global culture understand, respect, love and honor different national traditions, ethnicities and customs. But they belong to a new multicultural "inter-nation" who have minimized the cultural taboos and the no-go zones. The "Internationals" live the universal values of love, light, contribution, laughter, joy, generosity, security, growth, health, excitement, openness, humanity, acceptance, tolerance, freedom, learning, evolution, fascination, spontaneity, reinvention, mixing, curiosity, boldness, prosperity, diversity, responsibility, accountability, knowledge, sharing and readiness to change. They understand there are no right or wrong ways, just different ways. They run toward new possibilities—not away from fear of loss. Why are you running?

As reported in *Business 2.0* (August 2005), Jeffrey Pfeffer, professor of organizational behavior at Stanford University's Graduate School of Business, says that recruitment, retention and utilization of global talent have become essential ele-

My personal call to action: I _____

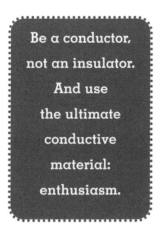

Be a conductor, not an insulator. And use the ultimate conductive material: enthusiasm.

ments of modern-day corporate success. However, he says, the global expertise provided by transnational workers must be nurtured carefully. "If only by force of habit, most organizations engage in 'homosocial reproduction'; because we naturally identify with people like ourselves, it takes extra effort to hire and promote those who are different."

Twice a year, Deloitte Consulting, one of the world's leading consulting firms, hires me to introduce new recruits to the concept of "personal branding." That's the science of turning yourself into a resource desired by one's colleagues and clients. I love these events because the audience is primarily under the age of twenty-five. At the end of every session I'm surrounded by people from every corner of the world. I look at their shining, eager faces. I listen to their earnest questions. I hear their uninhibited laughter. I feel their infinite hope and ambition. I sense their nascent power. And irrespective of their origins, I know I'm surrounded by one culture, indivisible—the culture of tomorrow.

In today's global economy you're not going to get better and faster on your own. Innovation will come only through meaningful relationships with other people or companies. In their book *Your Next Business Strategy*, John Hagel and John Seeley Brown state that the global economy offers opportunities to build networks of like-minded firms not only to share resources but also to learn from each other. The upshot—we'll design better products, solve problems faster, and gain more control over manufacturing if we share ideas with creative people from around the world.

So learn about individual cultures. Visit foreign lands. Talk to people from other countries. Do it physically, do it digitally, but do it. Understand what makes us all different. More important, understand what makes us all the same. Find the vein that runs through all of us and tap into it. Be a conductor, not an insulator. And use the ultimate conductive material—enthusiasm.

As you may have noticed throughout this book, I use the "point-and-tell" technique to communicate my messages: I make a point and then I tell a story to illustrate my point. Remember, people may forget points, but they never forget great stories. What's more, stories get through to the heart while points get stuck in the mind. Every valuable point needs a story to drive it home.

My personal call to action: I _____

So here is mine. In May 2005 I was asked to conduct a motivational program with 120 salespeople from Merck Frosst, the giant pharmaceutical company. The program was delivered at a resort about an hour's drive north of Montreal, in the French-speaking province of Quebec, Canada. About two-thirds of the audience were fully bilingual, about a quarter understood English, and a few didn't understand it at all. My program was three hours long. They were a great group and I delivered my message with my customary zest and vigor.

At the close of the program I ended the way I usually do—with a request for delegates to share their key takeaway from the program. I went around the room asking people to verbalize their learning from the day. Finally I focused on a young man who had been sitting directly in front of me. I had left him for last because he had listened to me with uncommon concentration the whole time. He had appeared to absorb every word I uttered. In fact, his unwavering attention was one of the reasons I felt so connected to the audience as a whole. He radiated style, success and charisma. The way in which his colleagues engaged him clearly branded him as a leader. A sixth sense told me that he would provide the most meaningful comment of the day to help me send everyone away on a high.

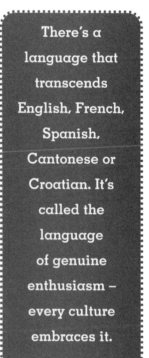

There's a language that transcends English, French, Spanish, Cantonese or Croatian. It's called the language of genuine enthusiasm – every culture embraces it.

"Pierre" I said, reading his name tag, "what is your key takeaway from the day?" Pierre just stared at me, not responding. Thinking that he hadn't heard me, I repeated the question a little louder and a little more slowly. Still no response. Then one of his colleagues said to me, "Mike, Pierre doesn't speak English."

"You must be joking," I thought to myself. "How could he have appeared to be so riveted for three hours without comprehending a word I'd said?" So I asked his colleague to ask Pierre why he had listened to me with such intensity when he didn't understand anything I'd said. A short dialogue ensued. Then his colleague told me, "Pierre says it didn't matter what you said. What mattered is how you said it. He says he loves your passion and joie de vivre. He says he learned a lot from just watching you." I gave Pierre a big *"Merci beaucoup."* He gave me a dazzling grin; then rose and embraced me. And the audience sprang into a spontaneous standing ovation.

My personal call to action: I _____

What's the moral of the story? There's a language that transcends English, French, Spanish, Cantonese or Croatian. It's called the language of genuine enthusiasm—every culture embraces it. With it you'll make friends and influence people everywhere. Without it, you'll live a life of isolation and mediocrity wherever you are. You may already be a global citizen navigating international waters with confidence, or you may be someone who has never thought beyond the boundaries of your province or state. I'm asking you, irrespective of your status, to think as if you are not bound by geography. I'm asking you to re-examine all that you've been told in the light of the new multicultural, international values. Use technology to reach out to distant nooks and crannies. Physically go to those faraway places. Become a purveyor of different perspectives. You'll be amazed at what you see, hear and receive from others.

Engage or Get Lost: I Want to Reach Out to Reach My Goal

Engage: to occupy the attention or efforts of a person; to secure for employment; to attract and hold fast; to bind as by pledge, promise, contract or oath; to become interlocked; to become involved.

~ Webster's Dictionary

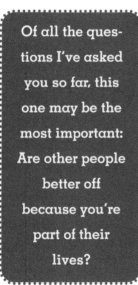

Of all the questions I've asked you so far, this one may be the most important: Are other people better off because you're part of their lives?

The only place where the loner succeeds is in comic books. If you're Superman, Batman or Spiderman, you might be able to make it on your own, but even then, life is an angst-filled experience. For the rest of us mortals, One is a puny number. On its own it's impotent. It needs to fire off other Ones in order to become powerful. One plus One can equal anything, but One by itself will end up being a fraction of what it could be.

The new superheroes are those who reach out to others. They're the connectors, the networkers, the social contributors. They're the ones who see everyone—family, company and community—as a partner. They're the ones who reach out to you when you're feeling overwhelmed. They're the ones who always seem upbeat, irrespective of circumstances. They're the ones who help you find a solution when none seems possible. They're the ones who

My personal call to action: I _____

organize the event that brings people together to support a cause. They're the ones who catalyze change in others. They understand that their own well-being is a direct function of how much well-being they create around themselves. So they reach out as an act of both contribution and self-preservation. They do it because they have to, because they want to, because they can.

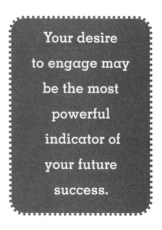

Your desire to engage may be the most powerful indicator of your future success.

Of all the questions I've asked you so far, these may be the most important: Are other people better off because you're part of their lives? Are you the one who is expanding their capacities? Are you the one who is enhancing their abilities? Are you the one who is enriching their perspective? True success is directly proportional to the size of the contribution you make to the people around you. Acknowledgment, fulfillment, connection and growth can accrue to you only if you're engaging others in the quest to be their best. And the good news is that if you're reading these words, you're walking along the right path. You're focusing on the right issues, and whatever you focus on, you move toward.

The return of faith and optimism is fueling the desire to engage. The more optimistic someone is, the more confident he's likely to be. And the more confident he is, the more likely he is to reach out rather than pull back. Think about it. If you're living in fear and pessimism, you're going to view others, especially strangers, as a threat. On the other hand, if you're positive about yourself and your future, you're going to view others, even strangers, as allies or resources in your quest to realize your goals.

I see it all the time. I make a living turning complete strangers into instant partners. For the duration of my program I partner with my audience to produce a transformational experience. Without the participants' willingness to contribute toward my success, I cannot make them successful. If they don't engage me, I cannot engage them, no matter how hard I try. It's reciprocal. My personal code demands that I always play full out. But if my delegates play only half-heartedly, I will flop. I can sense my audience's desire to engage the moment I stand up in front of them. If it's high, I cannot fail. If it's low, I know it's going to be a titanic struggle to lift them up.

Your desire to engage may be the most powerful indicator of your future success. If you bind yourself to life by pledge, promise, contract or oath, life has no

My personal call to action: I _____

> Voters are nine times more likely than non-voters to believe that their involvement can make a difference in society. They are four times more likely to have "meaningful moments."

choice but to engage you. It's an equal deal: You expect a lot from life and life expects a lot from you. The challenge is to stay engaged all the time, especially when adversity strikes, others turn against you or you momentarily lose your way. That's when your desire to engage becomes your lifeline. If you lose it, you're lost.

Think about the people around you who are disengaged. Describe them to yourself. Are they bitter, cynical, tired, angry, apathetic, frustrated, anxious? Exactly. They're lost. They've given up, so others give up on them. Until they get enough mojo to re-engage, they're not going anywhere. And remember, engagement is an all-or-nothing thing. You can't kind of, sort-of, semi-engage. You engage or you don't. It's like voting—you do or you don't.

Speaking of voting, here's some fascinating data on the difference between engagement and disengagement on a political level. According to data released by the Census Bureau, in the 2004 presidential election more than 125 million Americans—64 percent of those aged eighteen and older—went to the polls.

The agency also found that turnout rates were closely correlated to the voter's age. A little more than 73 percent of those between 65 and 74 said they voted, the highest rate for any age group. Those between the ages of 18 and 24 had the lowest, with 47 percent reporting going to the polls. Between those two groups, turnout rates increased steadily with age. Of those between 55 and 64, 73 percent said they voted, compared with 69 percent of those between 45 and 54, 64 percent of those between 35 and 44, and 56 percent of those between 25 and 34.

The numbers also indicate that turnout rates are closely tied to levels of formal education. Those with a bachelor's degree or an advanced degree voted at much higher rates (80 percent) than those with just a high-school diploma (56 percent) and those without a diploma or its equivalent (40 percent.). The agency also reported that the employed were more likely go to the polls (66 percent) than the unemployed (51 percent).

The Environics data also indicate that politically engaged Americans are not just more interested in political issues than are the disengaged, but in general

My personal call to action: I _____

they appear to feel more strongly connected to other people, both those close to them and those in society at large. Specifically, voters score much higher on a trend called "civic engagement." This means they believe that active involvement in the political process can make a difference in society.

For your own "helper's high" give at least two favors for every one you ask for.

Similarly, voters on both sides of the partisan divide have high scores on the trend "meaningful moments." This is a tendency to cherish the ordinary moments in everyday life over once-in-a-lifetime, grand-scale events. This means that voters are much more likely to take the time to cultivate meaningful connections with other people, even with strangers they happen to meet during the day.

These two trends suggest that politically engaged Americans, whatever their ideology, not only feel connected to their society by civic duty, but make an effort to foster a kind of emotional goodwill toward those around them. They emphasize the importance of community and approach social life in a spirit of responsibility and contribution. For example, voters are nine times more likely than non-voters to believe that their involvement can make a difference in society. They are four times more likely to have "meaningful moments." They are three times more likely to express "ecological concern"—which means they reject the notion that economic advancement should be allowed at the expense of environmental protection. They are twice as likely to believe that other cultures have a lot to teach us. They are also 50 percent more likely to be involved in their community.

Here's something even more fascinating: Voters are more than twice as likely as non-voters to commit to diet and exercise in order to feel better and have a healthy, wholesome lifestyle. Voters are also six times as likely as non-voters to believe that they can organize and control the direction of their future, even when it feels like forces are beyond their immediate control.

The bottom line is that people who feel engaged with their communities tend to be healthier, happier and more in control of their lives. Apathy kills. Isolation will make you sick. The effort required to reach out and make a difference always yields the highest dividends. Luck favors the sociable and the gregarious. Have you noticed that the people around you who are most engaged in their community tend to be the happiest and most successful of their peers? How about you? Are you tapping into the communal power source, or is your social well running dry?

My personal call to action: I _____

The person with the best friends wins.

According to *The Globe and Mail* (January 15, 2005), scientists using brain scans have found evidence that human beings are "hard-wired" to help each other. Overdosing on altruism may have a hidden perk—researchers call it the "helper's high," the same kind of endorphin rush that runners get as they lope along a trail. A growing number of studies suggests that this high can give the immune system a boost, speed recovery from surgery and cut down on restless nights. The challenge, of course, is to help others consistently, by ritualizing it.

Here's another fact to underestimate at your peril: Most people want to help. Margaret Heffernan, author and columnist for *Fast Company* magazine, states that when students asked fellow passengers on the New York subway system to give up their seats for them, 86 percent of New Yorkers obliged without question. Asking for help is a gift to the helper. "It's better to give than to receive" is more than a cliché—it's the truth. So reach out for help and make sure that you reciprocate in return. As someone who is constantly asking for favors, delivering favors and studying how the people around me give and receive favors, I can tell you we're in a hot "favor-trading" market. People who get this truth and who are good at trading favors will thrive. So seize every opportunity to ask for help. But for your own "helper's high" give at least two favors for every one you ask for, not to the same individual, but to your community at large.

In Canada, Environics tracks a cluster of trends that point to a strong surge toward social engagement among Canadians. For example, from 2001 to 2004 "social learning" has increased by 14 percent. This means an enhanced attraction to and interest in diversity. Diversity is perceived as a source of personal enrichment, a way to satisfy a hunger for discovery and exploration and to extend a network of contacts. This trend is also associated with a respect for other people and cultures, as well as a heightened social conscience.

The trend "networking" is also up strongly, increasing by 13 percent from 2001 to 2004. This is a desire to belong to a network or networks of people who communicate with each other and do things together, both physically and digitally. Those folks who are in sync with the momentum of change understand that there is strength in numbers. They understand that the more people they have in their network, the greater their chance of being aware of opportunities that are camouflaged to the less well-connected.

My personal call to action: I _____

I'll make a confession to you right now, seeing as you're over halfway through the book: The main reason why I write books is to make new friends. "Whoa! That's a really effort-intensive way to meet new people," you may be thinking. And you may be right, but name one thing in your life, besides your attitude and your health, that's more crucial to your happiness. The person with the best friends wins. If you're reading these words, you're a person I'd like to have as part of my network. So e-mail me at mike.lipkin@environics.ca or, even better, call me at 416-969-2811. I'd like to talk to you. I'd like to hear from you. I'd like to hear what trends you think will be transforming the world in the next twelve months. I'm serious—let's communicate ASAP.

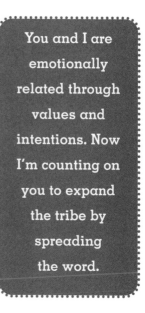

You and I are emotionally related through values and intentions. Now I'm counting on you to expand the tribe by spreading the word.

Are you wealthy? I'm not talking about your financial net worth. I'm talking about the amount of "social capital" you've accumulated in your lifetime. Social capital is the number of meaningful connections you've established with a wide range of people in your professional and personal life. It's the equity you've built up with others through your contributions, conversations and credentials. It's the trust that others have in you because of your past actions. It's the number and size of deposits you've made in the "relationship bank account." Most important, it's how much "currency of reciprocation" you've generated with others, which means how motivated others are to help you when you need it because of how you've helped them in the past. True insurance doesn't come from an insurance company; it comes from having helped as many people as possible so that they will step up for you during your time of need.

Here's another great trend: "flexible definition of family." This means willingness to accept nontraditional definitions of *family*, such as common-law marriages. It's a belief that family should be defined by emotional links rather than by the legal formalities of institutions. It's also a belief that society should be open to new definitions of what constitutes a family. This trend is up by 18 percent from 2001 to 2004, which means that we're feeling a lot more connected to a lot more people. We're opening up our tribes to allow in more members. And now there's a new tribe: people who share Mike Lipkin's passion for life and leadership on the Cusp of change. Guess what? You're part of it. Welcome! You and I are

My personal call to action: I _____

emotionally related through values and intentions. Now I'm counting on you to expand the tribe by spreading the word.

The moral of the "Engage or Get Lost" story is that you and I need to become the ultimate tribe member in multiple tribes. We need to view our success as a direct function of the success of the multiple tribes in our lives—family, friends, community, company, country, planet. We need to see ourselves as the people who do the most to contribute to the tribe. Then we need to act on that. Remember, sow your thoughts, reap your feelings. Sow your feelings, reap your actions. Sow your actions, reap your habits. Sow your habits, reap your character. Sow your character, reap your happiness.

To end this section and segue into the next, here are Lipkin's ten actions to become the ultimate tribe member on Lipkin's reality show, Keeper of The Flame:

1. Give more than others think is wise. Give so it hurts a little.
2. See everyone as a gift, a friend and a teacher.
3. Make sure everyone else sees you as a gift, a friend and a teacher.
4. Do whatever it takes to be that gift, friend and teacher.
5. Deliver optimism. Be the reason why people are more hopeful.
6. Introduce others to new possibilities. Think, "What if?"
7. Rise above your moods. Be consistent, like the sun rising every morning.
8. Radiate your affection, gratitude and respect. Compliment genuinely.
9. Get over disappointment instantly. Forgive quickly. Learn and let go.
10. Build your mojo every day. Resilience always wins in the end.

My personal call to action: I _____

Personal Notes

Part Three

Reaching For The Torch:

Mastering The Six Nuclear Dimensions to Become a Keeper of The Flame

If you were in front of me right now, I would salute you.

WOULD EVEN EMBRACE YOU, IF THAT WAS ACCEPTABLE TO YOU.
I like you because you share my values. You share my curiosity, my tenacity, my desire to do whatever it takes to be fully you. You've fought off the distractions. You've thought through the issues. You've completed your commitments to action on every page. You've made some breakthroughs, and there are many more to come. You're a long-hauler. "Bravo!" I say to you. "Bravo!"

I'm going to pause for a minute of celebration before I continue. And so should you. You're part of the elite ten-thousandth of Americans and Canadians. What do I mean? Approximately 330 million people live in Canada and the U.S. This book will sell about 33,000 copies. That means one out of every 10,000 people will read this book. Including you. You are not just one in a thousand—you are one in ten thousand. In fact, by getting to this point you're closer to one in 100,000, because 90 percent of people who buy a book never get past the first few pages.

Congratulations! How does it feel? If you could see me now, you'd see me smiling as I type these words on a warm summer evening. It's a rush—I'm on fire! And I sense that you are too. I also know it could be half a year, two years or even five years before you read what I'm writing. Just know that I planted the seeds for your breakthroughs in August 2005. Whenever you read these words, the common element that binds us together across the timeline is that it's happening now. I'm writing these words now and you're reading these words now. How cool is that? When you live in the now, there is only the present—the gift that you and I are sharing in this instant.

My personal call to action: I _____

131

> The future belongs to only one kind of person: people who focus all their energy in the best way on what they do best to help others become their best.

So let's look back briefly on our journey so far: You know what a Keeper of The Flame is. You know there is no such thing as ordinary. You know about the eighth deadly sin and how to avoid it. You've learned about the Cusp of change. You understand the power of trust. You've been introduced to the five themes characterizing every Keeper of The Flame's story. You've been reminded that there is no small stuff. You've been challenged to live brilliantly. You know you have to love change. You're aware of the five signals and the nine Life-Transforming Trends. We've come a long way together. But it's all been preparatory to the real motivation for your investment so far: cracking the Keeper of The Flame code so you can inspire others on the Cusp of change.

If you're like most of the people I research, you feel as though you're close to breaking through in certain core success areas. You're so close you can hear the code clicking into place. These are your "power zones." You're on the verge of victory, yet there's still something getting in the way. It's like the detour or roadblock just before you reach your destination. You can almost see it, feel it, touch it, but there's one more challenge you have to overcome—a challenge that could still upset everything.

In your other core success areas you feel as though you're still in a no-go zone. It's as if the more you try to move toward your goals, the more they recede into the distance. And then when you feel as though you're eventually making progress, it turns out to be a mirage. Frustration, resignation, exasperation, desperation are your unwelcome companions in these areas. It drives you crazy because you know you need to succeed in these areas in order to direct your energy elsewhere. The more time you spend in these "struggle zones," the less time you have to become a Keeper of The Flame in the domains where you know you can shine.

You've just studied the nine Life-Transforming Trends. So you know the future belongs to only a certain kind of people: people who focus all their energy in the best way on what they do best to help others become their best. Read that phrase again. It has four components:

People who focus all their energy: If you're not focusing all your energy on the task at hand, you cannot become a Keeper of The Flame. Distraction dilutes your

personal power. Every thousandth counts. If you're not fully there the spoils go to someone who is. You're focused or you're second, third, fourth or nowhere. The challenges are too big and the competition is too good to thrive without total, unadulterated focus.

People who focus all their energy *in the best way*: It's one thing to focus your energy, it's another thing to know how to focus your energy in the best way. We all have a unique strategy that maximizes the impact of our personal energy. It's like our fingerprints or our DNA: ours alone. If you understand your unique strategy, you will achieve the highest ROE—return on energy.

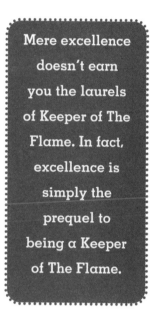

Mere excellence doesn't earn you the laurels of Keeper of The Flame. In fact, excellence is simply the prequel to being a Keeper of The Flame.

People who focus all their energy in the best way *on what they do best:* You are a genius. How do I know? Because we all have an exceptional natural capacity for one specific activity. It may be driving a car or organizing an event or programming software, repairing machines or making people laugh. What's your exceptional natural capacity? If you're like most of the people I research, you don't exactly know. That means you're not focusing all your energy on developing it. That means you're not self-actualizing. That means it's very difficult for you to become a Keeper of The Flame, because you don't even know what truly lights your fire. On the other hand, if you know what your genius is, it's easier to keep fueling it so you become brighter and hotter to the people around you.

People who focus all their energy in the best way on what they do best *to help others become their best:* The end goal is always to catalyze others' success. That's the North Star. That's the constant motivation guiding Keepers of The Flame. Those who have it will always prevail in the end. Those who don't will never quite make it to their personal promised land.

Okay, it's time to crack the code. It's time to understand the Six Nuclear Dimensions and how to master them to become a Keeper of The Flame. Remember, from here on, our joint mission is not just to excel. Someone who excels is someone whose performance may be superior to others. Her excellence means that she is usually at the front of the pack. She is one of "the leaders." But mere excellence doesn't earn you the laurels of Keeper of The Flame. In fact, excellence is simply the prequel to being a Keeper of The Flame.

My personal call to action: I _____

We're after much bigger game. We're after a quality of performance that is legendary. It's the performance that introduces you to what's possible. It's the standard of delivery that reminds people what dreams are made of. It's the kind of actions that excite them into action. It's the sights and sounds that stir their hearts and inspire them at a primal level. It's what we feel when we experience an act of great love, courage, skill, generosity, creativity, energy or connection. It's a call to our higher selves that we cannot deny.

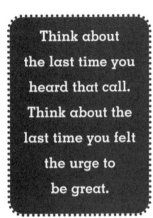

Think about the last time you heard that call. Think about the last time you felt the urge to be great.

Think about the last time you heard that call. Think about the last time you felt the urge to be great. Think about the last person who made you feel like a champion or a hero. Think of a time when you knew you were performing at your highest level. Think of those times when you know you helped and empowered others to be the best they could be. Think of the contributions you've made to others and the lives you've enriched. Now think about what it would be like to make that level of performance the level you play at every day. It is possible. In fact, it's the way thousands of people around you are already living their lives.

I see them wherever I go. They're my clients. They're my partners. They're my colleagues. They're participants in my seminars. They're my fellow citizens. They're in the stores I visit and the restaurants I eat at. They're in the planes I fly on and with the charities I support. They're front-line people and they're captains of industry. They're teachers, doctors, salespeople, technicians, entrepreneurs, office workers and civil servants. They're people who are bound together by a platinum thread—they've made the decision to be stellar. Sometimes it's been a conscious choice, but most of the time it's simply who they are and how they act. Being anything less would be unthinkable. They're not driven by external accolades; their exceptionality is embedded in their psyche. Whatever they do, they make it their masterpiece.

They're people like Angie Jun, who came to Canada from South Korea in 1977. I met Angie at the end of 2004 when she bought a small dry-cleaning business in Forest Hill Village, a couple of miles from my house. I had responded to a "$1.95 per shirt" special, but from the moment I encountered Angie I felt I was in the presence of someone special. She's a small, trim, impeccably tailored woman with a pixie face and irresistible energy. Before taking over the

My personal call to action: I _____

dry-cleaning business, she had run a convenience store in north Toronto for 26 years. She says, "I loved doing this. I loved my customers. They used to come to me and talk to me about all their problems. Then I used my savings to buy this cleaning business at the end of 2004. There is a lot of stress in this business but I try to do my best every day. . . . I always just listen to difficult customers because they always have something on their minds—that is why they complain. If I am able to do something, then I say, 'I can, yes, I can.' If I am unable, then I say, 'I can't, no, I can't.' I love being and speaking with all the people in my business. The most important value with customers is trust."

Angie's relish for her customers shows not just in the way she handles them in her store, but also in the individual drop-offs she makes after she closes every night. Of all the people I'll describe in this book, Angie Jun may be the most compelling Keeper of The Flame I know. I also know that Angie didn't need to read a book on how to become motivated. Being customer-centric is as natural to her as breathing. But who knows? Once she reads this book she could take herself to a whole new level of "Angie-ness." Stay tuned . . .

Here's what I believe: Whether you're Angie Jun or Jackie Smith or Mike Lipkin, life is meant to be lived at a stellar level, where you're shining as brightly as you possibly can. That's where your light inspires others to do the same. It may be that your light is of a softer shade than mine. It may be that it's not accompanied by thunder and fireworks. It may be that your music is gentler on the ear and your energy softer to the touch. That's simply a matter of style. What really counts is that you heed Henry David Thoreau's warning, "Most men lead lives of quiet desperation and go to the grave with the song still in them." The antidote to that fate, of course, is to live as though you plan to leave nothing unused. It's to live in such a way that when it's time to go, you can say, "I became all I was meant to be. I did all I was meant to do. I gave all I was meant to give."

As we make the sublime real, let's move from the ideal to the practical. I'd like to introduce you to the concept of *Nuclear Dimensions*. A Nuclear Dimension

> Live as though you plan to leave nothing unused. Live in such a way that when it's time to go, you can say, "I became all I was meant to be. I did all I was meant to do. I gave all I was meant to give."

My personal call to action: I _____

135

is a core component of your lifestyle that determines the quality of your life and the lives of all the people you interact with every day. If you get the Nuclear Dimensions of your life right, you'll integrate insight, balance and energy to become a Keeper of The Flame. You'll feel that you're living in your high-performance zone. Others will feel your integration, and they'll be both inspired and empowered by your example. The virtuous cycle will have been initiated— and my work will be done.

So what are the core components of your lifestyle that determine the quality of your life and the lives of all those people you interact with every day? What are the central parts of your life that control your sense of contentment, confidence, capacity and connection to others? Think about what's most important to you.

I've identified six Nuclear Dimensions that we need to master to become Keepers of The Flame. I've listed them in order of priority, although each one is vital to living a life that is an inspiration to others:

The Six Nuclear Dimensions

1.	**Focal:**	How you direct your energy, time and resources
2.	**Strategic:**	How you build your Personal Manifesto
3.	**Mental:**	How you learn and grow every day
4.	**Emotional:**	How you master The Seven Power Emotions
5.	**Action:**	Living your Everyday Empowering Ritual
6.	**Social:**	Earning kudos through your Personal Charisma, your Personal Team and your Personal Network

After fourteen years of studying the best of the best, I believe that these are the six Nuclear Dimensions that help make them so. As we explore each one, I'll provide you with key insights gleaned from our research and my interaction with literally thousands of champions from around the world.

Before we go any further, though, I'm asking you to participate fully in all the exercises I ask you to complete. Writing this book has helped me improve my delivery on all six Nuclear Dimensions. Simply writing down my thoughts

My personal call to action: I _____

in an open-ended manner has sharpened my thinking and revealed a whole new vista of possibilities. By reading my words you've helped me communicate with myself and, most important, you've given me a purpose. This book has dominated my waking hours for an entire year. I've processed every book, magazine, newspaper and conversation through this filter: How can I include this insight in my book to make it even more relevant to my readers? It's been a magnificent obsession. Now it's up to you to leverage my work to sharpen your thinking, open up your network of possibilities and increase your power as a mentor to others.

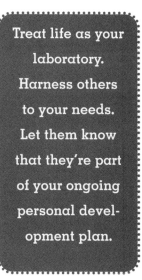

Treat life as your laboratory. Harness others to your needs. Let them know that they're part of your ongoing personal development plan.

So think through each Nuclear Dimension and customize it to fit your unique situation and challenges. Don't hurry—this is not a drive-through. Take as long as you need. Then test your thinking by acting out your theories. Treat life as your laboratory. Harness others to your needs. Let them know that they're part of your ongoing personal development plan. You'll be amazed at how many people will want to contribute even more.

No one has a plan that's just right for you. Like me, they may have relevant, proven strategies for success, but there's no one-size-fits-all. It's up to you to customize them to yield maximum dividends. Tell me, what could be more important to your success and happiness than having specific plans to get the most out of your life? And tell me another thing, what could be more important than helping the people closest to you build a specific plan for their success and happiness?

You know the answer, I know the answer—we all know the answer. Yet more than 99 percent of all people never build specific plans. This is not a theoretical number; it's based on my experience with almost two hundred focus groups over the past six years. I ask people how many of them have a written plan for success and happiness. Maybe one percent answer yes. The rest let life happen to them. They let the current drag them along until one day they wake up and they're miles from where they wanted to be. Sound familiar?

In line with the general theme of the whole book, I'm going to make these Nuclear Dimensions wonderfully simple. I want you to get the message as you read the words. I want to excite you into action, but I also want you to struggle

My personal call to action: I _____

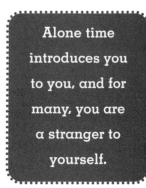

Alone time introduces you to you, and for many, you are a stranger to yourself.

just a bit. Any time you try to describe your route to success and happiness, it's going to be challenging. You've probably never done it before, so don't expect the words to just pop into your brain. Every living thing requires some time to gestate before it's born. The neat thing is, when you wake up with a headache in the morning, you'll know it's not a hangover—it's simply tired mental muscles.

At the same time, don't stress about the answers. The beauty of these assignments is that you're in control of the timeline. So give yourself the gift of time, but also set yourself a deadline. A deadline disciplines your thinking and provides just the right amount of urgency to make it happen. I had to publish this book in January 2006 so I'd have a program to build my business on for the rest of the year. Nothing motivates me more than the knowledge that my career depends on these words.

So take it easy, take it slow, but take the time. There will be moments when the thoughts flow to you in abundant streams. Other times, the flow will dry up. It doesn't matter. You need both the flow and the slow to create brilliance. There were times during the writing of this book when I produced over three thousand words a day, and other times when I produced a couple of hundred. Always, though, "alone time" delivered results. Alone time introduces you to you, and for many, you are a stranger to yourself. How deep is that? I ask you (smiling).

Okay, to quote Walt Disney, all neat and pretty? Then on with the show!

My personal call to action: I _____

Your Focal Nuclear Dimension:

 ## How you direct your energy, time and resources

The F-man cometh. Focus equals power. Focus equals concentration. Focus equals strength. Focus equals your reality. Focus equals your future. What you focus on is what you are becoming. What you focus on is what you're moving toward. What you focus on is what you're feeling right now. Focus is the spinal column that runs through every other Nuclear Dimension. If it's strong and healthy, you can do anything. Without it, life is a heck of a lot more difficult.

Here's another simile: Focus is like a mental magic wand. It can instantly change your moods and your morale. It can turn pleasure into pain or pain into pleasure. It can fill you with certainty or doubt, delight or dread, love or hate. Right now, think about some things that could go wrong in your work. Come on, list at least three possible problems. Good. Now think about a person who is causing you grief. Think about a person who is frustrating you. Think about someone who stands for everything you don't like. Good. Now think about the actions you hate taking. Think about the tasks that drive you nuts but are inescapable. Good. Now think about a time when you embarrassed or humiliated yourself. Think about a mistake you made that cost you big time. Good.

Or maybe not so good. Right now you're feeling a little fragile. You're cognizant of what's wrong: what went wrong, what's going wrong and what could go wrong. My directions have led you into a personal sand trap. But at least it was conscious—you know why you're feeling

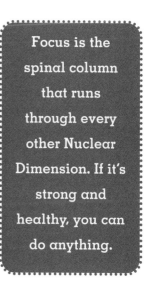

> Focus is the spinal column that runs through every other Nuclear Dimension. If it's strong and healthy, you can do anything.

not so good. How often have you just slipped into a bout of the blues or self-doubt without knowing why? Now you know. You allowed your focus to turn on you. You allowed the dark side to take over for a little while before your instinctive life force fought back and reclaimed your focal high ground.

Now let's switch gears. Think of a person who would do anything for you. Think of three people you really love being with. Think of your best client or customer. Think of a recent big win at work. Think of one undeniable reason

My personal call to action: I _____

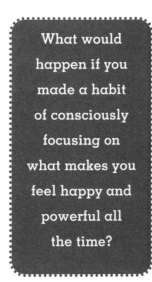

> What would happen if you made a habit of consciously focusing on what makes you feel happy and powerful all the time?

why you will be phenomenally successful this year. Think of one reason why you are truly blessed. Think of one reason why life has been miraculous for you. Think of the best meal you've had this year. Think about the person closest to you smiling at you with adoration. Think about why you're a gift to your friends and family. Think of someone who always makes you smile. Think about a hot bath on a cold night with your life partner, spouse or intimate friend. Think about a breath of mountain air on a sunny spring morning. Inhale deeply. Exhale. Good.

How are you feeling now? Much better than just a minute or so before, right? Why? Because you focused on the magic, not the tragic. You consciously directed your imagination toward a mental reality that you found desirable. So what would happen if you made a habit of consciously focusing on what makes you feel happy and powerful all the time? I'll tell you what would happen—you'd be happier and more powerful more of the time. No one can be up all the time, but those who strengthen their focus muscles enjoy a lot more uptime.

You and I are given 168 hours a week to live. In my case I'll spend about 49 hours sleeping—that's non-negotiable. If I don't sleep, I can't burn brightly when I'm awake. But the other 119 hours—17 hours a day—are fully focused on burning bright and strong so that I light up everyone around me. How many people do you know who can say they spend 17 hours a day focusing on inspiring others? And, by the way, that's not overstatement. My job is to talk to people about inspiration. It's to research inspiration. It's to write about inspiration. It's to help others plan for inspiration. Inspiration saturates everything I do. Most important, it's a conscious focal point for my time, energy and resources.

Even during the fourteen hours a week when I'm watching TV or DVDs on my home theater system, I'm thinking about how I can use what I'm watching to inspire someone. Some of my best lines are from great movies. Seriously—I watch movies with a notebook, ready to scribble down great lines as I hear them.

Like you, I have to spend a big chunk of time on tasks and chores that can be unappealing, unpleasant and unavoidable. I estimate I spend at least three hours a day on those tasks, about 18 percent of my waking time. It's called running a

My personal call to action: I _____

business. It's the array of administrative tasks that must be completed, conflicts that must be resolved, money that must be managed, debts that must be collected, time that must be spent in airports, negotiations that must be conducted, regulations that must be met, problems that must be solved. But even then I'm asking myself how I can use every situation to inspire others. And every time I ask, I get an answer. To quote Napoleon Hill, "Every adversity, every setback, every heartache carries within itself the seeds of an equal or greater benefit."

So, inspiration is my gig. What's yours? What's your magnificent obsession? What's the focal point of your time, energy and resources that will make you a model to the people around you? Think a while before you move on. Write it down. Write down what you want to achieve with it. Write down what you love most about it. Write down why you're uniquely talented to achieve it. Write down how the people around you will benefit from it.

Imagine a propeller with four blades joined at the centre. Each blade is a separate element of your focal plan. The center is your Sweet Spot, the place where you're moving toward an outcome that thrills you (first blade), doing something that you're passionate about (second blade), using your genius (third blade), and benefiting the people around you (fourth blade). Let's build your propeller that will drive you forward.

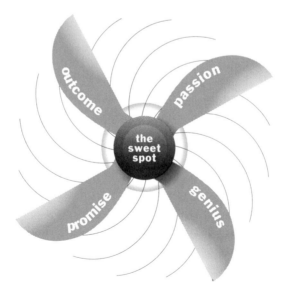

✖ First Blade: Your thrilling outcome

In the next twelve months, what are the one to three outcomes you want to achieve that would thrill you? They should be personal and professional. But don't go for more than three. Beyond three, focus gets dissipated. In imagining these outcomes you need to be as specific as possible. You need to be able to see them as clearly as you see these words. You need to feel them, hear them, taste them, smell them. They need to be as real to you as the seat you're sitting on or the shoes you're standing in. Here are mine:

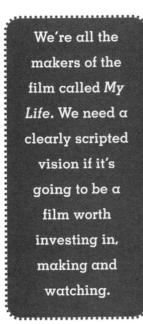

We're all the makers of the film called *My Life*. We need a clearly scripted vision if it's going to be a film worth investing in, making and watching.

Professional: I want to talk to 100,000 people live. I want to sell 33,000 books, CDs and DVDs. I want to directly or indirectly influence a million people to do one thing they would never have done to fulfill one goal they would never have fulfilled. I can see their shining eyes. I can hear their laughter. I can feel their warmth. I can taste their joy.

Personal: I want to weigh 175 pounds, have a cholesterol level of 3.3 and a resting heart rate of 50. At the chronological age of forty-eight I want my physical age to be thirty-eight. I also want a powerful set of abdominal muscles to protect my damaged lower back with a sheath of strength and support. I can see myself at that weight. I can feel the vitality of a healthy cardiac and neurological system. I'm already enjoying the energy and well-being that comes with being only thirty-eight years old.

By the time you read these words I'll have achieved my thrilling outcomes and set new ones. It's already happened. I'm in lag time. I know with total certainty that I'll achieve them. How do you think that makes me feel? How would that kind of certainty make you feel? How many more ventures would you launch if you knew you couldn't fail? Exactly.

So define your thrilling outcomes. Make them come alive in the fertile soil of your imagination. You have no idea what can grow from there. I have practiced this discipline every year since 1992, when I emerged from my bout of clinical depression. And do you want to hear something amazing? Every year

My personal call to action: I _____

for the past fourteen years, I have overachieved my out-comes. Imagination, said Einstein, is more important than knowledge, because imagination is what you do with your knowledge. Just imagine where you could go!

Passion is the highest-octane fuel.

In an interview with *The Financial Post* (February 26, 2005), Michael MacMillan, CEO of Alliance Atlantis, half-owner of the world's most successful TV series, CSI: Crime Scene Investigation, stated, "Like a filmmaker's skills, you have to have a clear vision, not be worried about what other people say, be enthusiastic, force yourself to change to get the goal and have a high tol-erance for contradictions and setbacks." I love that. We're all the makers of the film called *My Life.* We need a clearly scripted vision if it's going to be a film worth investing in, making and watching. As soon as you're ready, describe your clear vision to someone around you. Then tell it to someone else and someone else. The more you talk about it, the more real it will become.

If you're a leader, make sure that you create a thrilling outcome that will give your people a sense of mission. People will give much more to something they want to devote their time and energy toward achieving.

Second Blade: Doing something you're passionate about

Passion is the highest-octane fuel. With enough passion you could probably drive all the way to your thrilling outcome without mastering any of the other Nuclear Dimensions. It could be a longer, bumpier journey filled with wrong turns and dead ends, but ultimately you would get to your destination.

Passion conquers all, partly because all are conquered by passion. What do I mean? Passion for the product or service that you are providing, or passion for the customer to whom you are providing the service, is rare. The majority of people are driven by necessity, not excitement. So when we're confronted with someone who is delighted to be serving us, we're smitten. We want more. We buy the other person's attitude toward us as much as we're buying the product or service. We want some of the other person's juice, and simply by associating with him, we get it.

Obviously there's no substitute for knowledge or competence. If you don't know what you're doing, you may not get a second chance. But this is not a

My personal call to action: I _____

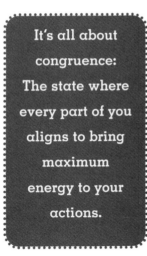

It's all about congruence: The state where every part of you aligns to bring maximum energy to your actions.

book about knowledge and competence. I take it for granted that you've mastered the fundamentals of your trade. You cannot become a Keeper of The Flame if you're still struggling with the basics. If you are, carry on reading, but get a firm grasp of the facts and figures driving your business. Like you, I have been confronted with people who are on fire but then do or say something that reveals their amateur status. After that it may be pleasant to watch or listen to them, but I'm not going to entrust great resources or responsibility to their care.

That caveat dealt with, let's carry on. Right now, on a scale of 1 to 10, if 1 is "I hate my job" and 10 is "I'm in professional nirvana," where are you on the professional-passion scale? Anything less than a 9 means you're ambivalent about what you're doing. You have a suspicion that something else, somewhere else may be better than where you are now. Even a nine may not be enough. In the business of being a Keeper of The Flame, anything lower than 9.9 out of 10 is a failing grade. I score 11 out of 10 on the passion scale. I'll always be awed at being able to do for money what I would do for free. I'm passionate about what I do because I'm passionate about getting people excited. I'm passionate about flicking people's ON switch. I'm passionate about the light that follows. What does it for you?

It's all about congruence: The state where every part of you aligns to bring maximum energy to your actions. We can feel when we're in the presence of congruence. It's so compelling because it fosters confidence and certainty—the two attributes we want most in the New Uncertainty.

There are three ways to become enamored of what you do. The first is to genuinely love your work. If you do, there is no difference between work and play. Your challenge is simply to channel your passion more powerfully so that there's minimal wasted mojo. In fact, if you genuinely love your work, I'm willing to bet that you're already a Keeper of The Flame. You're just looking for ways to burn a little brighter.

The second way to love what you do is to change your perception about what you're doing. Remember, love is a verb as well as a noun. You may be focusing on what's wrong or what's painful. Or you may be fixated on a person who is painful. Change your focus; change your reality. This requires toughness

My personal call to action: I _____

and discipline, because your brain is always going to be drawn to the negative. It's a survival skill. But if aspects of your work are so appealing that you can get past the negatives, stick with it.

There is a visualization technique called reframing. That's when you rearrange the context of your environment to deliver a different meaning to you. For example, writing this book will take me well over 1500 hours. If I had chosen to perceive this project as an excruciating mental marathon, I would never even have started. When I chose to perceive the book as an opportunity to crystallize my thinking, upgrade my technology, connect with thousands of people and create a masterpiece, I became far more likely to love what I'm doing. Does this make sense to you? How can you reframe your work so that it delivers a different meaning to you? Once you've figured that out, you need to constantly refocus on your reframing.

The third way to love what you do is to change what you do. But here's another Lipkinism:

Never run from something – run *to* something. If you run from something, it will follow you; you take you wherever you go.

So study your options. Take the time to truly understand what you love to do and where you will be allowed to do it. Above all, don't get frustrated. Frustration smothers passion. Remember, "God's delays are not God's denials." Everything is happening just the way it's supposed to. Just as you can't hurry the evolution of a caterpillar into a butterfly, you can't schedule an appointment with destiny. It will happen when it's supposed to happen. The lesson here is that you need to be alert to the moment when it presents itself to you. You need to sense that it's right for you. You need the courage to pursue it. Then you need to grab it and stick with it. Most important, if you feel at your deepest level that it's right, let no one talk you out of it. Remember the eighth deadly sin, regret.

Once again, help the people around you uncover their passion. Based on all my research, at least 75 percent of people are not acutely conscious of their passion. They're operating by rote. If you can reconnect them to their passion in a way that aligns with the business, you'll witness a renewed surge of motivation and productivity.

My personal call to action: I _____

✖ Third Blade: Using your genius

Just as the sun rises every morning, you have the genius within you. You have something you can do so well, that you could be one of the great ones of all time. This is not hyperbole. To quote Shakespeare, "Be not afraid of greatness: Some are born great, some achieve greatness and some have greatness thrust upon them." Lipkin's interpretation of Shakespeare's meaning is that everyone has greatness. Some are fortunate enough to begin using it from birth. Others learn to use it over time. And others are forced into using it by a crisis or emergency. The point is that the greatness is there from the beginning. The quality of your life is a direct function of how long it takes you to discover and develop it.

> Greatness is there from the beginning. The quality of your life is a direct function of how long it takes you to discover and develop it.

I was thirty-four years old when I discovered my greatness. It took a year of clinical depression, a stroke of luck and a Nobel prize–winning author to motivate me to leave the advertising business, where I was good, but not great.

At the end of 1991, as I was nearing the end of my year-long episode of depression, I heard about a book called *Darkness Visible*, by William Styron, the author who won a Nobel prize for his novel *Sophie's Choice*. In the book, Styron described his struggle with and eventual triumph over depression. I read the book just as I was regaining my joie de vivre. It helped me make sense of the mental chaos I had just been through. It also motivated me to chronicle my experiences as a way of putting them behind me. I submitted my writing to a local magazine, which published the story. The response was so great that I turned my story into a book, *Lost and Found, My Journey to Hell and Back*. The book sold over 50,000 copies, making it one of the bestselling South African books ever. What followed were hundreds of requests to talk about the book and share its messages.

I discovered that I was damn good at speaking, and damn good at getting through to people. Intuitively I knew just what to say and how to say it. And the more I spoke, the better I became, the more books I wrote, the more seminars I delivered, the more cachet I generated, the wider my influence and the more people I helped. Today I believe I'm as good as anyone in the world at exciting

My personal call to action: I _____

people into action. But I'm a long way from how good I'm going to be. Every time I speak I can feel myself getting better. I'm constantly focusing on how to take my delivery up by even one one-thousandth.

That's my story. What's yours? How are you developing your greatness? Have you even discovered it? Right here, right now, describe your genius to me as though your entire career depended on it—it does. If you cannot articulate your genius in compelling terms to someone else, you have no chance of understanding it yourself. If all you do as a result of this book is define your genius in a uniquely compelling statement, your investment may have been worthwhile. Here's how I define my genius: "I'm a communicator. I use my passion and insights to establish instant rapport. I use the written and spoken word to excite people. I use my confidence to give others confidence. I transfer my skills to others easily so they pay it forward." It took me an hour to find those forty-three words. Now it's time for you to find yours. In fifty words or less, describe your genius and send it to me at mike.lipkin@environics.ca. It may be one of the most important things you do this year. Once again, don't rush—think.

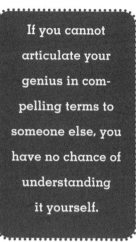

If you cannot articulate your genius in compelling terms to someone else, you have no chance of understanding it yourself.

By the way, the origin of the word genius can be traced back to Roman mythology. In Roman times a family or individual was said to have a guardian spirit, or genius. Whenever a person performed brilliantly, whether athletically or intellectually, it was said that their genius had guided them. Let yours do the same . . .

Here's an "aha!" that's so obvious you may not have thought of it: Over the course of a human lifetime, personal success is a direct function of how much time is invested in skills that can be improved by rigorous training as opposed to those that you have to be born with. In my case, I'll never be great at financial accounting or business process re-engineering. It's just not in me—I could spend years being taught those skills and I would never learn them. On the other hand, when it comes to oral or written communication, I get it immediately. Even the smallest insight can lead to major improvements in me. Play to your genius. Invest as much time as you can where you're going to get the highest return. It makes sense in business and it makes sense in life.

As always, help the people around you discover their genius as well. I'm always amazed at how few people have even thought about the one component

My personal call to action: I _____

that could help take them to their highest level. Time after time, in my seminars and focus groups, I hear, "I don't know. I've never thought about it before." Well, it's time to think about it now. It's time to help your colleagues, peers, friends and family members pinpoint their inner greatness so they can express it and pay it forward . . .

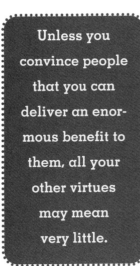 Fourth Blade: Your personal promise – benefiting the people around you

Here's a hard truth: Unless you convince people that you can deliver an enormous benefit to them, all your other virtues may mean very little. Your promise is where your passion and genius come together to reward others in the most meaningful manner. If your promise isn't meaningful to others, your value to them may be minimal.

Remember, we're living in a winner-takes-all environment. If you want to live well, being one of the best isn't good enough. Excellence guarantees you nothing—it's brilliance or bust. What's more, in an age when we have no time, if you cannot express your meaningful promise succinctly the first time around, there won't be a second chance. If you don't get someone's attention from the get-go, you're just an interruption. And once she forms an opinion of you, it's almost impossible for you to change it.

> Unless you convince people that you can deliver an enormous benefit to them, all your other virtues may mean very little.

So what's the personal promise that makes you invaluable to your stakeholders? What reward do you deliver that is uniquely and utterly you? What advantage do you bring to others that will motivate them to crave your contribution? What's your spark that lights their fire? Why are you the go-to guy or girl?

Let me translate my message into dollars: Having a powerful personal promise is worth over $500,000 a year to me. Fifty little words are the reason why I win at least fifty assignments I would not otherwise have won. What do I mean? After five years of marketing myself in the U.S. and Canada, I've established a profile as a top-tier, research-based motivator. I've been successful in getting my name onto many decision-makers' top-five lists of candidates for specific assignments. Top five, however, is

My personal call to action: I _____

a long, long way from a win. In at least two-thirds of all interviews for an assignment, I'm asked a version of this question: "Michael, why should we hire you rather than the other four candidates we're considering?"

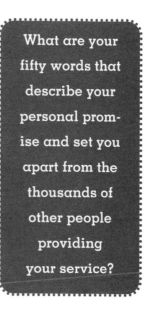

What are your fifty words that describe your personal promise and set you apart from the thousands of other people providing your service?

Here's my response, which I deliver with enthusiastic conviction and theatrical flair: "I will give your people the proprietary insights that will open up their minds and get them so excited they'll do those things they never would have done to get the results they never would have got. And not only that, their success will inspire everyone around them to do the same."

Whenever I utter these words there's always a few seconds of silence from the client as she absorbs what I've just said. Then there's a smile, followed by, "Wow! That sounds great." At least 40 percent of the time it's my ability to express my promise in ten supercharged seconds that clinches the deal for me. I'm also helped by the fact that my competitors haven't taken the time to express their message as effectively. If, after reading these words, they decide to follow my example, I'll just have to invent a new competitive edge.

What are the fifty words that describe your personal promise and set you apart from the thousands of other people providing your service? Write them down and send them to me. This is another really simple exercise that will give you the tiny edge that yields huge returns. Seriously, when I ask people in my seminars what their personal promise is, they tell me, "I'm reliable"; "I'm professional"; "I have integrity"; "I'm creative"; "I'm experienced"; "I'm a good leader"; or "I'm a good listener." People expect all those attributes from you—they're called hygiene factors. Without them there's no way you can be excellent. What I'm asking you to do is go on the offensive. Create a benefit that is meaningful, memorable and motivational. Experiment with it. Have some fun. Get some feedback. Then, when you've got one, embrace it. Talk it, walk it—and change it when it's time.

Once again, coach the people around you into articulating their promise in a way that makes others want what they have to offer. By coaching them you'll be entrenching the learning in your own mind. Pay it forward and you'll be paid very well.

My personal call to action: I _____

Your Sweet Spot: The convergence of outcome, passion, genius and promise

Keepers of The Flame live in their Sweet Spot, and their power comes from their alignment. They're fueled by an internal synergy that makes the whole greater than the sum of the parts. That's why many of them seem larger than life. They aren't losing their life force through ambivalence or conflict. They're augmenting their energy with the exhilaration of living at their highest level. For them, inspiring others on the Cusp of change is the only place they want to be.

▶ If you live in your Sweet Spot, I don't think you can ask for anything more for yourself. That's about as close to nirvana as anyone has a right to be. But it comes with both a caution and a responsibility. The caution is that Sweet Spots don't stay sweet without constant refreshment and reinvention. The responsibility is that if you're in the Sweet Spot, much has been given to you. In return, much is expected from you. Deliver.

My personal call to action: I _____

Your Strategic Nuclear Dimension:
✗ Crafting your Personal Manifesto

Have you ever been through an experience that's a clone of a bad dream, except it's happening while you're definitely awake? Here's one of mine. One of my most valued professional affiliations is with the Rotman School of Business of the University of Toronto. The school hires me to deliver sessions on motivation and team-building as part of their executive education programs. In any given year I'll deliver about twenty seminars for them. It's an important connection for me because of the credibility, the contacts and the learning I derive from the association.

On February 17, 2004, I was in my office fine-tuning a presentation scheduled for the following day. At 5:45 p.m. my phone rang. It was a representative of the school asking where I was. "In my office," I responded, stealing a quick glance at my calendar on Outlook. Nothing was booked. "You're supposed to be here," the representative said. "We've got you delivering a program this evening, beginning at 6:00 p.m." For some reason I hadn't recorded the engagement. "I'm on my way," I sputtered, my chest going tight with panic.

I grabbed the nearest bunch of handouts I could find and hurtled out the door. Fortunately the school is only about two miles from my office, but it's in the middle of town, with heavy traffic. I jumped into a passing cab and began to catastrophize: How could I not have recorded the engagement? What would happen if I didn't deliver a great program because of this mishap? Would the school think that I was unprofessional? Would this be the end of a treasured relationship?

I arrived at the school at 6:10 p.m. The head of the program, Professor Joe D'Cruz, was waiting outside the lecture theater as I arrived. With a look that managed to convey both amusement and annoyance, he asked me wryly, "Ready?" With my most reassuring smile, I nodded and we entered the room.

I looked at the forty people staring back at me. There was the mixture of expectancy and mild agitation that accompanies situations in which something's clearly not going to plan. They were obviously senior executives, and their faces conveyed their disapproval of my lateness. Meanwhile, my brain was scrambling. I had this group for two hours and I didn't have a clue who I was speaking to. I didn't know what industry they were in or what company they were from. I

My personal call to action: I _____

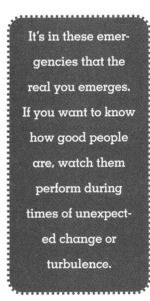

It's in these emergencies that the real you emerges. If you want to know how good people are, watch them perform during times of unexpected change or turbulence.

prayed that Joe would mention the company or the industry during his introduction. And, at the very last moment, he did. They were from CIBC Mortgages, one of the leading mortgage providers in Canada. I had done work for that organization, I had many friends there and I knew the industry well.

That was all I needed. In a heartbeat my consternation morphed into confidence. I took control. I knew I was where I was meant to be. I knew that everything was happening just the way it was meant to happen. I knew I was being given an opportunity to walk my talk by instantly getting into the high-performance zone. I was filled with a flush of well-being. My adrenaline-fueled enthusiasm surged. I embraced the audience with my eyes, told them how thrilled I was to be there with them, and let them know that the next two hours were going to be their most enjoyable learning experience ever. They caught my excitement. They forgot the late start, and the session was rated as "exceptional" by more than 90 percent of the audience.

Why do I tell you this story? Because it's just another version of your story. We're all subject to crises, surprises and shocks for which we're unprepared. Sometimes we create the emergency ourselves. And sometimes it comes upon us like a sudden storm. No matter how composed or courageous we are, we each go through moments of alarm and fright. We're human, with all the faults and frailties that come with that condition. As Woody Allen once said, "I've had many problems in my life and most of them have never happened."

In every case, though, the end result is a function of how quickly and effectively you respond to the challenge at hand. What's more, it's in these emergencies that the real you emerges. If you want to know how good people are, watch them perform during times of unexpected change or turbulence. Keepers of The Flame are at their best when things are at their worst. That's when they reach within to find the resolve and resources to perform at their highest level.

That's the point: If you're looking outside for answers during times of massive, sudden change, you may be looking in the wrong direction. In fact, you're likely to become even more confused. What lies outside of you is nothing compared to what lies within you. But in order to access your personal power, you

My personal call to action: I _____

have to know how to find it. You have to know how to channel it. You have to know how to express it—over and over again.

Smart clients buy the person first, the company second.

In other words, you need a strategy. A strategy is a method for consistently obtaining a specific result. A strategy is a way of finding and applying the most powerful resources to achieve the success that's right for you, and for the people you serve. On the Cusp of change, a strategy is your lifeline. It's what makes you decisive when others are doubtful. It's the difference between not knowing where to turn and knowing exactly where to go. Consciously or unconsciously, all Keepers of The Flame have a strategy that guides them through the unknown.

How would you describe your strategy for success? This question is as important as any I've asked you so far. One of the biggest themes permeating my conversations with leadership groups across the United States and Canada is the importance of the individual representative in building relationships with clients. Smart clients buy the person first, the company second. The smart clients know that it's the individual who is their gateway to the resources offered by the company. They know it's the individual's knowledge, passion and commitment to them that will determine the caliber of the overall value they receive. So the smart clients do as much due diligence on the individual—or the team—servicing their business as they do on the company with whom they're signing the contract.

So let's role-play. Imagine I'm a key decision maker about to award your company with its biggest assignment ever. You are the person designated to manage the account. So before I sign on the dotted line, I want to get a sense of who I'm entrusting my business to. I want to understand your strategy for success the way I understand your company's strategy for success. Give me your Personal Manifesto—a public declaration of your strategy.

As you compose your Personal Manifesto, think about what approaches have worked for you in the past. Think about the approaches that yielded the best results for the people you served. Most important, think about what methods or systems are most likely to work in the future. Revisit the nine Life-Transforming Trends. Anticipate the changes that are likely to happen in your world. Leverage your Sweet Spot. And write your strategy for success in words that uniquely express your voice.

My personal call to action: I _____

Here's Mike Lipkin's seven part Personal Manifesto:

1. **I attract positive energy to me** by conditioning the highest level of personal vitality within me.

2. **I sustain a still mind and a strong heart** by staying connected to my higher power, especially in turbulent times.

3. **I pursue pre-eminence** by taking every chance to learn new ways of multiplying positive energy and transferring it to others.

4. **I seek out extreme situations** where I can accelerate breakthroughs and inspire others on the Cusp of change.

5. **I use my gift of persuasion** to help others grow themselves through communication and teamwork.

6. **I leverage my global exposure** to enrich others' perspectives so they see more, understand more and achieve more.

7. **I partner with the best people** to create new possibilities that change the world one individual at a time.

It's taken me thirteen years as a researcher, motivator and coach to develop my Personal Manifesto. I'm constantly refining it as I migrate from one level to the next. It has become both my rudder and my filter. It guides my actions while defining the meaning that I attach to what's happening around me. In *pivotal moments* I've developed the habit of evaluating my actions and my thoughts against my Personal Manifesto. I consciously ask myself whether I'm "on strategy" or off it. Then I course-correct as I go along.

A *pivotal moment* is any situation in which your actions can have a significant impact on both your success and happiness and the success and happiness of others. I believe we encounter several pivotal moments every day. Most people are unaware of the potential offered by such a moment, so they pass it by or they underperform. How many times have you heard people talk about "big opportunities"—those rare or once-in-a-lifetime chances that may or may not materialize? Well, I believe that pivotal moments are the real big opportu-

My personal call to action: I _____

nities, because they'll occur today, tomorrow and the next day. In the next seventy-two hours, be hyper-alert for a pivotal moment. When it happens, be your personal best. Evaluate your performance against your Personal Manifesto. Grade yourself, learn, adapt, improvise—grow.

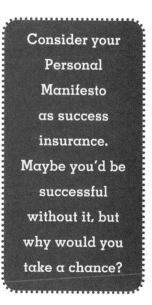

Consider your Personal Manifesto as success insurance. Maybe you'd be successful without it, but why would you take a chance?

One of the most enduring and powerful examples of a Personal Manifesto was written by William Griffin Wilson in 1938—the first draft of the Twelve Steps, the heart of the Alcoholics Anonymous program of recovery and a path described as a miracle by the many who have followed it. In the *Toronto Star* of July 2, 2005, Graeme Cunningham, associate professor of psychiatry at McMaster University in Hamilton, Ontario, states, "Traditional psychiatry says, 'What can I do to help you?' AA says, 'What do you need to do to change yourself and how can we assist you with that?'" The steps are practiced by each person in his or her own way; they are not regulated. Cunningham believes that the explosion of twelve-step programs in the last two decades—aimed at helping those addicted to everything from narcotics and gambling to overeating and sex—shows that people everywhere are searching for a workable blueprint for living.

Here's my message to you: Don't wait for the pain to become too great before you reach for a twelve-step program. If you put off writing your Personal Manifesto, life will force you to come to terms with a reality that is unreceptive to your interests. Then you'll be forced to create a Personal Manifesto while you're experiencing adversity—you'll be in a negative place, you'll be defensive, you won't be at your play-full-out best. So be prepared for the moment that will test you like no other. It could come sooner than you think. In 1938 it took William Griffin Wilson just thirty minutes to write his draft of the Twelve Steps. What can you do in that time?

So back to the opening story of this chapter. It was my Personal Manifesto that empowered me to adjust my mindset and attitude toward an extreme situation. The moment I passed through the initial shock of being taken by surprise, my strategy kicked in and I turned a potential moment of misery into a magical one.

My personal call to action: I _____

Without a Personal Manifesto the winds of change will blow you about like a kite without a tail. You'll be dependent on others for support and motivation. Your personal success will be as much a matter of coincidence as due to your own capability. Most important, you'll lose numerous opportunities to showcase yourself at your best. And every time that happens, it's another lost opportunity to inspire someone else to be magnificent in a pivotal moment.

I'll share something else with you: Just knowing that you have a Personal Manifesto gives you added confidence. It's an asset that makes you distinctive. It also enhances your interaction with others. Any time you share it, you make it more real. You make yourself more interesting and you position yourself as someone who is trustworthy in topsy-turvy times. So consider your Personal Manifesto as success insurance. Maybe you'd be successful without it, but why would you take a chance? What's more, unlike conventional insurance, which you hope you'll never need, you know you'll often find yourself in situations where you need to draw on the power of your Personal Manifesto.

So begin crafting your Personal Manifesto now. Yes, now. Begin it. Don't go any further without writing down a line that expresses the best method for you to get the results you want. Then come back to it later—add to it, subtract from it, polish it. And when you're ready, send it to me. Share it with others. Get their feedback. Help them craft theirs. Practice becoming a Keeper of The Flame.

As you may have noticed already, every Nuclear Dimension is interdependent with every other one. Your focus drives your strategy, which drives your emotions, which drive your learning, which drives your actions . . . and the sequence continues. It's about consistency: Every link in the chain makes every other link stronger.

It's also about integrity, defined as "the state of being whole, entire or undiminished" (Webster's Dictionary). You and I cannot restore anyone else to the state of being whole, entire or undiminished. That's an intensely personal task that requires courage, faith and forgiveness. But we can do it for ourselves. We can transform every experience that we've been through into positive energy that enlarges our capacity for growth and renewal. And as our flame burns more brightly, we give others encouragement to do the same.

My personal call to action: I _____

Right now I know you may be feeling a little overwhelmed at all the thinking and internal exploration I'm asking you to do. That's natural. In fact, if you weren't feeling challenged I wouldn't have done my job. So break the assignment into chunks. Like assembling the pieces of a jigsaw puzzle, start putting them together one piece at a time. Buy yourself a journal or, if you're totally digitized, open a Word file. Find a few minutes in your day to record your thoughts. Group them loosely into the Nuclear Dimensions I'm providing you with. Simply writing down your thoughts will help you clarify them. It will also give you a sense of perspective and control. Over time, as you become more practiced, it will all come together for you. It's in the doing that the real learning occurs.

My personal call to action: I _____

Your Mental Nuclear Dimension:
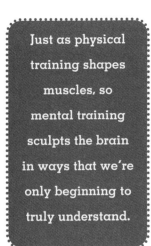 How you learn and grow every day

"How old would you be if you didn't know how old you were?" asked Satchel Paige. "Forever young," I replied. "For as long as I love to learn, I'll never get old."

Keepers of The Flame feed their minds just as they feed their bodies. They do it every day, they do it consciously, they know what's good for them and they're discerning about what they consume. They know that while the body matures early, learning helps the mind keep growing forever. They also know that anyone who stops learning is old, whether they're nineteen or ninety.

Learning is your talent's lifeblood. You can have impeccable character, you can have colossal natural ability, you can have deep expertise and experience. But it's constant learning that nurtures that character, ability and expertise. We all know groundhog people who have thirty years of experience that's really one year of learning repeated another twenty-nine times. Those unfortunate souls equate learning with pain, so they're condemned to the tyranny of living by routine, seeking the familiar as a buffer against change. Year by year they become more obsolete, until they vaporize into the sunset.

More and more evidence supports the fact that the brain, like the rest of the body, can be altered intentionally. Just as physical training shapes muscles, so mental training sculpts the brain in ways that we're only beginning to truly understand. Neuroplasticity is the term applied to the brain's recently discovered ability to change its structure and function, in particular by expanding or strengthening circuits that are used and by shrinking or weakening those that are rarely engaged. So if you're prepared to commit to learning, your brain will oblige by expanding its capacity to absorb and process what you feed it. Learning will even protect your brain, deep into old age. As reported in *USA Today* (January 25, 2005), according to research at Albert Einstein College in New York, minds in motion stay sharp. Seniors who were the most active, both men-

> Just as physical training shapes muscles, so mental training sculpts the brain in ways that we're only beginning to truly understand.

My personal call to action: I _____

tally and physically, reduced their risk of developing dementia by 63 percent compared to the least active seniors.

Why would you not expand the greatest asset you have—your mind? What could be more vital than expanding your mental ability to function at its highest level? The fact that so many people don't even think about this question is a national tragedy. The fact that so many—including you—are aware of it is why I live my life in wonder, gratitude and hunger for more, always more.

In the world of Keepers of The Flame, reasonable doesn't cut it.

The platinum thread running through the fabric of every Keeper of The Flame I know is their willingness to pay any price necessary for personal growth. For almost all of them, life without growth is death. That's how you can tell the Keepers of The Flame. They're the ones asking questions, registering for new courses, buying the latest books, listening to their peers with fascinated concentration. They're the ones risking failure and defying the fear of looking stupid, the ones admitting they're wrong so they can move on. They're the ones who are aware of the wonder and thrill of the new "aha!," who have the courage to challenge the status quo and the humility to see everyone as their teacher. They're the ones upon whom all progress depends because they're always looking for the better way.

Are you one of these people? If you're in sync with the social trends, you have to be. But there's a chasm of difference between wanting to learn and being a passionate lifelong student in perpetual pursuit of the next epiphany. I'm not exaggerating the commitment required to learn at the level demanded of you if you want to lead or influence others. No, it isn't reasonable—because what will be asked of you will not be reasonable. Reasonable is for wimps. Reasonable is easy. Reasonable is the minimum daily requirements that you have to meet just to survive. In the world of Keepers of The Flame, reasonable doesn't cut it. Crazy, never-been-done-before, extraordinary, astonishing, breathtaking, superhuman, "How does she do that?"–phenomenal is what we're talking about here.

I like the Webster's Dictionary definition of learning: "to gain a habit by experience or exposure to example." That's what we're talking about here—developing a philosophy of learning that becomes as much a part of you as any of your senses. It's your philosophy of learning that's your real sixth sense, because it helps you get more out of all the other senses. If the unexamined life, to quote

My personal call to action: I _____

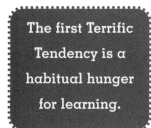

The first Terrific Tendency is a habitual hunger for learning.

Socrates, is not worth living, a habitual hunger for learning makes life one long, appetizing adventure. But that's just the beginning . . .

All our research indicates that when it comes to learning, Keepers of The Flame have seven Terrific Tendencies. We've already discussed the first one—**a** habitual hunger for learning. That's a tendency that can't be taught; it has to be developed from within. Until your hunger strikes you won't feast on anything. I developed my hunger for learning about inspiration as a result of my clinical depression. My original motivation was defensive—I was never going back down there again. It evolved into a lifelong healthy addiction as I experienced the power of my knowledge to transform both myself and others. Unlike your stomach, your brain has an infinite appetite. And the more you know, the more you realize how much you don't know, the more motivated you are to learn more . . and the marvelous momentum continues. What whets your appetite?

■The **2nd** Terrific Tendency of Keepers of The Flame is an understanding of their most effective mode of learning. They know what makes them learn best and they thrust themselves into those situations as often as they can. Let me ask you: When do you learn best? Is it when you're by yourself, quietly studying and thinking? Is it when you're conversing or interacting with others? Or is it when you're actually doing something, learning as you go along? Is it when things are calm and peaceful or is it when all hell is breaking loose and you're forced to find a solution fast?

And, by the way, at what time of day do you learn best? Are you a morning or afternoon or night-time learner? I recently delivered an after-dinner program for the courier company DHL. At about 9:45 p.m. I asked a delegate sitting in front of me when he learned best. "In about fifteen minutes," he responded. "What are you talking about?" I asked with a laugh. "I'm the night-shift guy and my shift usually starts at 10:00 p.m.," he replied.

I learn best by being in the moment. I can learn to communicate better only by communicating better when in front of stakeholders. I can learn to write better only by writing better for my readers. I can rehearse all I want to, but nothing

My personal call to action: I _____

comes near the impact of the live delivery or writing words that people will actually pay to read. That's where the rush comes from. That's where I get the juice. I'm in competition for attention with everything else in someone's life. For me to earn a few hours of your lifetime when you could be doing anything else, I have to be take-your-breath-away awesome. Anything else just doesn't cut it.

I have to talk three to five times a week, fifty weeks a year. If I miss even a week I can feel my edge becoming blunted. If I don't have a speaking opportunity I'll create one by talking for free. That's the difference between learning and knowledge. Knowledge, once gained, may be yours forever. Learning is knowledge in action, and it's far more perishable. The difference between fresh and stale can be twenty-four hours. That's why the Mental Nuclear Dimension needs to be a conscious part of your daily life. In a winner-takes-all world, anyone less than just-baked fresh will be rejected in favor of someone who is. So how hot are you? How crisp is your point of view? If life is a feast, you need to provide the goodies.

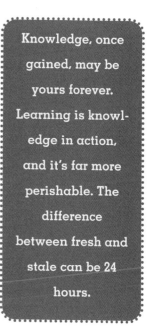

Knowledge, once gained, may be yours forever. Learning is knowledge in action, and it's far more perishable. The difference between fresh and stale can be 24 hours.

■The **3rd** Terrific Tendency is the willingness to unlearn obsolete thoughts and actions. Keepers of The Flame let go of lessons that don't serve them any more. They know that every time they learn something they have to lose something. As technology changes, as media change, as their market changes, as their clients change—they change. They know that their way is not *the* right way, it's just a way that's right for the specific moment or person. They'd rather be successful than right. They believe that *right* is any time a lesson has been learned. They're not psychologically or emotionally attached to a fixed point of view.

Watch the people who are most effective in your marketplace. They're the ones who are constantly shifting their positions as they absorb new information. They don't block new influences or ideas. They open themselves up to opportunity, so

My personal call to action: I _____

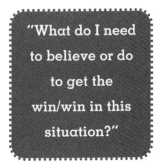

"What do I need to believe or do to get the win/win in this situation?"

opportunities open up for them. They're not out to prove the superiority of their thinking, they're out to achieve superior results. Whatever gets in the way of that goal is discarded. They'll change their stance in a heartbeat if they believe the evidence demands they must.

Here's a powerful thought for when you're confronted by evidence that seems to contradict an existing paradigm: "What do I need to believe or do to get the win/win in this situation?" If your existing beliefs or behaviors are right for that situation, hold on to them. If they're not, change them—or change the situation.

Here's another powerful thought for when you're confronted by someone who has a very different point of view from yours: "What happens if she's right?" The moment you ask yourself that question, two things happen. You open up to others, and others open up to you because they immediately sense you're open to them. There's a time to be rigid and a time to go with the flow. Keepers of The Flame know when to put a stake in the ground and when to burn it.

I've given you no absolute mandates in this book. I've simply offered you the insights and strategies I believe to be true, based on my global research, experience and beliefs. You decide what serves you. Use what does, and throw the rest away. It's your call.

■The **4th** Terrific Tendency is a talent for asking extraordinary questions. "In the Beginner's Mind, there are many possibilities," said Shunryu Suzuki, "but in the Expert's there are few." Keepers of The Flame consciously sustain their "Beginner's Mind" through questions. Like me, they come from the Socratic school of learning. Socrates was renowned for his ability to ask questions that guided his students to truths. Real wisdom means living the questions, not finding the answers. Answers are creatures with a very brief half-life. Because they're a function of a changing environment, as the environment changes, so do they. On the other hand, questions help facilitate change by opening up new ideas and possibilities. The word *educate* comes from the Latin verb *educare*, to draw out. When you ask great questions you develop other people, because they find the answers that are right for the moment. And because

My personal call to action: I _____

it's they who have found the answers, they own them. The best compliment anyone can pay you is "Wow, what a great question! I never thought of it that way before."

So what kind of questions are you asking? Are they openers or closers? Do they lift people up or do they bring them down? Are they empowering or disempowering? The quality of your life is a direct function of the quality of the questions you ask. Here are some examples of poor-quality questions: Why does this always have to happen to me? How come I can never do this? Why is life so tough? Why do people have to be so unpleasant? Why does it always have to be so difficult? Why does this have to happen now? Why do things keep getting worse? What for? Why bother? What's the point, anyway? Why can't they leave us alone? Why can't he make up his mind? What will happen if I fail?

These are poor-quality questions because they lead to poor-quality answers. A question is like a mental flashlight, illuminating the area you point it toward. If you point it toward areas of doubt, anxiety and resignation, that's exactly what you'll see. Poor questions are like blinkers—they narrow your vision so you see only the negative potential of the situation or person.

On the other hand, extraordinary questions ignite the imagination because they spark connections that were not apparent before the question. They open up your mind because they let so much more light in. Throughout this book I've asked you questions that helped you perceive your reality differently. I didn't instill an entirely new set of discoveries in your mind. There are no theories of relativity or quantum leaps in these pages, just a series of questions, observations and insights linked together by the theme of inspiring others on the Cusp of change. Each of them is intended to open up another mental artery to increase the flow of stimulation to your brain.

Here are some examples of extraordinary questions: What if we . . . ? What's the upside of . . . ? How could we . . . ? What's the best thing about . . . ? What would happen if . . . ? Where's the opportunity in . . . ? What can we do to . . . ? What's the best way to . . . ? How can I help to . . . ? What value can we bring . . . ? What's the most direct way to . . . ?

A question becomes extraordinary any time it opens up new options or opportunities. Sometimes it's the brilliance of the question, other times it's the timing. Other times it's knowing how to ask the question in relation to others. Every time, though, extraordinary questions are inspired by the desire to build, stretch, enhance, contribute, innovate, sculpt, grow, create.

My personal call to action: I _____

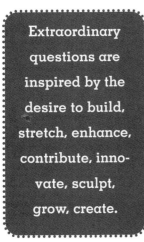

Extraordinary questions are inspired by the desire to build, stretch, enhance, contribute, innovate, sculpt, grow, create.

Keepers of The Flame have an instinctive understanding of when to ask the question and how to ask the question in such a way that it elicits the most fruitful response.

I'm at my best when I'm riffing with my audience in interactive dialogues around the issues I'm addressing in my sessions. The only way I can encourage people to open up in front of their peers is by asking extraordinary questions that make it easy for them to respond. Then I have to add value to what I've just heard, diving even deeper into the response with another question that yields even more insight while celebrating the courage and smarts of the person who has just responded.

Here's a classic illustration of that situation: In July 2004 I conducted a program for the sales force of General Mills Canada Inc. It was at a resort called Deerhurst, about 200 miles north of Toronto. I concluded my session with the following extraordinary question: "What is the biggest 'aha!' that you're taking away from the past two days?" I looked at the 350 faces in front of me. A man raised his hand at the back of the room, I nodded at him and he stood up. "I'm not going to play small any more," he said. The rest of the group felt the significance and power of his statement. I went with the emotional flow. "Wow!" I responded with enthusiasm. "That's awesome. What do you mean?" He paused for a moment, then said, "I have the power. I'm going to do whatever it takes to build the business. When I get back to my territory, my customers will feel the difference." As he finished, his colleagues exploded into a standing ovation. Those two questions and two answers created a magical moment that was the highlight of the entire conference. Extraordinary questions yield extraordinary responses!

■The **5th** Terrific Tendency is disciplined awareness. Whether they're working or playing, Keepers of The Flame are constantly processing their experiences through the filters of their focus and strategy. Listen to a Keeper of The Flame the next time you're with one. They simply cannot escape their self-imposed mission. They're always circling back to how the activity of the moment is helping them take both their focal and strategic Nuclear Dimensions to the next level.

My personal call to action: I _____

You never know when and you never know how life will provide you with the next lesson. What you do know is that if you're not aware of it, it will be wasted on you. Or, if it's a lesson you have to learn, it will keep being revisited on you until you pay attention. Remember this Lipkinism:

The wise person does immediately what the fool does eventually. Nothing is wasted on a Keeper of The Flame. Watch the ones you know – their antennae are always working. They're always placing their now in the context of their outcome, passion, genius, promise or Personal Manifesto.

Sometimes this Terrific Tendency can be an occupational hazard. Keepers of The Flame find it difficult to be frivolous. While they can be funny, charismatic and engaging, they cannot switch off. They're always thinking, always tracking the patterns, always driving to a new and improved way. This is the tendency that makes them so successful, but it's also the tendency that drives the people around them crazy. It's a fascination bordering on fixation. Disciplined awareness is a powerful tool, but it takes a toll on Keepers of The Flame and the people around them. It means that you can never truly relax and think about nothing. Whether it's on the beach or in the boardroom, your mind doesn't have an OFF button.

On the other hand, disciplined awareness enriches every experience: observing fellow commuters on the subway in the crush of Monday morning rush hour; savoring the first Starbucks of the day; solving the final clue that completes the crossword; having a telephone conversation with a friend that really clicks; sharing a joke with a stranger in an elevator; reading something that gets to you, or something that worries you; listening to someone who gets it or to someone who doesn't; winning the deal or not winning the deal; being accepted and being rejected; things going right and things going wrong.

My point is that with disciplined awareness nothing is ever pointless. Everything has learning embedded within it because everything is always happening at multiple levels. What you see is just the veneer. It's what's behind the veneer that counts. And it's your disciplined awareness that shows you what to look for and how to interpret it.

This book is a result of my disciplined awareness. My clients hire me for one primary purpose: to inspire their people to achieve more with less in the face of

My personal call to action: I _____

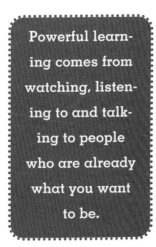

Powerful learning comes from watching, listening to and talking to people who are already what you want to be.

massive change. It struck me that I could never connect with these people the way their peers could. So I created a program called "The Insights of Champions." It features the top 1 to 10 percent of the client's personnel sharing their personal best practices through a combination of video, Internet and live presentations. Other staff can see first-hand how close they are to brilliance. It becomes real and everyone steps it up a notch. They take their team to the next level. Momentum is built and sustained. My clients win—and so do I.

This is called "modeling outstanding behavior." Powerful learning comes from watching, listening to and talking to people who are already what you want to be. That's why I'm so lucky; my whole life is spent with people who are the best in the world at motivating and communicating with others. I'm always talking to leaders, event planners, fellow speakers and audience members who are brilliant. On my iPod, which I listen to before every presentation, I've downloaded the great speakers of all time, from Martin Luther King to John F. Kennedy to Winston Churchill to Nelson Mandela to C.S. Lewis to Arnold Schwarzenegger (just kidding on that last one). My point is that learning is about having a champion to model yourself after who is both real and inspirational. Find as many of your own as you can.

This book is an extension of "The Insights of Champions." It's my attempt to show as many people as I can how close they are to being outstanding and what small steps they need to take to go all the way. What can your disciplined awareness alert you to? By the way, I'm assuming that you're already working on your outcome, passion, genius, promise and Personal Manifesto. If you're not, you cannot hope to have disciplined awareness.

■The **6th** Terrific Tendency is that Keepers of The Flame have an eclectic choice of influences. What do I mean? The best learners select their enlightenment from a wide variety of sources. They aren't followers of one specific system. They traverse different cultural, social and philosophical hemispheres. They're at the vanguard of the global citizenship trend. They consciously seek out new people, new concepts and new

My personal call to action: I _____

experiences to stretch their perception of the world. They want to discover and celebrate diverse world views. They know that once their mind is stretched it can never go back to its original dimensions.

I brand myself as a messenger from another reality. Like a bee cross-pollinating its sources of food as it flies from plant to plant, I cross-pollinate the minds of the people I serve. My worth is a direct function of the variety of places I visit and people I meet. So I'm allergic to homogeneity. I don't need to be with people who agree with me. I'm a motivational nomad in search of the next idea that contradicts my own.

My diversity curriculum is built into my work schedule and my lifestyle. In any given year I'll visit fifteen countries and interface with over 100,000 people. If your schedule is less kinetic than mine, you need to establish a formal way of expanding your exposure to diversity. If you don't, you're only seeing a fraction of the life picture. So reach out to colleagues at work who come from far away. Join community associations where you know you'll encounter diverse cultures. Use your resources to visit countries you've always wanted to visit. Read the books. Listen to the CDs. Use Google. Borrow from everyone; lend to everyone.

■The **7th** Terrific Tendency is follow-through. Keepers of The Flame follow through on their commitment to learning. They actually read the books, take the courses and complete their assignments. Follow-through precedes the breakthrough. There are no quick fixes. Learning is the fusion of theory and application. It's the arduous reprogramming of mind and body to perform at a certain level in a certain situation.

In order for me to perform at a world-class level in front of audiences who are benchmarking me against the great ones, it's not enough that I know what I'm doing. It's not even enough that I'm experienced at what I do. I have to feel what I'm doing at a molecular level. Every cell needs to be coalescing with every other cell to blow my audience away. The learning needs to be as much a part of me as my DNA. And that kind of saturation comes only with massive, relentless, whatever-it-takes follow-through. What's the level of your follow-through? Could I bet my life on it? Are you betting yours? I promise you that someone, somewhere, is. Don't let them down.

My personal call to action: I _____

Your Emotional Nuclear Dimension:
Mastering the Seven Power Emotions

An African chief was teaching his grandchildren about life. He said to them, "A battle is raging inside me . . . it is a terrible fight between two lions. One lion represents fear, anger, envy, sorrow, regret, greed, arrogance, self-pity, guilt, resentment, inferiority, lies, false pride, superiority and ego. The other stands for joy, peace, love, hope, sharing, serenity, humility, kindness, benevolence, friendship, empathy, generosity, truth, compassion and faith."

The old man fixed the children with a firm stare. "This same fight is going on inside you, and inside every other person too."

They thought about it for a minute and then one child asked his grandfather, "Which lion will win?"

The chief replied, "The one you feed."

How are you feeling? I mean right now. Seriously, describe your mood to me. Why am I asking you to do this? Because here is the truest Lipkinism since page 165:

> **Your mood determines your mojo. In other words, at any given moment what you feel is what you do. How you feel is how you do it. Motion comes from emotion. Your sentiment shapes your speech. Or, to quote Shakespeare, "A heavy heart bears not a nimble tongue."**

"When dealing with people, remember you are not dealing with creatures of logic, but creatures of emotion," said Dale Carnegie. "Remember that you are one of those people," says Mike Lipkin.

As I write this I'm both excited and scared. I'm relaxed and I'm on edge. I'm certain of success and I have my doubts. I'm passionate about what I'm doing and it's also a struggle. I'm grateful and I want more. I'm connected to others and I feel as if I'm on my own. I'm proud of what I've achieved and I feel as if I'm just starting out. I feel safe and I feel that it could all implode in a heartbeat.

My personal call to action: I _____

I'm always walking an emotional tightrope; my moods are constantly shifting. An hour is the new day. So much is flowing through my mind that sometimes it threatens to sweep me away. I'm holding on by my fingertips. But you know what? I wouldn't have it any other way. It's the breadth of my emotions that takes my breath away. It's the array of feelings I have to navigate every hour that gives me the juice. Intensity equals life. That's how I feel about what I feel. And, by the way, notice how my feelings about my feelings are driven by my Sweet Spot and my Personal Manifesto. Once again, it's all about consistency.

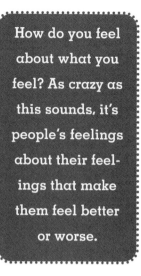

How do you feel about what you feel? As crazy as this sounds, it's people's feelings about their feelings that make them feel better or worse.

How do you feel about what you feel? As crazy as this sounds, it's people's feelings about their feelings that make them feel better or worse. How many times have you heard variations on these themes?—I shouldn't be feeling this way; I don't know why I feel like this; I feel guilty about feeling happy; I'm upset about feeling angry; It hurts me to feel sorry for him; I'm worried that I'm not worried; It's hard for me to take it easy . . .

Your Emotional Nuclear Dimension is about understanding and controlling the distinctive emotional character of your life. True quality of life is really the quality of the emotions you experience most often. I've interviewed people who have everything and yet they're poor because they live in negative emotional states. I've met smart people who are useless because they're at the mercy of their moods. On the other hand, I've lived and worked with people who have very little and yet they're emotionally rich. It may be their character or it may be their culture, but they're conditioned for happiness.

Keepers of The Flame have got it all together. They're talented, they're skilled and they're emotionally powerful. There is a big difference between being emotionally intelligent and emotionally powerful. I've interviewed emotionally intelligent people who are volatile in their personal emotions. They understand their emotions and the emotions of others, but they are less skilled in mastering those emotions during times of intense adversity or crisis. How many intelligent people do you know who cannot control their emotions under stress? Emotionally powerful people, on the other hand, are at their best under pressure. Tough times are their personal best time—that's when they shine.

My personal call to action: I _____

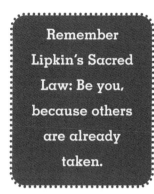

They complement their emotional intelligence with the conscious pursuit of "Power Emotions."

A Power Emotion is any feeling that enhances your capacity to succeed in the moment. Keepers of The Flame have the understanding, the strength and the conditioning to tap into the most appropriate situational Power Emotion. They seek out trying situations because they understand that life is just one test after another. They know that before they can graduate to the next level they have to pass the test that's in front of them today. The more challenging the tests they set for themselves, the more emotionally powerful they become.

Some people have a greater emotional range than others. I know people who were born to love or laugh, smile, celebrate, console, hug, sing. Others are more shy, constrained or cerebral. Remember Lipkin's Sacred Law: Be you, because others are already taken. Feel what's good for you, but understand what feels good for others. Never judge. One person's pleasure is another person's pain. In the world of emotions, there are no absolutes.

In *The National Post* of April 25, 2005, Dr. Hendrie Weisinger, psychologist and author of *The Emotionally Intelligent Financial Advisor*, states that we need to anticipate the emotions of the people we're going to encounter and to be on guard against AADD—anger, anxiety, depression and dejection—all of which qualify as highly contagious emotional viruses. He says that if the market is crashing and frantic clients are calling, financial advisors need to "emotionally immunize" themselves against their distress, to be aware of their own emotions and consciously maintain equilibrium.

Whether you're a financial advisor or any other kind of advisor, your primary role as a Keeper of The Flame is to help others transform emotional pathology into emotional positivity. In any of the twenty-eight countries in which I've worked, the most successful people are those who continually radiate courage, optimism, respect, wonder, excitement, love and lightness. These are seven Power Emotions that characterize the Keepers of The Flame whom I've had the privilege of interviewing. I've listed them in order of their power—one follows the other. As you review them, evaluate yourself in terms of each Power Emotion and ask yourself what you need to do to acquire it, get more of it and pass it on to others.

My personal call to action: I _____

Power Emotion 1: Courage Lipkin's definition of

courage: *the foremost Power Emotion; the gift that you give to yourself; the raw material of character and self-esteem; fear's Siamese twin; the antidote to regret; the source of confidence.*

Courage is the first Power Emotion because it's the Power Emotion from which all others spring. Courage helps you do what you know you have to do when you have to do it, even when you don't want to or are afraid you may not be able to do it. Courage is when you act in accordance with your principles in spite of criticism, resistance or risk. Courage is a gift you give to yourself. No one else can give it to you, and no one else can take it away.

To others, courage is an admirable quality. But to Keepers of The Flame it's a way of life. Their conscience gives them a sense of what is right or wrong in any situation, compelling them to take the right action. Courage is what helps them obey their conscience when it's tough to do so. Anyone can do the right thing when the cost is low. It's when there's a price to be paid that courage manifests itself. It's in those moments that heroes are made. It's in those moments that you and I build our character and self-esteem. Those moments become deposits into our future success—or withdrawals that will hold us back.

No matter how many times you exercise courage, you'll always feel fear.

No matter how many times you exercise courage, you'll always feel fear. That's another definition of courage: doing what you fear so the fear disappears. Without fear there can be no courage. At its core, every great story is a story of courage versus fear, over and over again. Lose your fear and you lose your vigilance. You lose your humility. You become reckless and careless. You suffer, and the people around you suffer.

Courage is a habit that is always a conscious choice. No matter how many times you exercise it, you always have to stare down the dragon within. You're always tempted to run away. Yet, even as you consider fleeing, you know it's not an option. You do what you know you have to do because the alternative will cause you more pain than anything the dragon can inflict. The mere act of facing

My personal call to action: I _____

the dragon defeats the dragon. Running from the dragon means that the dragon wins, and that means defeat at the level of your soul. To quote Senator John McCain, "You can live with pain. You can live with embarrassment. Remorse is an awful companion. The one fear we must all guard against is the fear of ourselves. Don't let the sensation of fear convince you that you're too weak to have courage. Fear is the opportunity for courage, not proof of cowardice."

Unlike optimism or respect, courage is "the greatness that cannot be taught," to quote David Halberstam. All I can do here is encourage you never to give in to your fear. If your conscience commands you to do something, do

it. I'll make a confession to you: Part of me is always afraid. I have a daily rendezvous with unease and disquiet. All the meditation and motivation in the world won't anesthetize me from my angst; it's too ingrained in my psyche. So I'm courageous not because I'm brave, but because I'm scared of giving in to my fear. I don't like it when I see others succumb to their fear. I'll despise myself if I do. And if I despise myself, it doesn't matter who else respects me.

What's your motivation for courage? Find it. Practice it. Condition it. The more you show courage, the greater the certainty that you'll be courageous when it counts. *Never, ever give in to your fear.*

If you've got courage, confidence is easier to acquire. Confidence is an offshoot of courage—a "mini-courage." And it can be learned, because it is situation specific. Confidence is when preparation meets practice to produce desired results. It's the knowledge that you can thrive in the future because of what you've done in the past. So, for example, I'm confident that this book will become a bestseller, because I've already written nine bestsellers since 1992. I'm confident that I will amaze, inspire and delight my next audience, because I've done it about 1500 times since 1993.

In the areas of writing and speaking I'm mega-confident. But I feed my confidence every time I write or speak. I feed it every time I receive a compliment or experience a breakthrough in my own mind. I feed it the way a mother feeds her baby—it's totally dependent on the care I give it. In turn, my well-being is totally dependent on how well my confidence continues to grow and develop. Where can you be mega-confident? How can you consistently feed your confidence?

My personal call to action: I _____

Power Emotion **2**: Optimism Lipkin's definition of

optimism: *the source of hope; seeing the opportunity in every difficulty; positive foresight; protection against giving up; the fusion of knowledge, preparation and attitude.*

Optimism has been a central theme throughout this book. It's both an external trend (the return of faith and optimism) and a Power Emotion that can be learned. It's as indispensable to being a Keeper of The Flame as courage. Without optimism you cannot sow hope. And without hope there's no chance of anyone catching fire.

At its core, optimism is the ability to transplant the present into the future. It's the ability to see things the way they can be. While pessimists see the difficulty in every opportunity, optimists see the opportunity in every difficulty. Optimism fuels inspiration; pessimism snuffs it out. Robert Jarvik, inventor of the artificial heart, states that "leaders have no concept of the odds against them." True optimism grows in direct proportion to the size of the challenge, because that's when it's most needed. If there's little risk of failure, you don't need optimism. It's when others are skeptical that the optimist shines through.

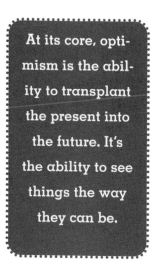

At its core, optimism is the ability to transplant the present into the future. It's the ability to see things the way they can be.

In the beginning, the optimist may even appear to be deluded. She's the one continually flying in the face of conventional wisdom, defying the naysayers, getting up off the canvas, rallying her troops, partners or investors—until one day she breaks through and everyone else sees what she saw all along. It's optimism that protects you against giving up or giving in.

My personal call to action: I _____

Here's a quick test to evaluate your ITO, or inclination to optimism.

Rate your feelings on a scale of 1 to 5 for each question

1 – pessimistic, 2 – doubtful, 3 – neutral, 4 – optimistic, 5 – totally certain of a positive outcome

When others say it cannot be done, I become ☐

When difficulties appear bigger than I thought, I become ☐

When I'm not getting the results I want, I become ☐

When I keep being rejected, I become ☐

When I feel I'm all alone, I become ☐

When others criticize my actions, I become ☐

When I have to risk a lot of money to pursue my objective, I become ☐

When I'm doing something I've never done before, I become ☐

When I'm really tired, I become ☐

When everyone is depending on me for their success, I become ☐

Total ☐

Anything less than 35 means that you're not overly optimistic. Anything less than 44 means that you're not functioning at the level of Keeper of The Flame optimism. If you scored 45 or more, you're incandescent with possibility! I want to talk to you. Call me at 416-969-2811—but only if you scored 45-plus.

My personal call to action: I _____

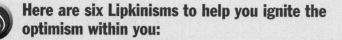

Here are six Lipkinisms to help you ignite the optimism within you:

1. **Listen to your instincts. Instincts tell you what to do before your head has a chance to figure it out.**

2. **Play to your strengths. Operate in the domain you know best. Do your homework. Know everything there is to know about the situation facing you. Don't trust your optimism on things you know nothing about. For example, I know nothing about real estate; I have no feel for the dynamics of that market. When it comes to self-development and motivation, on the other hand, I'll stake everything on my call.**

3. **Ensure your team is strong so they'll support you in the crunch moments. You need people who believe in you no matter what.**

4. **Develop your network and build far-flung alliances. Get different perspectives from a diversity of sources.**

5. **Protect yourself against fatigue and burnout. Tiredness makes pessimists of us all. Do whatever it takes to stay fresh, vital and strong.**

6. **Walk away from your own position if the evidence suggests you should. Ego must serve optimism, not sabotage it.**

The ultimate poster girl for the power of optimism is Trisha Meili, the Central Park jogger who was given the last rites after her rape and savage beating in New York sixteen years ago. According to *USA Today* (June 29, 2005), only the soles of her feet were left without bruises. Multiple gashes split Meili's scalp; an eye socket was fractured in twenty-one places. She could not breathe on her own, lost most of her blood and had severe brain damage.

My personal call to action: I _____

Doctors doubted that the twenty-eight-year-old would live. But she didn't just survive, she thrived. Today she is a motivational speaker and a volunteer who works with others recovering from traumatic changes. Meili cites five ingredients that contributed to her remarkable recovery:

- **"Can-do" optimism and goal setting:** Meili set daily goals and drove herself relentlessly. Even small changes would reinforce her sense of progress.

- **Emphasis on the present:** "I didn't wallow in 'what ifs' and 'if onlys'," she says. She knew she was in the fight of her life. "I felt I couldn't afford to dissolve in rage about the past or ruminate about the future."

- **Bravery:** She faced the hardest things head on. "I had to face this dragon," she recalls, and she fought the beast with every memory and cognitive exercise at hand.

- **Willingness to accept help:** Meili had taken pride in always being the strong one, but she quickly realized that she couldn't make it without throngs of helpers. She held on to all the outstretched hands, with gratitude.

- **Spirituality and life-changing growth:** A lapsed Catholic, Meili came to believe that "there is a higher power of some sort . . . I do feel that I saw God's grace in all the people who reached out to me." Gradually Meili felt an urge to "pay forward" this outpouring of support by helping others.

Meili's is a story of "mega-recovery." She says it heartens her to realize she can make a difference in the lives of others. "It doesn't matter what I could have been. What matters is who I am right now." Sixteen words that we should all live by.

Power Emotion **3**: Respect Lipkin's definition of

respect: *celebration of the potential of everyone around you to contribute to your personal growth and success; honoring every person as a fellow Keeper of The Flame; leaving every facility better than you found it; treating the elements of your personal environment with the care and deference they deserve.*

You can always tell Keepers of The Flame by the courtesy they accord to others. Irrespective of their social position, they handle the people around them like most-honored guests. Everything about them radiates a sense of reverence for

My personal call to action: I _____

the other person. It's in their stance, their voice, their eyes. It's not synthetic. The respect that Keepers of The Flame have for others springs from their inclination to look for reasons to admire the people around them.

Respect also means doing away with standards of "right" and "wrong" when it comes to the customs, points of view and principles of others. There's no right and wrong, there's just different—and different means deference. It means seeing the other person as a partner in the mutual quest for brilliance and inspiration on the Cusp of change.

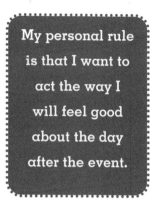

My personal rule is that I want to act the way I will feel good about the day after the event.

Respect applies to things as well as to people. Keepers of The Flame have a relationship with everything around them that borders on adoration. Think of the best people you know. Think of the way they interact with food, machines, clothing, or their physical environment. Watch a true craftsman with his tools, a sailor with his boat, or an athlete with her equipment. They understand that there is an interchange of energy between everyone and everything. Treat everything with respect and the respect will flow back abundantly. It's called reciprocal harmony, and it's a beautiful thing.

On the other hand, think of the last time you witnessed an expression of disrespect for a person, a thing or the environment. Whether we are directly implicated or not, it's always disturbing. Any act of disrespect has an aspect of violation. It diminishes the other person or thing. If we're part of it, even if it's only in the role of observer, we are diminished along with it. Unless, of course, we take action. That leads to crucial questions: When should we intervene and when should we turn away? I know that you know the answers to those questions. It depends on you, the situation, and the act of disrespect. But as a rule, we should act when we know what to do, with adequate respect for our own well-being and safety. My personal rule is that I want to act in a way I will feel good about the day after the event.

You cannot give to others what you do not give to yourself. Respect is an inside job. Keepers of The Flame sustain their dignity by honoring who they are, where they are and where they've come from. Listen to the Keepers of The Flame around you. You will not hear them denigrating themselves. You will not hear them minimize their achievements. You will not hear the language of self-loathing. What you will hear is pride, strength, independence and self-esteem.

My personal call to action: I _____

Everyone messes up. Paradoxically, Keepers of The Flame mess up more than others, because they're trying more things, risking themselves more and engaging more people. Their ability to keep on keeping on is a direct function of how they treat themselves after the mess-up. The respect they have for their own ability to persevere, adapt, innovate, improvise, withstand, recover and learn sustains their stamina and self-belief.

Every week I do something that amazes me because, in retrospect, it was so clear that it would fail. However, anything is obvious with the 20/20 vision of hindsight. I'm often tempted to hurl all kinds of abuse at myself. I'm often tempted to become angry about what I've done. I've learned, though, that I don't do self-abuse or anger very well. I've learned that I have the ability to hurt me more than anyone or anything else. And, just as important, I've learned that self-disrespect is a habit that is too easily formed. Once you succumb to that habit, you begin disrespecting others.

Respect is the conduit to self-control. If you honor the value of you, your world and all the people in it, you have to do what you believe is right for all parties. You will not act out of malice or self-indulgence. Trust me when I tell you that your instincts will serve you well. Yes, you will make mistakes, but they will be mistakes that build your world, not bring it down.

Respect for yourself, your environment and others will also keep you humble. In fact, Webster's Dictionary defines humility as being "courteously respectful." I love that. It means that respect, combined with courtesy, will defend you against hubris. It will also help you sustain your politeness, that most Canadian of traits.

One final comment on respect: It's an all-the-time emotion. If you want to strengthen your respect muscles, practice being respectful when you're agitated, in a hurry, angry or fatigued. That's when you need respect the most. And that's when it will serve you the best, because that's when it will save you from yourself. The greatest threat to our sense of self-esteem is *stressed behavior*—the actions we take in crises, crunch moments or trying situations. If you act poorly or abuse others in any way, your actions will come back to haunt you over and over again. We manufacture our own nightmares through our lapses in the defining moments. It's in those moments that our characters are forged.

▶ So make ultimate respect—for yourself, your environment and your fellow humans—your default position. Make the question "How do I demonstrate my esteem for this person?" your instinctive guide when dealing with anyone, anywhere.

My personal call to action: I _____

Power Emotion 4: Wonder Lipkin's definition of

wonder: *continual fascination with life's everyday dramas; a deep appreciation for others and their contribution; a celebration of your gifts; a heightened alertness to common miracles; constant admiration and amazement.*

Here's the secret of eternal youth: Live your life in a continual state of wonder. Be amazed by everything, over and over again. I call it "experienced naïveté"— the ability to use your experience to reinforce your sense of awe and insulate you against becoming jaded and blasé. It goes to the underlying theme permeating every page of this book: There is no ordinary. At some level, everything in our lives has the power to astound and delight us.

Think of the Keepers of The Flame you know. Aren't they perpetually child-like in their sense of awe? Aren't they continually exclaiming about their amazement at what's happening around them? Aren't they the ones who remind everyone else around them of the significance of everyday events?

Wonder is an elevated state of gratitude. It's a sense of being part of the greatest drama ever produced. It's like being the hero in your own blockbuster movie, surrounded by a cast of thousands of quality co-stars on a set designed by divine talent. That's how I feel almost all the time. I have so many powerful interactions with so many different elements that I often have to pause to savor each encounter fully. Think about events that have happened over the past twenty-four hours. Think about why you should regard them with wonder; think about what and whom you should admire; think about the gifts you had the opportunity to use and the actions of others that are worthy of your appreciation.

If you think about those moments, they will come. I often amuse people with my exclamations of wonder. My favorite question is "Isn't that amazing?" It's an expression of my fascination with what I've just heard or seen. It's also the question that elicits the best response from my audiences. Whenever I hear something interesting from someone, I utter that question. Immediately I see people start paying attention as if they've missed something. And they have. They weren't listening for what was amazing, so they didn't hear it. When I explain why I thought what I heard was amazing, I see heads nod in agreement. So here's my message: See and listen with eyes and ears of wonder.

My personal call to action: I _____

A miracle is as much about what doesn't happen as about what does.

Speak in a tone of wonder. Use words of wonder. Be wonder-full. In the next twenty-four hours look for the wonder, listen for the wonder, talk about the wonder. And help others do the same.

There is no sadder sight than someone who has lost their capacity for wonder. There's a heaviness to those people, an aura of resignation and fatigue around them. They've become sluggish because, when they lost their sense of wonder, their energy lost its octane. They've stopped living and begun existing. Reconnecting them with their sense of wonder is like mouth-to-mouth for the soul.

On August 2, 2005, an Air France Airbus carrying 297 passengers and 12 crew from Paris overshot a runway at Pearson Airport in Toronto, crashing into a ravine. All 309 people scrambled to safety seconds before the airliner burst into flames. "Miracle on AF358" stated the headline in *The National Post* the next day, referring to the plane's flight number. I agree that it was a miracle, but I also believe it was just another miracle on top of all the other miracles I experienced that day. You see, I believe a miracle is as much about what doesn't happen as about what does. So, for example, the fact that I can write these words unimpeded on my new high-powered laptop is a miracle. The fact that I drove two hundred miles today without an accident is a miracle. The fact that my forty-eight-year-old body got through a grueling sixty-minute workout in a state-of-the-art gym today—without complaint—is a miracle. The fact that Robert Half International, a world leader in staffing services, hired me to coach their people today is a miracle. The fact that I got to meet and interact with over 120 talented people in a single day is a miracle. The fact that you're reading these words is a miracle.

And if you think I'm investing these everyday events with too much significance, think about what could happen at any moment. Think about the devastating impact on our lives when one of these "everyday miracles" doesn't happen. Think about the parts of the world where this kind of normality is still a faraway pipe dream. Think about the close calls you've had where you almost lost it all. Think about what could have been, admire what is, dream about what could be. Smile in celebration and breathe deeply. Revel in your great fortune.

My personal call to action: I _____

Power Emotion **5**: Excitement Lipkin's definition of

excitement: *human electricity; enhancement of your intelligence; when you are stimulated into action because of the passion you attach to the action; the motivation derived from pleasurable anticipation of a future event; the fire sparked by visualization of a future goal; the power to succeed.*

You've got the courage, the optimism, the respect and the wonder. You're clearly a person who has the right stuff. You're a model to others. You're a leader, an influencer and an achiever. But without the fifth Power Emotion you cannot hum at your highest frequency. Without excitement you're not using all of your capacity. Excitement and its companion emotions, enthusiasm, joy and passion, are the conduit between the good you and the brilliant you. Excitement turns on your genius. It's like human electricity. It lights up not just you, but all the people you serve. Think about what happens to you when you're around a genuinely excited person. Don't you feel more alive? Aren't you motivated into thinking or acting a certain way? Don't you feel uplifted? So here's another Lipkinism:

> **Consciously or unconsciously, the people around you are listening for your excitement before they do what you want them to do. If you're excited you will incite others into action. If you're not, it's a crapshoot – maybe they will act and maybe they won't.**

Excitement is even more compelling because it's so rare. So few people are genuinely turned on by what they do for a living. Even fewer understand the need to show that they're turned on. And only a fraction are willing to consistently demonstrate their excitement through what they say and do every day. Are you one of them? If I were with you, would I say to myself, "This person is on fire! She's passionate about her work"? (By the way, you don't need to be a showman to show your excitement. You can show it any way that's right for you, but show it you must, over and over again.)

Excitement bypasses rational barriers. When we're with a person who is transparently passionate about what she's doing and why she's doing it, we experience her emotion vicariously. That means we feel or enjoy her excitement

My personal call to action: I _____

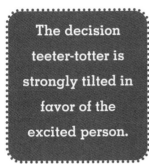

The decision teeter-totter is strongly tilted in favor of the excited person.

through imagined participation in the experience. It's the positive intensity of the other person's emotion that transports us to where the other person wants us to go. Excitement makes it easier for us to rehearse the pleasure we'll feel before we take action. It also makes it easier for us to give ourselves permission to go to the next level. Human beings are infinitely inventive when it comes to finding reasons to embrace or to avoid something. The decision teeter-totter is strongly tilted in favor of the excited person.

I'll share something powerful with you: After researching almost half a million people since 2000, I believe that people want to believe in other people. They want to believe in champions, heroes and icons because there is a champion, hero or icon within each of us just waiting to break out. But we can't become what we can't see. We need models to show us what can be done. We need warnings about what could happen, but we also need examples of what's possible. Excitement helps us become living models of what's possible, not walking warnings about what could happen.

So far I've focused mainly on how compelling excitement can be to others. But here's why excitement is really one of the seven Power Emotions: It makes you clever and creative. It raises your IQ. It increases your mental resources. Think about your performance when you're excited about something. Isn't it far superior to your performance in a more subdued or negative state? Don't you have access to many more internal resources? I would not survive without my ability to access excitement on demand. Before every talk, before every writing session, I focus on why I should be excited in the moment. I think about my Sweet Spot and my Personal Manifesto. I think about the dreamlike privilege of being a mentor to thousands through these words, I visualize you making your dream happen through these words, I put myself into the hearts of all the people benefiting from these words—and I become exhilarated. The thoughts flow into words, the words flow into sentences, the sentences flow into pages and the pages flow into—a book.

When the excitement expires, so does everything else. If I'm not fired up, I burn out. That's why consciously accessing your excitement is so vital to becoming a Keeper of The Flame. You cannot rely on other people or the outside world to give it to you. Most people are struggling just to keep it together. The outside world is in chaos. You are the POET, the Purveyor Of Excitement Today.

My personal call to action: I _____

So here are Lipkin's five ways to become a POET:

1. Consciously live in your Sweet Spot. Keep your outcome, passion, genius and promise at the top of your mind all the time. Ask yourself how your current activities or thoughts are contributing toward your Sweet Spot. If they aren't, change them.

2. Ask this question as though you mean it: What's exciting about this? Believe in the question; believe in the answers.

3. Practice being excited about the small things as well as the big things. Develop your excitement muscles. Look for the excitement potential in everything. Think it. Feel it. Imagine it. Link it to the never-ending chain of exciting consequences. Make each link more fantastic than the previous one. I'm doing this right now: You're reading this book. You'll tell twenty people what you've read. They'll buy the book and tell twenty others. They'll all pay it forward. They'll spread the message. Thousands of people will tap into their reservoir of excitement. Thousands of lives will be enhanced. Thousands of people will be "Lipkined." I'll live my dream and so will they . . .

4. Act as though you're excited even if you're not. Thoughts and actions are mutually reinforcing. Motion creates emotion and emotion comes from motion. Practice exciting others and being excited by others in return. Make excitement a habit.

5. Immerse yourself in people, activities and things that excite you. Surround yourself with turned-on folk. Read inspiring words. Listen to music and speech that enthuses you. Absorb all you can; give all you can.

My personal call to action: I _____

Power Emotion 6: Love

Lipkin's definition of love: *both a verb and a noun; the ultimate engagement; personal strength; the antidote to selfishness; an umbilical connection to others; a willingness to do more for others than one would do for oneself; an enduring source of energy and inspiration; being simultaneously vulnerable and powerful; a prolific generator of pleasure and pain.*

Love hurts. It hurts so bad and it hurts so good. It hurts so bad because we want to keep and protect what we love. If it's taken away or threatened, we feel the pain at our deepest level. It hurts so good because love enriches our lives so intensely that we struggle to absorb it all. We feel as though we're unworthy, like mortals feasting at a banquet of the gods. We're also scared that, even when it's good, it could leave us at any time.

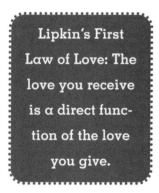

Lipkin's First Law of Love: The love you receive is a direct function of the love you give.

If you're one of the 60 percent of Americans and Canadians over thirty, you've probably loved someone who didn't reciprocate your affections. Or perhaps you loved someone who loved you back, then shifted their love to someone else. Or maybe you're one of the 45 million Americans and Canadians who've been separated, divorced or widowed. In other words, you've had your heart broken, or at least cracked, at some stage. You've been let down, disappointed or betrayed. Consciously or unconsciously, you've inflicted pain on others and they have inflicted pain on you. In other words, love is a risky business. It's risky both in our personal lives and in our professional lives. Life partners and spouses leave. Business partners and valued clients leave. Marriages dissolve and businesses become insolvent. It can all go so right and it can all go so wrong. According to all my research, the number one reason why people are afraid of love is that they are afraid of losing it.

How about you? Are you willing to love as though you'll never be hurt or are you circumspect? Do you love spontaneously and generously? Or do you put up an emotional firewall between you and potential partners because of the pain you've been through in the past? I'm not telling you to ignore your lessons from the past, but here's Lipkin's First Law of Love: The love you receive is a direct function of the love you give. If you stop or slow down the flow of love from you, you stop or slow down the flow of love to you. The risk is never that

My personal call to action: I _____

you'll give too much love to others. It's in being able to keep on giving when it's not given back. Love is never "lost"—it's simply redirected. If you give self-lessly, you know that love always enriches the person who receives it. Remember the words of Dicky Fox, Jerry Maguire's mentor: "If you don't love everybody, you can't sell anybody."

Here's Lipkin's Second Law of Love: Love as though you've never been hurt. Whatever your past experiences, make the decision to love freshly from today. Learn from your mistakes, but do not allow your mistakes to dry up your sup-ply of love. To love is to live, to live is to love, and there is no in-between state. Right now, if you're not loving someone or some cause/activity that's benefiting others, you're leading a half-life. Physically you may have a pulse, but emo-tionally you're a dead person walking.

"Whoa!" I can hear you thinking. "Them's fiery words, Mr. Lipkin!" Exactly. Love is to the mind as oxygen is to the body; you cannot live without it. So don't wait for it to come to you. The most important trip you'll ever take in life is to go and build love wherever you can, with whomever you can, whenever you can. If you love fully and truly, you can never regret. It's when we withhold our love or fail to follow through on our love that we suffer greatly.

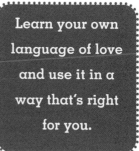

Learn your own language of love and use it in a way that's right for you.

After interacting with more than a million people over the past thirteen years, I can tell you what you already know: People imbued with love have an aura that evokes a reciprocal love from others. They are love-ly—their beauty appeals to the heart as well as to the eye. Like gravity, love exerts a pull that cannot be resisted. Humans sense the presence of love at a primal level, the way they sense the presence of fear. And whereas humans shrink from fear, they're instinctively drawn to love. And when so many channels of communication pre-vent face-to-face contact, the demand for love is at an all-time high.

Love is a magnet that draws the best emotions out of other people. That's why it's the hallmark of Keepers of The Flame. Whereas excitement is an acute emo-tion that spikes in response to the thought or the moment, love permeates you like blood, sweat and marrow. It has a look, a sound and a scent. It's tactile. Like its owner, love has stood the test of time. It has withstood the threats, the disap-pointments, the shocks, the losses, the sacrifices. That's why the older the love, the more powerful it becomes. It's 100-proof benevolence in the face of a world that seems bereft of it.

My personal call to action: I _____

Courage, optimism, respect, wonder and excitement will make you a "situational" Keeper of The Flame, meaning that in situations where those emotions are required, you will shine. But without love, none of the other Power Emotions are sustainable. Love is the enduring source of energy and inspiration. It's an unconditional commitment to hold fast, hug slow, stay true, give back, pay it forward and make the other person or thing better, whatever it takes. Love doesn't hold back, it doesn't split hairs, it isn't ambivalent. It surges, not trickles, and once it's turned on, it keeps on flowing.

Who do you love? What do you love? What is your enduring source of energy and inspiration? Are you willing to make a public announcement? Are you willing to be vulnerable? Are you willing to be transparent? Can you even articulate your range of loves? Have you told the people around you what you love? Do you know what they love? This my request to you: Be open. Say what you believe; believe what you say. Learn your own language of love and use it in a way that's right for you. Take every chance to let people know what you love, why you love it, why they should love and why you love them. I'll go first.

- I love the people who read my books and come to my seminars.
- I love living in a society where anything is possible, I'm free from fear and the rules of fair play prevail.
- I love my wife and my three children.
- I love the higher power that gave me my gifts and the ability to develop them.
- I love the look on people's faces when they get excited.
- I love living my dream.
- I love seeing and hearing great words.
- I love my body that does everything I ask of it, and more.
- I love every day and the discoveries it brings.
- I love anyone who is a Seeker of The Flame—anyone who strives to inspire others on the Cusp of change.

So develop your own love vocabulary. This is a way of both verbal and non-verbal communication that imprints your love on everyone around you. It's your collection of words and gestures that clearly demonstrate your feelings to others. This whole book has been a thesaurus of my verbal love vocabulary.

My personal call to action: I _____

If I ever have the privilege of talking to you face to face, you'll also see my non-verbal love vocabulary:

- I'm always open, ready to embrace you.
- I lean forward into our conversation.
- I smile with my whole face.
- I look at you in such a way that you feel my respect, affection and commitment.
- I celebrate you with all my energy and congruence—everything about me says that I'm thrilled to be with you.

By the way, if you want a crash course on nonverbal love vocabulary, watch a dog. I have a street breed called Toby. She's a cross between a Maltese/poodle and a Staffordshire terrier. She's also the most expressive creature I know. She's always ready to embrace me, she always looks at me with ultimate love, and everything about her always tells me that she's thrilled to be with me. Toby has taught me another powerful lesson as well. This is so important that I want you to pause before you read it, and think about it for a moment afterwards:

> ▶ In matters of love, do not be subtle. Leave no room for doubt. Don't make the other person guess your feelings. Be categorical. Overcome your inhibitions to ensure that others really get your feelings and commitment toward them. Tell them over and over again. Then follow through with consistent action.

In this age of being overwhelmed, people are emotionally fragile. Love, appreciation and support form the emotional triad that will rally people to your side. The more you deliver the triad, the stronger you become and the more you attract the triad to yourself. Keepers of The Flame are always net providers of love. They're always depositing more than they receive. It's their goodwill that creates their good karma. It's a one-sided contract for them, with all the obligations on their side. They're not good Samaritans, though. They don't love just because it's the right thing to do for others. They love because it's the right thing to do for themselves. The objects of their love offer them the opportunity to get better at loving. And the more they love, the more they receive.

My personal call to action: I _____

I'll conclude this section with Mother Teresa's words on love: "There is more hunger for love and appreciation in this world than for bread. It's not how much you do, but how much love you put into the doing that matters. We can do no great things; only small things with great love."

Power Emotion 7: Lightness Lipkin's definition of

lightness: *taking yourself lightly; traveling farther, higher, longer; turning past negativity into present positivity; laughing in the face of adversity; letting go of what doesn't work to embrace what will; turning tragedy into comedy; lifting others up; making every interaction inspirational.*

So you've got the courage to do what you fear. You've got the optimism to always expect the most favorable result from every situation. You respect and honor the people and the environment around you. You live each day with a sense of wonder. You turn on your excitement at will. You're a true love-meister. You're one emotionally powerful dude (or dudette)!

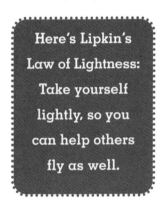

Here's Lipkin's Law of Lightness: Take yourself lightly, so you can help others fly as well.

But all those Power Emotions can weigh heavily on you. By definition, if you're running on the six Power Emotions we've discussed, you're going to be imagining more, feeling more, carrying more, anticipating more, doing more and giving more than your average fellow global citizen. Without lightness to counterbalance your substance, you could be struggling to keep your Flame alight.

Quick, think of the qualities associated with lightness: flight, unsinkability, speed, agility, nimbleness, resilience, humor, forgiveness, flexibility, portability, weightlessness, sociability, affability, painlessness, effortlessness, ease, tranquility, grace, poise.

Now think of qualities that are the opposite of lightness: heaviness, darkness, encumbrance, baggage, overweight, drag, slowness, gravity, seriousness, shadow, gloom, bulk, crisis.

What qualities best describe you? Would others describe you as light or heavy? Would they say that you weigh them down or lift them up? Here's Lipkin's Law of Lightness: Take yourself lightly, so you can help others fly as

My personal call to action: I _____

well. Of all the insights I've shared with you so far, this may be the one that takes you the farthest: If you travel lightly you need less fuel. You can travel farther and longer. What's more, the lighter you are, the higher you fly, the greater your view, the smaller your obstacles and the more inspiring your example.

I have never met a Keeper of The Flame who didn't have a lightness about him or her. They all have the ability to laugh in the face of adversity or enrich their perspective through humor. As Churchill said, "I like a man who smiles when he fights." Keepers of The Flame have mastered their lightness of being because they know three things: First, they cannot sustain their pace and their contribution if they're weighed down by too much baggage. Second, they know that others will not want to be around them if they're heavy. Third, they know that they can't embrace change with their arms full of the past.

Lightness is the Power Emotion that inoculates you against anger, resentment, regret, bitterness, blame and self-reproach. It's the ability to redirect the memories of your past to portray any event as a source of comedy, not tragedy. Isn't that what comedy really is—tragedy filtered through the insight of hindsight? How many times has someone said to you, "Don't worry, you'll laugh about this tomorrow"? Well, why wait? Laugh about it now. Help your people laugh about it. Chances are, unless you're in medicine or the military, it's not a case of life or death. Interpret the situation accordingly.

As reported in *The Globe and Mail* of March 4, 2005, even NASA is looking for a sense of humor as one of the personality traits of its future astronauts, believing that candidates who have a funny bone are more flexible, more creative and better able to deal with stress. Of course, if you're going to be crammed into a spaceship for days or weeks at a time with someone else, it helps if your fellow astronaut is good company. And I've never met anyone without a sense of humor who is good company.

Here's my anti-promise to you: If you don't make the people around you smile, they will leave you. I'm referring to both your personal and professional partners. Life is just too intense to have to cope with "insiders" who make the situation even worse. In focus group after focus group, people tell me: "I can deal with all the external challenges. But it's my boss who is driving me crazy. He's the one causing the real crisis. Everything is urgent. Everything is serious. It seems as though he can't handle his job so he's pass-

My personal call to action: I _____

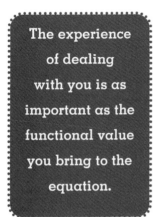

The experience of dealing with you is as important as the functional value you bring to the equation.

ing the stress on to me." I call this phenomenon the Leadership Paradox—the very people who should be alleviating their people's stress are the ones causing it. The problem is that they're being heavy when they need to be light. If you lead or manage people, make sure you're the reliever, not the stressor.

The experience of dealing with you is as important as the functional value you bring to the equation. The emotional state that you put people in is the real value you deliver as a Keeper of The Flame. When people leave their meeting or conversation with you, are they more fired up than they were before? Are they happier as a result of meeting with you? Are they more confident because of their interaction with you? If your genuine answers are yes, yes and yes, you're a lightness conductor.

My friend and client David Goodman is the quintessential example of the power of lightness. David is the president of Dynamic Mutual Funds, one of Canada's most successful mutual fund companies. He is also one of the most intense, competitive people in corporate Canada. He says that the title of his autobiography—were he ever to write one—would be *Something to Prove*. And yet David is also one of the funniest CEOs I've had the pleasure of working with. It's not just his natural sense of humor; it's the fact that he is so committed to developing that sense of humor. He recently completed a one-week course on stand-up comedy offered by Humber College in Toronto. He told me that one of his proudest achievements was placing second in a competition for "stand-up comics with day jobs." The $200 cheque he received as prize money is proudly displayed in a frame on his office wall. What message do you think that sends to his people? What message are you sending to your people?

By now I hope you're sold on the virtue of lightness. What you may still be uncertain about is how you actually achieve lightness.

Here are Lipkin's eight ways to lighten up:

1. Turn your greatest sources of anger, resentment or bitterness into the funniest things that have ever happened to you. Laugh out loud. It's over. There's no use crying about it, so you might as well laugh.

My personal call to action: I _____

2. If you have a sense of humor, develop it. Get some coaching on how to enhance it. If you think you don't have a sense of humor, get some feedback from the people around you. Develop one. And always laugh at the humor of others.

3. Keep your perspective. Don't invest things with a life-or-death seriousness. Pretend you're in a movie theater watching a film about your life as it happens—and make it a comedy.

4. See yourself as not just a manager but as a motivator, whether you have people reporting to you or not. Practice lifting people up even when you're down. You'll find that lifting others up transports you to higher ground as well.

5. When you're communicating with people who depend on your optimism and encouragement, keep your angst to yourself. Always be a source of new possibilities. But have an "inner circle" with whom you can break down and cry sometimes.

6. Never ever vent your negative mood on others. It's the mark of a petty tyrant. If someone vents on you, just know that it's not about you. Maintain your grace and dignity. Respectfully let the other person know what they've just done, then walk away.

7. Model lightness by studying it in others. Experiment. Adopt. Adapt. Fly. Take others along for the ride.

8. Let go of anger at people who have wronged you. Revenge isn't sweet; it will just make you bitter. The most rewarding thing you can do for yourself is forgive others. Don't do it for them, do it for yourself—and everyone will be healthier and happier.

As a final note, here is a heads-up from someone who's been there. When you begin sliding into depression, your lightness will be your first casualty. If you feel your light going out, take action—fast. Even if he's your brother, he's going to find you heavy. And once you've been branded as "heavy company," the people around you will do anything to avoid carrying your burden.

My personal call to action: I _____

Your Action Nuclear Dimension:

 ## Living your Everyday Empowering Ritual

Everyday Empowering Ritual (EER): the actions you take every day that are central to your success and have the greatest power to inspire others; a code of conduct that is true for you; the actions that help you play the life game by your rules; the place you go for inner guidance and certainty.

Person of action: someone who is decisive, consistent and knowledgeable; someone who has the self-assurance to back himself in the face of criticism; someone who always follows through on promises; someone who always wants to do more for others than others think is wise; someone who is self-aware; someone who is brilliant at their specialty.

"Action is eloquence," said Shakespeare. "Talk doesn't cook rice," goes an old Chinese saying. "You must do the thing you think you cannot do," declared Eleanor Roosevelt. "Action is the antidote to despair," counseled Joan Baez. "Today is your day! Your mountain is waiting, so get on your way," commanded Dr. Seuss. "As I grow older I pay less attention to what men say. I just watch what they do," noted Andrew Carnegie.

What is your mantra on action? If I watched you, what would I think? Do your deeds speak for you? Are you renowned for your results or are you notorious for your rhetoric? Do you have a daily plan of action or are you at the mercy of your environment? Here's another Lipkinism to kick off this chapter:

> **Action doesn't always create happiness, but there can be no happiness without action.**

In line with my commitment never to ask you to do something I wouldn't do, here's my action mantra: "I play full out every day. I leave nothing behind. I perform every Nuclear Dimension at my personal best. I give my everything to everyone. I am the sum of all my actions. If not now, then when? If not me, then who?" Write down your action mantra and e-mail it to me ASAP. The first rule of action is that the best time is always now. An imperfect action today is always superior to a perfect action tomorrow.

My personal call to action: I _____

My action mantra is the only thing between me and the last bogeyman in my life: regret. As long as I follow my mantra, I'm safe. If I falter . . . well, I don't even want to go there. My mantra is my lifeline. It's what helps me keep reaching for the torch. It's what helps me write this book, give my talks, handle the pressure and fill my reservoir of inspiration for the people I serve.

Welcome to execution time. This is where we translate focus, strategy, learning and emotions into results. This is the part that's real. It's the visible application of all the insights you've gained up to now. It's the part that can help you become a Keeper of The Flame, even if you started the book on this page. Actions spark inspiration as frequently as inspiration sparks action. Action is what makes the world go round. Everything else is just preparation. Action is where mind, heart, spirit and body coalesce to create proof of what's possible. This is where the Keeper of The Flame shines her light brightest, because she knows others are watching.

It's also action that fuels the Keeper's flame. Until you act, all your potential remains locked within you. It's action that unleashes your personal power. The best actions generate the best results, less effective actions generate less compelling results, and zero action generates zero results. Of course there is a time to do nothing. There's a time to be still, to be quiet, to be patient, to think, to plan. Then there is a time for action. The challenge is to know when to do what. You're the best judge of your preparation-to-action ratio.

However, when you're not acting, are you preparing? Are you anticipating? Are you enhancing your readiness to act? Or are you just drifting? Are you waiting in a state of inertia for something or someone else to propel you forward, or are you driven by your own propeller (see page 141)? The vast majority of people whom I interview spend too much time in a state of inaction. They're constrained by their doubts when all they need is to take a single action. Remember this Lipkinism:

> **Action will remove the doubts that thinking cannot solve. You can't do everything right away, but you can do one thing right now. Find out what it is, then do it. Then the next, and the next. That's exactly what I'm doing right now. I'm writing one word, then the next, and the next. And here's Lipkin's Law of Writing: Every word opens a pathway for the next word. Each word is like a step, and with every step I take, I see further ahead of me where I need to go.**

My personal call to action: I _____

Someone has to make it safer for others to follow. Is that someone you?

Fortune favors people who act decisively in the face of risk. Luck accrues to people who defy convention. The prize goes to people who act with imagination and flair. Success is attracted to people who are willing to go to the edge and jump into the unknown. Fortune, luck, prizes and success align with these kinds of people because all progress depends on someone actually doing something. Inevitably that something has to be done in the face of imperfect data and uncertain consequences. Someone has to go first and keep on going. Someone has to subject himself to criticism, failure and even ridicule. Someone has to make it safer for others to follow. Is that someone you?

Here's a staggering insight from Brian Guthrie, director of innovation and knowledge management at the Conference Board of Canada: "There are 3,000 ideas for every one commercial success, so the challenge of innovation is not so much coming up with new ideas as it is driving those ideas into reality." Yup, you can dream all you want, but someone has to wake up and make it happen. Once again, is that someone you?

Take this ten-point action test before you go any further.

Rate yourself on a scale of 1 to 5

1 = never, 2 = rarely, 3 = sometimes, 4 = often, 5 = daily

1. I have a personal code of conduct that guides my actions. ☐

2. I'm aware of the impact my actions are having on others. ☐

3. I'm usually the first to act. ☐

4. I do more than others think is wise. ☐

5. I'm willing to take a risk by acting boldly. ☐

My personal call to action: I _____

6. I follow through immediately on my promises to others. ❏

7. I exercise my mind, body and soul every day. ❏

8. I am brilliant at my specialty. ❏

9. Through my actions I show how passionate I am about I'm doing. ❏

10. I always persist in the face of setbacks or rejection. ❏

■ **Total** ❏

If you scored 45 or more, you're a true person of action. You're on fire! You're already living brilliantly. Maybe what you do is explicit or maybe it's instinctive, but this chapter will help take you to a perfect 50 by helping you define and execute your Nuclear Actions every day.

If you scored between 39 and 44, you're on the Cusp of a breakthrough. To become a person of action, you need to kick it up a notch where it matters most. This chapter will help you do whatever it takes to play at your highest level.

If you scored less than 39, it's time to step up. It's time to do some important work. But it's also time to get excited, because you're ready to bring more of yourself to everything you do. You're ready to be worthy of your gifts.

The highest compliment anyone can pay me is "Mike Lipkin knows what he's doing. I can count on him to help me get what I want. He will always come through for me." Replace my name with yours and tell me how you would feel if all your stakeholders believed this truth about you. Are you feeling proud, certain, motivated, warm, powerful, committed, strong, significant, valued, connected, successful? I am. I know that if I can get my stakeholders to believe this truth about me, I will have achieved both their trust and their loyalty. What's more, because my stakeholders will have so few people in their lives who can play this role for them, they'll talk about my contribution to their stakeholders. Their happiness grows, my acclaim spreads, I get to help even more people, and

My personal call to action: I _____

the world becomes more pumped, prosperous and powerful—one person at a time. All the insights that I share with you in this chapter are aimed at helping you achieve this position in the minds of the people you serve.

Think about the things other people do that excite and delight you the most. Here is my top ten list:

1. They do what they said they were going to do when they said they were going to do it. Follow-through is a rare and beautiful thing.

2. They do more than I expect them to do—for the sheer joy of doing it.

3. They take huge pride in what they do; they radiate passion.

4. They never get tired, bored or stale. The longer the game, the more energized they become. For them, every day is the first day.

5. They tailor their actions specifically to my wants and likes. They make me feel that I'm the only one that matters in the moment.

6. They do what they do with a skill and artistry that take my breath away.

7. They pay attention to the big picture and also to the small details. When I deal with them I never have to worry about anything falling through the cracks.

8. They're unswervingly consistent. They keep getting better, to both their benefit and mine.

9. They never, ever take me or my business for granted. They earn and re-earn their spurs with every interaction.

10. They're remarkably resilient. They take a beating and keep on beating. They don't waste time feeling sorry for themselves or carrying grudges.

How many of these kinds of people are on your side? Are you one of them? Remember, like attracts like. You're far more likely to hang with these kinds of folk if you're part of their tribe. And, just like every tribe, these people of action have rituals. Specifically, they have **Everyday Empowering Rituals** (EERs). It's to an exploration of those rituals that we will now turn.

First of all, what's a ritual? All living creatures have an instinct for ritual, or

My personal call to action: I _____

behavior that provides meaning, structure and support. Over the years, many of our rituals—religious, social, legal, familial, corporate—have been prescribed for us by our culture. Many of these rituals have become so ingrained in us that they've lost their power to ignite our flame. Their primary role is to anchor us to our traditions so we don't get swept away by change. Think about the amount of literature or theater that has originated around this theme: the ritual of the old versus the influence of the new, the threat of disruption versus craving for the status quo.

Think about the rituals that anchor you to tradition. If you're like any of the million people to whom I've spoken since 1993, you observe many rituals as an integral part of your lifestyle. Think about how many of them you adopted from your family, your community or your company. Now think about how many of your rituals you have personally, consciously created to help you play at your personal best. Write them down. Evaluate their power to invoke the untold you, the all-you-were-meant-to-be you. If you're like 99 percent of the people I work with, you're having difficulty writing anything down right now.

Let me be clear: We all need the guidance, comfort and symbolic meaning provided by the rituals that have shaped our lives. Other than one caution, I have nothing to say to you about your traditional rituals; they may be as much a part of you as your DNA. My caution to you is simple: Make sure that your traditional rituals are serving you. Don't just go through the motions to please people around you or because you've always done them. Don't numb down. Make every ritual a powerful rite that moves you to where you want to go.

Your Everyday Empowering Ritual (EER)

I have three questions for you:

1. How many rituals have you consciously created that are individually designed to help you live at your personal best while inspiring everyone around you to do the same?

2. How often do you participate in them?

3. How committed are you to them?

Everyone has their own everyday rituals. Not all of them are empowering. Very few of them are consciously designed to help the individual practicing them to become her personal best.

My personal call to action: I _____

Here are some everyday rituals performed by people who have attended my programs:

- have a shower upon awakening
- have a coffee after the shower or on the commute to work
- listen to or watch the morning news or read the morning paper
- check e-mails
- attend meetings
- call business and personal acquaintances
- carry out daily tasks, both professional and personal
- visit a regular lunchtime venue
- call spouse, partner or children
- spend time with family and friends
- watch TV
- meditate
- work out
- pray
- enjoy a nighttime alcoholic beverage
- read a few pages of a book before bedtime

Sound familiar? That's the whole point of rituals: They immerse us in the familiar so we can buffer ourselves against the weird, the bizarre, the strange and the scary uncontrollables that threaten our well-being every day. They make our lives as routine as possible so we can minimize disorder and stress. Even the onerous routines have the appeal of being predictable in a world that is increasingly less so.

The danger is that we put on blinkers so we don't have to see what we don't want to see. The danger is that we anesthetize ourselves so we don't have to feel what we don't want to feel. And, in the age of the iPod, when we never have to change CDs, the danger is that we lay down our own soundtrack so we don't have to hear what we don't want to hear. The net result is a fabricated reality that shrinks our range of possibilities and potential for breakthrough. Humans are a lot like koi fish; their maximum size is determined by both heredity *and* environment. And just as koi will not grow any larger than their pond can support, so humans will not grow beyond the boundaries of their rituals.

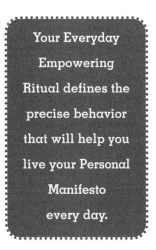

Your Everyday Empowering Ritual defines the precise behavior that will help you live your Personal Manifesto every day.

Your Everyday Empowering Ritual is designed to help you expand your boundaries every day in a way that is true for you. It's a technique that empowers you to simultaneously expand your growth, your effectiveness and your certainty. It's a shift from a mindset of personal defense to one of personal development. It's the difference between a half-life and a life-and-a-half. Here's another Lipkinism:

> **Happy ever after begins and ends today. If you want a great life, live today greatly.**

Remember your Personal Manifesto? It defines your overall strategy for success in life. Your Everyday Empowering Ritual defines the precise behavior that will help you live your Personal Manifesto every day. After working through your Strategic Nuclear Dimension, you crafted a Personal Manifesto, right? If not, craft it now. Review your Strategic Nuclear Dimension again. Write it in pencil in the space provided on the next page. It doesn't have to be perfect; in fact, sometimes your first response is your best response because it's intuitive. You can always go back and refine it until it feels exactly right for you. Do it now. Remember Helen Keller's famous line: "Ideas without action are worthless." I promise that the mere act of thinking about your Personal Manifesto and writing it down will strengthen your bias toward action.

By way of illustration, here is my Personal Manifesto again:

◆ I attract positive energy to me by conditioning the highest level of personal vitality within me.

◆ I sustain a still mind and a strong heart by staying connected to my higher power, especially in turbulent times.

My personal call to action: I _____

◆ I pursue pre-eminence by taking every chance to learn new ways of multiplying positive energy and transferring it to others.

◆ I seek out extreme situations where I can accelerate breakthroughs and inspire others on the Cusp of change.

◆ I use my gift of persuasion to help others grow themselves through communication and teamwork.

◆ I leverage my global exposure to enrich others' perspectives so they see more, understand more and achieve more.

◆ I partner with the best people to create new possibilities that change the world one individual at a time.

Now write yours:

_____

_____

_____

_____

_____

_____

_____

_____

_____

My personal call to action: I _____

Outstanding! Now let's create our Everyday Empowering Ritual together. I'll model the process by showing you how mine flows out of my Personal Manifesto. Then I want you to create yours and send it to me. That action alone will help make it real for you. By the way, there's another reason why I'm sharing my EER with you: Over 30,000 people will read these words. I am making a point-of-no-return public commitment to a certain code of conduct. In a world ruled by six degrees of separation, our paths will definitely intersect sometime soon. You will see me behaving in a certain way. I may or may not see you seeing me. You will put me to the test, and I'd better pass it, or I will incur your contempt for not walking my talk. That would be the beginning of the end for me. So here is the first of two core Lipkinisms:

 If the right person says the right thing about your performance, you will thrive. If the right person says the wrong thing about your performance, you will slide. Whatever the wrong person says doesn't matter.

Here is the second core Lipkinism:

Someone is always watching, and what you do speaks so loudly I can't hear what you're saying. So no matter what happens, make it look like it's easy, you're in control, you're happy to be where you are, with whomever you're with. As I joke to my audiences, learn to sweat from the neck down. Or, in the very wise words of Q, James Bond's beloved gadget man, "Never let them see you bleed."

Here is a true story of these two Lipkinisms in action. On a recent Thursday evening I flew from Toronto to Vancouver to deliver a program. I had had one of those days when it took all I had just to keep up with the losers, and I was facing a five-hour flight departing at 8:00 p.m. I was feeling shattered—and I don't say that lightly—as I stood in the business-class check-in line like a dead man waiting. All of a sudden I heard my name called out by a woman who had been in my program five months before. "Aren't you Mike Lipkin?" she asked. "Yes," I replied curtly. "Shouldn't you be smiling?" she asked brightly. I immediately went through a change of state as her words triggered a consciously upbeat mood. "If you talk the talk," I reminded myself, "you'd better walk the walk."

My personal call to action: I _____

If you're a Seeker of The Flame you're going to be held to the same standards as I am. Remember, people judge themselves by their intentions, but they judge you by what they see you do consistently. There are no time-outs for Keepers of The Flame. So here's my EER:

Mike Lipkin's Everyday Empowering Ritual

◆ Every day I will celebrate my gifts by playing full out. I will always finish stronger than I started. I will turn it on, especially in the face of adversity.

◆ Every day I will feast on the knowledge resources around me. I will learn from my partners, my clients, my research, the media and passers-by. I will attract the next insight to me by always being ready for it.

◆ Every day I will do something I've never done before. I will build the discipline of mastering fear and fatigue. I will always forgive myself and others when we screw up. I will always travel light.

◆ Every day I will work out for one hour. I will swim one day, cycle the next, for 365 days a year—no excuses. I will relish the sweat, the burn, the endorphins and the permission my workout gives me to savor my favorite food and drink without guilt.

◆ Every day I will find quiet time to still my mind and strengthen my heart through communion with my higher power. I will always remember that inspiration comes through me, not from me.

◆ Every day I will spend half my time talking to others. I will make every meeting, conversation and conference call a tour de force. I will use every interaction to make people feel better about themselves after being with me.

◆ Every day I will give others more then they expect. I will collect other people's smiles by acting spontaneously to surprise and delight them.

My personal call to action: I _____

◆ Every day I will show the people closest to me how much I love them. I will find new ways to express my love. I will immunize my family against taking anyone for granted.

◆ Every day I will laugh loud and long at whatever I can. I will find time to play and party. I will be a joy sauce to spice up everyone's daily fare. I will magnetize positive energy to me by being consistently positive, especially in the face of negativity.

◆ Every day I will honor myself and respect the people I serve by living in my Sweet Spot. I will upgrade my tomorrows by upgrading my genius and my promise today.

◆ Every day I will take everything that happens to me and use it to build my mojo, my resilience and my enthusiasm. I will live in gratitude and wonder.

Are you excited? I defy you to read my EER and not feel the juice those words hold. I've also written them in "Lipkin-speak." Lipkin-speak is my signature vocabulary—the words I love using because of their emotional impact on both me and the people I serve. You may resonate with a different kind of language. Identify it and use it. The actual words you use generate the power that drives your motivation. And the more you use them, the better you'll become. So have some fun with your EER. As always, send it to me within forty-eight hours of reading these words. Beyond that time frame, your motivation will wither and other priorities will cannibalize your attention. In the space below, take a first cut at drafting your EER. Don't worry if it's imperfect; it's a start. When you've finished it, send it to me . . .

_____

_____

_____

_____

My personal call to action: I _____

_____

_____

_____

_____

_____

_____

_____

_____

_____

_____

_____

_____

_____

_____

_____

_____

_____

My personal call to action: I _____

Of all the things I've shared with you so far, it's my EER that most helps me handle the escalating stress that's the ever-present companion of Keepers of The Flame. The more inspirational you become, the more problems you will be given to solve, the more other people will want to draw on your resources and the higher the standards you will be asked to meet. My EER actually changes the way I respond to stress, turning it into the raw material that helps me turn each day into a masterpiece. It has become a source of inspiration, not exasperation. I know one thing about my future: It's going to be filled with "stress-flation." Whatever I've been through, it's only a rehearsal for what's coming. My EER helps me get into a state of readiness. Bring it on!

> The more inspirational you become, the more problems you will be given to solve, the more other people will want to draw on your resources and the higher the standards you will be asked to meet.

Here's a little cautionary note about rituals. There is such a thing as a fatal ritual, and it's called the holiday season. According to the Journal of the American Heart Association, researchers examined 53 million deaths from natural causes in the United States from 1973 to 2001. They discovered that the number of deaths from heart disease reaches a peak during the Christmas/New Year period. David Phillips, the leader of the research team, said that during the holidays in particular, people tend to abruptly change their eating, drinking, exercise, sleep and work patterns, which can have an impact on heart health. According to Dr. Nalin Ahluwalia, head of the emergency department at York Central Hospital in Richmond Hill, Ontario, the holiday season is a "high stress time—high emotional stress, anxiety, and financial stress." So be especially committed to your EER when it's most difficult to follow it. It may save your life.

"Wellness Plans Return $3 for Every $1 Spent," according to USA Today, August 1, 2005. The article referred to the ROH—return on health—achieved by companies that invest in their employees' health. While I applaud the companies making the investment, my message to you is "Don't wait for someone to give you a 'wellness plan.'" Design your own and have the discipline to live it every day. That's what my EER is to me. Together with my Sweet Spot and my Personal Manifesto, it forms the triad that empowers me to constantly play the role of coach, mentor, motivator and stand-up philosopher.

My personal call to action: I _____

Throughout this book I've been inviting you to do what you may never have done before: Step outside of yourself to evaluate yourself with a fresh set of senses. I know you'll discover powerful resources currently lying dormant. I know these exercises work because of the feedback I've received from thousands of Seekers of The Flame over the past decade. They are the ones who did something. They took the time, wrote the words, followed through, fine-tuned their Nuclear Dimensions and reaped their rewards. Be one of them. Here's the final Lipkinism of this chapter:

> **There are so many things that we wish we had done yesterday, so few that we feel like doing today, so much that depends on our actions tomorrow. Think about it. Creating your EER is a simple exercise that can be completed in such a short time and gives such powerful benefits. Why wouldn't you complete it? Think beyond the few hours you'll invest to the competitive advantage you'll gain.**

Time and time again I'm amazed at how few people have an intimate understanding of their inner resources. Use their ignorance to your benefit. Then take it to the next level by treating your Sweet Spot, your Personal Manifesto and your Everyday Empowering Ritual as a contract between the you of today and the you of tomorrow. The you of tomorrow is as dependent on the you of today as any other dependants you may have. Don't let the you of tomorrow down. She or he will never forgive you when it's too late and your song remains forever unsung.

My personal call to action: I _____

Your Social Nuclear Dimension:

 Earning kudos through your Personal Charisma, your Personal Team and your Personal Network

Lipkin's definition of the Social Nuclear Dimension: the expanded you; the perception that others have of you; the connections you've made; the contributions you've made; the profile you've created within your company, your industry, your community; the reciprocal commitment you've built with the people in your greater social circle; your overall value as a person, as a professional and as a catalyst for others' success.

If you live and work in the company of other people, this is the Nuclear Dimension we've been driving toward since page one. You can have all the personal power that comes from being focused, strategic, mentally-hungry, emotionally-powerful and action-oriented, but if you're not socially synced up with your communal circle, isolation will always get in your way. We all know

My personal call to action: I _____

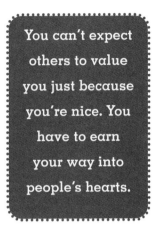

You can't expect others to value you just because you're nice. You have to earn your way into people's hearts.

people who seem to have it all together but something's missing. Some small discordant note ruins their personal symphony. They don't harmonize with their peers. They don't maximize their contribution. They don't grow trust. They lose their fire and burn out.

On the other hand, we've all experienced the great pleasure of living and working with people who are socially gifted. They're smart, they're fashionable; they're the go-to people, they're generous, they're connected with the right people; they seem to make everyone around them successful; they're winners who have stood the test of time. You love being around them because they make you feel so alive. They're true Keepers of The Flame. Their fire warms everyone around them. It lights the way for others in dark times and provides direction in the dizzying dazzle of change.

Your Social Nuclear Dimension is where all your other Nuclear Dimensions are translated into kudos. I define *kudos* as other people's celebration of your contribution to their success. Kudos goes beyond mere recognition or credit. It contains equal parts of admiration, adoration and appreciation. It's given to you by other people when you achieve something extraordinary that has a clear and valuable benefit to them. The greater the achievements, the more frequent the achievements, the clearer the value of the achievements to others, the more kudos you receive.

There you have it, Lipkin's personal motto: Contribution, Communication and the Pursuit of Kudos. What do I mean? You cannot build your Social Nuclear Dimension unless you can demonstrate your value to your communal circle. There is no free ride. You can't expect others to value you just because you're nice. You have to *earn* your way into people's hearts. That's why we can discuss your social Nuclear Dimension only after you've mastered the other five.

So first you must *contribute*. Then you must *communicate* your contribution in a skilled, appropriate manner. That's not bragging; it's personal branding. Until others understand and appreciate the importance of your role in their life, your kudos will never rise to its fullest potential. According to our research, one of the biggest reasons why people become alienated from others is their failure to receive the recognition or encouragement they crave. Here is another big "aha!": 90 percent of people are not proactive in seeking opportunities to

My personal call to action: I _____

recognize and reward others. The same percentage are also poor at communicating their virtues to others. They're too caught up in their own private struggles to publicly express their strengths.

So talk your walk. Talk at full volume. Talk as long as you need to broadcast your benefits to your world. Talk until you know others have heard. But also talk to others about their own virtues. Let them know that you know the impact they're making on your life. Seize every opportunity to compliment and coach them. It's Lipkin's Relationship Rule: Talking is how we exchange emotions with one another. The more free-flowing the conversation, the healthier the emotions, the healthier the relationship. When it comes to relationships, silence isn't always golden. In fact, when one party stops talking, it's the beginning of the end.

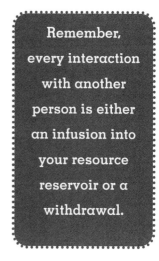

Remember, every interaction with another person is either an infusion into your resource reservoir or a withdrawal.

Kudos and reciprocation go hand in hand. They're the golden siblings of social currency. People have a built-in need to reciprocate the gifts they've received from others, not because they're motivated to do the right thing, but because they know their future relationship depends on it. Think about how you feel about people who don't reciprocate the contributions you've made to them in the past. The moment you become convinced that the other person won't reciprocate your past help, you shut down that relationship. You may be forced to coexist with that person, but all potential for future connection is severed.

Keepers of The Flame achieve more because they've done more to motivate more people to reciprocate their giving. They're at the front of the line when it comes to receiving the attention of those they've helped in the past. Reciprocation is their secret reservoir of resources for success. That's why Keepers of The Flame always seem to be so self-assured in challenging situations. They know they can call on so many quality people to help them rise to the occasion. Remember, every interaction with another person is either an infusion into your resource reservoir or a withdrawal. Too many withdrawals and it's game over for you. What's more, all of us at some time will hit a losing streak—that's life. When you take the dive, remember, it's almost impossible to come out of it alone. Without the goodwill of good people motivated to pick you up, you could be in for a long walk in the dark.

My personal call to action: I _____

Take this test to estimate how much kudos you've earned in your communal circle.

Rate yourself on a scale of 1 to 5
1 = I disagree, 2 = I have no idea, 3 = I might be, 4 = I think I am, 5 = I know I am

■ I am best in class (or very close to it) at what I do. ☐

■ I can clearly describe the main benefit I deliver to others. ☐

■ I know exactly how I want others to perceive me. ☐

■ I act in a way that reinforces the way I want others to see me. ☐

■ I tell others about the main benefit I deliver to them. ☐

■ I've established a strong position in the minds of others. ☐

■ I'm renowned for my generosity in time and resources to others. ☐

■ I'm known as a great team player. ☐

■ I belong to a strong team at work. ☐

■ I have built a wide network of friends, business associates and community representatives. ☐

■ I am constantly building my network by making new contacts. ☐

■ I nurture my existing relationships. ☐

■ I'm always thinking about how I can add value to others. ☐

■ I have a specific plan for building my profile in my personal and business community. ☐

■ **Total** ☐

My personal call to action: I _____

If you scored 60-plus, congratulations. If your responses accurately reflect your reality, you are already a social champion. This chapter will be even more valuable to you because you clearly understand the power of what I'm about to share with you. You're also skilled in applying the lessons you're about to learn. Share them with as many people as you can.

If you scored between 50 and 59, you're on the Cusp of social brilliance. This chapter will give you the insights you need to connect and contribute to others so you can become a Keeper of the Social Flame.

If you scored less than 50, your social muscles are not as strong as they need to be. Treat this chapter as the beginning of a lifelong workout.

Building your Personal Charisma: Helping others get what they want

Charisma: that special power or personal quality that gives an individual influence or authority over large numbers of people ~Webster's Dictionary

A few rare people are lucky enough to be born with overdeveloped charisma glands. They are the ones who've won the genetic lottery. Without seeming to make any effort, they radiate a power that inspires others to help and support them. I don't know about you, but in spite of all my global travels, I don't know many people with this kind of power. In fact, I can't think of a single person who was born with this gift. How about you? I'm willing to bet that you also don't have first-hand contact with many of these almost mythical creatures.

I don't know any movie stars or heads of state, so that may explain my lack of first-hand contact with divinely inspired charisma. But I do know thousands of people who have worked very hard to build their influence and credibility with others. Some of these folks are more extroverted, like me, and some are more muted. Some find it easier to connect with other people, others find it more of a strain. But here's my counterintuitive discovery: Charisma is not a function of personal charm. That's very short-lived, and it can even cause a backlash when you don't live up to the heightened expectations that others have of you. Rather, charisma is a simple function of how effectively you help others get what they want in a way that no one else can. I cannot say it any more clearly than that. People who are outstanding at helping you get what you want

My personal call to action: I _____

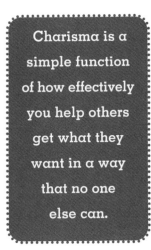

Charisma is a simple function of how effectively you help others get what they want in a way that no one else can.

will have a special power over you. They will own your loyalty, your affection and your business. You will seek them out, you'll do what they want you to do, and you'll sing their praises to everyone around you. I call that charisma.

If you lead other people, helping others get what they need in a memorable way is a powerful method of building a culture of charisma throughout your team or organization. Jeffrey Fox, author of *How to Become a Great Boss: The Rules for Getting and Keeping the Best Employees*, says that stories of bosses who look out for their employees can be inspirational to other staff members. And stories are what it's all about—they connect with people at the heart level. What's more, stories tend to get bigger over time. Do something small but memorable for your people today, and watch it become a heroic tale tomorrow.

As far as you're concerned, I know you think Mike Lipkin has charisma. How do I know that? You believe my insights will help you get what you want. In fact, you've already got a little of what you want from this book. You've had some realizations, you've made some breakthroughs, you've experienced some excitement, and you've shared some of your mojo with others. Am I right? I must be, or you wouldn't still be with me in these final few pages. I followed a specific plan to build my charisma with you. Here it is:

Lipkin's Nine Step Charisma Blueprint of how to exert power and authority over people you find very desirable:

1. Identify the specific people you want to influence. You cannot be all things to all people. In my case, I identified people like you—people who want to grow, learn, contribute, achieve, explore, reinvent, create and stay forever young. The subtitle on the cover of this book identifies you: someone who wants to learn how to inspire others on the Cusp of change.

My personal call to action: I _____

2. **Learn all you can about them.** As per the nine Life-Transforming Trends, I understand the challenges facing you as you seek to inspire others on the Cusp of change. I'm constantly researching people like you. I talk to people like you, interview people like you, watch people like you. I am someone like you. I know you. Maybe we've met and maybe we haven't; that's not important. What's important is that we share a common passion: the passion to inspire others to be the best they can in times of change.

3. **Be the best you can at helping them get one important thing they want.** In line with my commitment to communicate my genius to you, I'll tell you that I am the best in the world at exciting people into actions that make them successful and inspire others to do the same. So if it's action-oriented excitement and inspiration you want, I'm the guy best equipped to give it to you. That's what I'm about: action-oriented excitement and inspiration. That's the single-minded promise I deliver to my stakeholders. I cannot do more for you and I won't do less. Every day, in every way, I'm enhancing my excitement and inspiration skills.

4. **Communicate your ability to help them get what they want.** This is the toughest part of the blueprint—getting their attention. When I came back to Canada in 2001 it took me three years to connect with certain stakeholders. But the more kudos I built with others, the more referrals I generated, the better known I became, the more I understood how to get through to my stakeholders, the more articles I wrote for magazines, the more airtime I received on TV, the more seminars I spoke at, the more hits I achieved on Google. It's all about creativity, perseverance and building presence. It's about living your Sweet Spot out loud. It's about equal parts patience and urgency. It's also about the one breakthrough with the key opinion leader who opens up the floodgates of kudos for you. Align yourself with people who influence the people you want to influence. If you believe in what you're doing, never, ever give up. Keep on experimenting, reinventing and innovating. The jackpot is just a shot away.

My personal call to action: I _____

5. **Develop a distinctive personal style that sets you apart.** Charisma is a function of how you help others get what they want, in a way that no one else can. That means you need a distinctive style and positioning that you build with every action. In my case, my positioning is that I'm a global nomad with access to cutting-edge social trend insights who excites people into action. My style is high-energy, direct, humorous, engaging and easily understood. In every interaction I do my best to reinforce both my positioning and my style. I engage my prospects by always driving the conversation toward the issues of motivation, teamwork and human brilliance.

The Wall Street Journal (February 8, 2005), states that successful networking requires self-confidence and the ability to find common ground with people who may be more powerful or more knowledgeable about a particular subject. Richard Edelman, CEO of the PR firm Edelman USA, felt insecure when he was seated next to Sergey Brin, cofounder of Google, at a dinner. "I didn't know enough to talk to him about technology," says Edelman. So he quickly turned to a subject he did know about, asking Mr. Brin how technology might be used to counter obesity. "You have to be curious and confident, but you can't be looking like a hustler—no matter how much you want to do business with someone," he says. It's about your authentic style, your expertise and your ability to control the focus of the interaction. Remember, the other person wants to enjoy the interaction by both talking with and learning from you. So take the lead with style, and delight in the other person's company.

6. **Look for the magic in everyone.** Whatever you look for is what you'll find. What's more, other people instinctively know what you're looking for in them. They know whether you like what you see or not. So look for the magic in everyone and, by the law of reciprocation, they'll look for the magic in you. You may encounter people who have temporarily lost their magic, or who are temporarily beyond your power to connect. Don't let their darkness overwhelm your light. Help them rediscover theirs.

My personal call to action: I _____

7. **When you're with them, take their breath away.** When someone gives you face-time, they're giving you a tiny chunk of their life. They're giving you something they can never get back. Honor the significance of their sacrifice and make it worthwhile. Deliver at a level that eclipses anything they've experienced before. I'm serious. At least 80 percent of my new business comes from clients who enthusiastically refer me to others because of how I performed when I was in front of them. Develop your own style and reinforce it with every action. Know exactly what qualities you want others to associate with you. Do whatever it takes to wow them with your message, your product or your service. Make it a habit and you'll discover that others become addicted to you.

8. **Follow through by staying visible and raising your game.** As hard as it is to take their breath away initially, it's even harder to do it a second time and the next and the next. But the truth is, charisma is a highly volatile substance. It can expire in a heartbeat. It requires constant stoking. That means enhancing your contribution every time you're in front of your stakeholders. It also means ensuring that you're constantly on their mind. That's why I write a new book every 18 months. It's a whole new story that I have to tell and a whole new relationship that I build with the same people. Here's what I've found out: However far I've come, I've just begun. The more I create, the more I'm capable of creating. Every connection leads to another connection.

9. **Build a team around you that feeds, supports and empowers you.** Even superheroes need teams. The most charismatic people always have a team of people around them who make it easier for them to stay on fire. They can concentrate on blowing away their clients because they're being juiced and supported by their nucleus of turned-on folk. How's your personal team? How many people do you have around you who are helping you become successful? Like lions, humans have to hunt together to be successful. So it's to the business of team-building that we now turn.

My personal call to action: I _____

Building your Personal Team:
How to become a brilliant player/coach

Lipkin's definition of a personal team: a tight band of people around you whose success is intertwined with yours; the people who help you play full out; the people whose complementary strengths make your impact even stronger; the people who recharge you in the tough moments; the people whom you're totally committed to helping; your partners in the game of winning.

Self Test Of all the questions I've asked you so far, these may be the most important.

Use a scale of 1 to 4   1 = no, 2 = I don't know, 3 = maybe, 4 = definitely

- Do the people that you want on your team want you on their team? ☐
- Do you see yourself as a team player? ☐
- Are you a skilled team builder? ☐
- Are you attracting the right people to be on your team? ☐
- Do the people on your team have skills that complement yours? ☐
- Does your team usually win? ☐
- Do you belong to multiple teams? ☐
- Can you play different roles on different teams? ☐
- Do you improve the performance of all the players on your team? ☐
- Do you enjoy playing on your teams? ☐
- **Total** ☐

My personal call to action: I _____

If you scored 35-plus, the following section will reinforce in theory what you're already doing in practice. If you scored between 30 and 34, you're a good team player on the Cusp of becoming great. If you scored less than 30, you're still thinking too much like a soloist.

This book is a response to a big request that I constantly receive from my clients: "Help us help our people become better team players. Unless we get people to play effectively together, we will not win. Too many people are protecting too many silos. People are afraid to trust each other. They're not prepared to risk anything for their colleagues. They're thinking *me*, not *we*." Sound familiar? Keepers of The Flame, on the other hand, think exactly the opposite. They're all about trust, responsible risk, sharing and openness.

If you build a reputation as a great team player, you will do well. If you build a reputation as a great team builder, you'll excel in the extreme. In this section, I'm going to give you Lipkin's Top Ten Steps to Becoming a Brilliant Player/Coach. These are the researched traits of champions who are recognized as both outstanding players and outstanding coaches/mentors to others. If you aspire to being a Keeper of The Flame, the role of player/coach is a role you have to learn to play. In today's climate everyone has to produce results. If you're not in the arena getting knocked down and getting up every time, you can't judge those who are. It's easy to shout encouragement from the safety of the sidelines. Only by consistently facing the same challenges that others face can you truly inspire them to greatness.

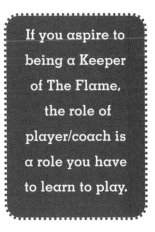

If you aspire to being a Keeper of The Flame, the role of player/coach is a role you have to learn to play.

At the same time, depending on your role, it's up to you to let your leaders know what's going on in the arena if they're not around. It's all about communication—up, down and eye to eye.

My personal call to action: I _____

Here are Lipkin's Top Ten Steps to Becoming a Brilliant Player/Coach. Ask yourself to what extent you're taking them.

1. Attract HIPER people to your team. Once you've ascertained whether your potential team members have the competence for the role, listen to your heart. Explore their HIPER factor: Humor, Integration, Passion, Empathy and Resilience. Without a sense of humor they may burn others out. Without personal integration they may not hold it together. Without passion they'll never influence anyone. Without empathy they may not connect with your customers and partners at the deepest level. And without resilience they may not withstand the daily barrage of rejections, setbacks and micro-disasters. Compile your personal checklist of core questions, and evaluate both your performance and others' performance against it every day.

2. Give them a MAD reason for playing full out every day. That's a Motivational Achievable Destination. Of course life is about the journey. But it's also about wanting to get to a certain place and knowing that we can get there. Since childhood we've been asking the classic question "Are we there yet?" I have found that the best people are goal-driven and impatient. They need to drive toward a specific result that motivates them highly. If you're the coach, give it to them. If you're a player, be the one who does the most to achieve it. If you're a player/coach, fire up your people by what you say and show them how to be a Keeper of The Flame by what you do.

3. Outplan, outplay, outsell, outpresent, outlast your competition. Create the game plan that gives your team the edge. It may be a big edge or, more likely, it may be small. That doesn't matter. Once you have it, become legendary at how you play it. Find the most compelling way to sell it, over and over again. Keep adjusting your pitch until it's just right. Then adjust it again and again. Seize every opportunity for you and your people to present the message. The more you present, the more presence you achieve and the more presents you will receive. Then make sure you lead from the front—at the end of the day, the end of the week, the end of the month and the end of the year.

My personal call to action: I _____

As the player/coach you have to set the highest standard for your people. Then you need to hold yourself to an even higher one. Remember the 90:10 rule: You have to perform at your personal best 90 percent of the time; your team members will forgive you the other 10 percent.

4. **Bring out the brilliance in your people by asking brilliant questions.** Don't look for answers, live the questions. Be the CQO—Chief Question Officer. Ask the questions that make your people think, grow, adapt, thrive. Question everything every day. Questions are universal; solutions are situational. Remember, there's always a better way to break through—it just hasn't been found yet. All progress depends on someone's asking a better question. Be that someone.

5. **Define your team's rules of engagement.** Every team needs an operating ethos, a way of getting things done, a style of execution that sets it apart and keeps it together. The rules of engagement are like an Everyday Empowering Ritual for the team. They guide each player on how to play with her fellow members. They set out the expectations the team has of each member. They give them the code for collective consistency while helping them focus on how they can maximize their contribution. So your team's rules of engagement must be tight enough to provide clarity and commitment, but loose enough to allow your people to unleash their individual brilliance.

6. **Prepare for the breakdown.** No matter how skilled, trained and motivated your people are, you know that the mistake, the disconnect and the crash are just around the corner. So be ready for them. Have an RRP—a Remarkable Recovery Program. All our research says that a breakdown that is well repaired makes a relationship far stronger than one that has never been tested. It's in the breakdown that you have the biggest opportunity to break through. As with a fire drill, keep reminding your people how high they need to raise their performance when the crisis hits. Just letting your people know that you consider a breakdown a marvelous opportunity to enhance the team's performance will change their attitude toward it when it happens.

My personal call to action: I _____

7. **Be the cheerleader-in-chief.** It's not good enough just being a leader; you have to be a cheerleader. Whatever your style, assume responsibility for rallying your team members in tough times. Be the self-appointed team motivator. By encouraging others you'll be more empowered as well. There are three kinds of people—those who run from difficulty, those who run toward it and those who help others run toward it. Be the reason why people who used to run from difficulty now run toward it. Build the habit of finding their key and turning it. This is what I do for a living. In difficult times I look for the other person's "leverage point"—the thing that motivates them to act. Then I press it as forcefully (and respectfully) as I can.

8. **Saturate your people with kudos.** There is no such thing as giving your people too much admiration and appreciation, as long as it's genuine and heartfelt. No one ever gets tired of hearing "Great job! Because . . ."; "Outstanding performance! Because . . ."; "You're awesome! Because . . ."; "That was amazing! Because . . ."; "I loved the way you did that! Because . . ."; "You rock! Because . . ."; "You blew me away! Because . . ."; "Encore! Because . . ." Practice paying people authentic compliments. Tell them what you think and tell them why you think it.

   One of the best compliments I ever received was paid to me by Salim Khoja, a partner of mine in the seminar business. In response to a standing ovation from 3,000 people at a seminar in Montreal, he said, "You were the best I've ever seen you today—because you got a standing ovation first thing in the morning, which very rarely happens. You reinforced our belief in you." So become a constant-kudos-generator and you'll always have outstanding people who want to play on your team. Remember the insight of David Livingstone, a University of Toronto professor who is leading a project on lifelong learning and work: "The extent to which we are motivated to share the knowledge that we have with our workmates, managers and others . . . is really conditioned by the extent to which we feel comfortable that the knowledge is going to be recognized and rewarded" (*The Globe and Mail*, June 18, 2005).

My personal call to action: I _____

9. **Make the hard call—any cut cuts deep.** At some point you're going to have to cut someone from the team. Do it when you have to do it. Do it decisively but do it respectfully. Do it in a way that reinforces your team's rules of engagement. Do whatever you can to make the person who has just been cut an ambassador for your team, not an adversary. This may be the hardest challenge facing any player/coach. Even though I've added and cut hundreds of people from my teams over the past thirty years, I'm still only batting about .250 on this action. The important point, though, is that my current team members see me doing my best to do the right thing. Play to win, but play fair.

10. **Promote your team to the world.** Grab every opportunity to advertise your team's achievements and the roles played by individual members. Become your team's P.T. Barnum. As the player/coach you're usually talking to more people, attending more events and being asked more questions. Find subtle ways to tastefully sing your team's praises. Your people crave outsiders' recognition of their success. They need to feel the pride that comes with playing on a team that is publicly acknowledged as the best of the best. In fact, if you do not achieve public acclaim for your team, you will lose your best players to the player/coaches that do. Remember this truth: Your stars need more than just your recognition—they want to be famous. Become their personal publicist. Yes, you may still lose some of them, but you'll become famous for making them famous, and that will make you a magnet for more stars.

Those are my ten core steps to building the extraordinary personal teams I have around me. Those are the steps that have attracted the following Keepers of The Flame to me (in alphabetical order): Michael Adams, Dean Baxendale, Brian Blosser, Erica Cerny, Sean Charters, Salim Khoja, Sheila Laredo, Simon Lewis, Hilary Lipkin, Martin Perelmuter and Bob White. Each of these eleven people has made a priceless contribution to my success. I honor them as I hope they honor me. Who are your core Keepers of The Flame? And how are you celebrating their contribution to your success?

My personal call to action: I _____

Weaving your Personal Network: Catch more opportunities

Lipkin's definition of a personal network: **weaving your personal worldwide web of quality people who are the constant recipients of your attention and gifts; your greatest assets in the hunt for new opportunities; people with whom you are mutual benefactors; people who are your eyes and ears in places where it counts.**

So you've built your personal team. Now it's time to weave your personal network so you can create more possibilities for your team, get the highest return on your personal charisma and improve the lives of thousands of other people.

> "How can I inspire the most people to help me inspire the most people?"

I'm not kidding. That has to be your motivation: To improve the lives of thousands of other people. If that's not your primary motivation, you will never be a champion networker. Think about it: If you can positively influence just ten people and they each positively influence just ten other people, that's a hundred people right there. In today's mobile, nomadic social environment, we all have the opportunity to positively influence ten new people every week, if not every day. In the age of personal URLs, blogging, online chatting, Googling, podcasting, streaming and linking, there are infinite ways to network and influence others.

I am an extreme example of a networker. In the next twelve months I'll talk to more than 100,000 people in more than ten countries. That means I'll directly influence 100,000 families. They'll communicate with at least ten other people. And that excludes my virtual impact over the Net. I'm getting to the point where I can't travel anywhere in the United States or Canada without meeting someone who has somehow intersected with me or my message. Yet I will never tire of being told by somebody that they changed their life for the better because of something I said to them. It's always a huge rush for me. And that's why I've included my personal coordinates throughout the book. I crave communication with you (mike.lipkin@environics.ca; 416-969-2811; www.mike-lipkin.com). E-mail or call me right now to tell me what you think.

The difference between you and me is only one of scale, not of significance. Influencing even one person is like influencing the whole world in miniature.

My personal call to action: I _____

We can never know the full extent of the consequences of the good things we do for others. So when you network, don't go in with a mindset like "How can I meet the people who can help me meet the people who can help me succeed?" Lipkin's networking mantra is "How can I inspire the most people to help me inspire the most people?"

When you're meeting people, they immediately sense whether it's to use them for your own advancement or to help them advance as well. Within seconds of meeting someone, one of three kinds of relationships is created: a one-off connection with no future potential; benefactor and beneficiary; or mutual benefactors in different ways. If you meet a Keeper of The Flame or if you are a Keeper of The Flame, you may engage in the second kind of relationship. But that's a form of social charity; it's a meeting of unequals that is probably not sustainable.

It's the third kind of relationship that social Keepers of The Flame are highly skilled at weaving. Their extraordinary personal networking skills help them build scale and amplify their impact. They even turn their beneficiaries into mutual benefactors because of the impact they have on them. They understand and apply Metcalf's Law of Networking: Every new quality member of your network exponentially increases the value of your entire network.

Here are Lipkin's seven insights into how Keepers of The Flame personally network.

1. **Make networking a major personal priority every day.** Invest the time, invest the resources, invest the effort to connect with others. Attend the events. Make the calls. Follow through on your promises. Know that every connection you make can help you change your world—one person at a time. Make friends with strangers; you never know when you're talking to an angel. Learn how to work a room. Reach out to people you haven't met yet. Be the one who initiates conversations. Get rid of your self-consciousness and inhibition—they're illusions. It's not about you anyway; it's about the people you're inviting into your network. Remember Dale Carnegie's immortal advice: If you want to be interesting to people, be interested in people. Develop a reputation as the person other people absolutely have to have at their event.

My personal call to action: I _____

In *The Globe and Mail* of September 3, 2005, Avner Mandelman, president of the highly regarded Toronto-based money management firm Giraffe Capital, sums up the value of making networking a daily priority as follows: "We apply our expertise only to stocks where we have exclusive information. How do we get it? We must either sleuth for it ourselves or cultivate informers to get the inside scoop." So, courtesy of Mandelman's insight, here's Lipkin's Essence of Networking Success: exclusive information obtained through the inside scoop provided by informers who value you as a member of their network.

2. **Become best in class through your achievements in one recognizable discipline.** The best networkers understand that they need to bring something valuable to others so they can achieve mutual benefactor status. Earn "bragging rights" so that you can promote your offering to others. Networking is like the stock market. It's a vast open exchange where you trade your value to others in return for their value to you. Sometimes you need to give more than you're getting in return; other times you will receive more than you give. Keepers of The Flame entrench themselves in the position of always giving more than they receive. My advice to you is that you shouldn't even begin to think about networking until you have a clear, compelling value proposition for the people you wish to network with.

3. **Become a "micro-celebrity" by profiling yourself as an authority in your field.** Build your reputation—speech by speech, article by article, interview by interview. Become a keynote speaker at your industry events. Write articles for your industry's trade journal. Volunteer to serve in your industry's association. Offer your services to a recognized charity where you're likely to meet like-minded souls. Become known for a specific, distinctive point of view. Use a personal publicist to get you exposure in the press and on TV or radio. Set up a website that is constantly being updated with items of interest to your community. Think about your business: How many people are willing to offer a point of view that is different from the mainstream? Very few. Become one of them and others will invite you to network with them.

My personal call to action: I _____

I speak from experience. All the steps I've outlined here are the steps I took to become someone other people approached rather than someone who was constantly approaching others. I've also discovered that, courtesy of Google et al., every time you publish something of interest it's picked up by the search engines and read by thousands more people than you originally targeted—all over the world.

4. **Get through by standing out, over and over again.** The right people are always going to be the busiest people. They're the ones everyone else is also trying to see. So don't take their lack of response as a personal affront. It's not you they're rejecting; it's your lack of visibility or relevance to their interests. Always remember that your message is being sent in a highly cluttered, noisy environment. If it's not truly outstanding it will not stand out, and you will not get through. So format your approach to make it irresistible to your target connection. Understand the issues, understand the person, understand what your competition is doing. Deliver your message with creativity, charm and grace. And remember, if you succeed in getting through the first (or second, third, fourth or fifth) time, it's a fluke! What do I mean? You haven't even begun until you've experienced five non-responses. Successful networkers know that persistence will eventually overcome resistance, as long as it's done with poise and charm. Many of my most valuable network members responded only after my twentieth approach. What's more, they responded because of my persistence— that's the trait they admired the most. So keep on trying until you get through. Keep evolving your approach. But if you get a message that you should stop—stop. Nothing can alienate someone more than unsolicited, unwanted intrusions.

5. **Set up opportunities by connecting members of your personal network with each other.** Become known as someone who knows people who can get things done. Often, I'll be asked to give a talk that I can't accept because of a prior engagement. In those instances I'll refer the prospect either to a speakers' bureau or to a fellow speaker. Either way I build kudos with the prospect, the speakers' bureau and my

My personal call to action: I _____

fellow speakers. The best networkers are like 24/7/365 Santa Clauses. They're always out there dispensing gifts, acting as opportunity brokers and game changers. Remember, by the law of reciprocity you'll be paid back tenfold. My entire business success since 2001 has been based on this model. Keith Ferrazzi, former chief marketing officer at Deloitte Consulting and Starwood Hotels and Resorts, networking guru and author of *Never Eat Alone*, says, "I'll sum up the key to success in one word: generosity." His point is that the more you do for people in your personal network, the more they will trust you and want to do things for you. Keep giving, and keep receiving with interest.

6. **Stay in touch by using quality communication and attention.** The best networkers ensure that they're constantly on their network's radar. They communicate frequently via all the media—e-mail, telephone, meetings. They have a specific plan of contact to ensure they connect with their fellow networkers in regular cycles. I'll be honest with you—this book is as much a tool to stay in touch with the members of my network as anything else. I produce a new book and audio program every eighteen months. I produce a new training program twice a year. And I send out a newsletter twice a year as well. I phone my "top 200" people every three months and my "top 500" people every six months. Thanks to the expertise of my digital navigator, Erica Cerny, and Outlook, I have all the cyber-help I need. There's no excuse not to stay in touch, but you have to have something valuable to say. Finally, when you're engaging your fellow networkers, play full out. Give them everything you have, and they'll return the favor.

7. **Don't just attend events, create them.** If you're the one creating the events that other people attend, you occupy the highest rung on the networking ladder. That's the ultimate test of the kudos you've generated with others: whether they're willing to give you their time in anticipation of a social, professional or learning return on that time. It could be an intimate personal dinner, a one-on-one private lunch or a major industry forum. The more complex the event, the more you need to enlist the help of professionals to ensure that it's executed flawlessly.

My personal call to action: I _____

Whatever the event, ensure that it's a first-class experience for the attendee or delegate. Just okay isn't okay. You never want to be the reason why someone feels they've wasted their time. You always want to be the reason why they feel enriched and exhilarated afterward.

You know you're becoming a champion networker when . . .

- People give you the early heads-up about potential opportunities.
- People call you for your point of view regarding their challenges.
- People invite you to speak at or contribute to their events.
- People refer other people to you because of the impact you've made on them.
- People are willing to come through for you in the crunch moments.
- People forgive you for your mistakes.
- People let you know they have very high expectations of you.
- People accept your calls, return your calls and even call you.
- People quote you in their presentations and conversations.
- People want to link their websites to yours.

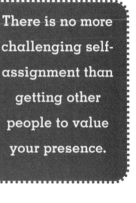

There is no more challenging self-assignment than getting other people to value your presence.

Networking is so simple in theory and so difficult in practice. There is no more challenging self-assignment than getting other people to value your presence. It takes time. It takes humility. It takes extreme commitment to contributing to others' success. It takes imagination. Most of all, it takes a love of making other people happy. That's something no one can give you. If you find networking a chore, you may never excel in your Social Nuclear Dimension. And that may be okay; no one can excel at all the Nuclear Dimensions. But make sure you align yourself with people who complement your strengths and your mediocrities.

My personal call to action: I _____

Human beings are not designed to be alone. We are all integral parts of other people's well-being.

Here's a final comment on mastering your Social Nuclear Dimension: Build your Personal Charisma, your Personal Team and your Personal Network not just for the kudos it will earn you. Build it because your very life depends on it. Vancouver physician Gabor Maté, writing for *The Globe and Mail* on June 11, 2005, quotes an Australian study that revealed that women who experienced a major stressor in their lives and who lacked intimate emotional support had a ninefold increase in their risk for breast cancer. Conversely, British researchers in 2004 showed that emotional connection can reduce by half the recurrence risk of heart attacks. Belinda Linden of the British Heart Foundation is quoted as saying that "a close relationship can play an important role in both preventing coronary heart disease and enhancing recovery from a heart attack."

Maté goes on to talk about those people who develop disease but who are surrounded by love. He states that, on closer inspection, many of these people are committed to supporting others but they don't extend the same love toward themselves. They keep their troubles inside, feeling they should be able to handle all their problems without assistance. Not opening themselves to be supported, they do not permit the love of others to flow into them. Echoing Maté's sentiments, Dr. Paul Appelbaum, president of the American Psychiatric Association, says, "Anxiety feeds on itself. Sharing the concern with others can be enormously helpful." Not sharing it can be enormously destructive.

Maté concludes by offering five questions that we need to ask ourselves at the end of every day:

- Have I reached out to anyone in an emotionally vulnerable way?
- Have I shared myself?
- Have I made it possible for others to share themselves with me?
- Have I taken care of others but ignored my own needs for understanding and acceptance?
- If I feel lonely, how have I created a life in which I am lacking intimate contact with others?

My personal call to action: I _____

I hope you can answer Maté's five questions in ways that make you healthier, both physically and mentally. Human beings are not designed to be alone. We are all integral parts of other people's well-being. Take care of yourself and take care of others by being the first to reach out, the first to ask for help, the first to give. By allowing someone else to help you, you just may be saving that person's life as well. Makes you think, doesn't it?

My personal call to action: I _____

Light Some Fires of Your Own

So here we are at the finish line. I've learned so much in writing to you. I hope you've learned as much in return. You've given me the gifts I value the most from other people: your time, your attention, your energy, your commitment and your company. It doesn't get better than that for me.

We're also at the starting line. Both of us are about to apply all the lessons we've learned. Both of us are about to light up the world, one person, one day at a time. I've lived with this book for over a year. It's been like a presence beside me 24/7. I've gone within and wrestled with the life-changing issues I've outlined in each of the Nuclear Dimensions. First there was struggle, then there was reflection, then

Without constant renewal, everyone ages and fades.

there was understanding. Next there was trial and error, and then there was mastery. Then it happens all over again. Things change, people change, and the master becomes the rookie—sometimes by accident, sometimes by design. Then the rookie grows into a different mastery, passes it on and begins as a rookie all over again. It's the five themes repeating themselves throughout our lifetime: being unaware—trial by fire—reaching for the torch—being Keeper of The Flame—having a fresh mind. Without constant renewal, everyone ages and fades.

There's no way to avoid the wrestling match with the issues that will define your destiny. There's no easy walk to self-actualization. There are no coaches or guides who haven't lost or become lost themselves. So I hope you completed the exercises I offered you. I hope you have a clearer understanding of your thrilling outcome, your passion, your genius and your personal promise so you can play in your Sweet Spot. I hope you've crafted your Personal Manifesto so you have the freedom of a tightly defined strategy, whatever circumstances you find yourself in. I hope you've defined how you're going to acquire the Seven Terrific Tendencies that will help you learn and grow every day. I hope you've created a way to master the Seven Power Emotions so you're always on fire, especially in the pivotal moments. I hope you've created your own Everyday Empowering Ritual so you can experience the certainty and joy of living according to your personal code of conduct. And I hope you've constructed a plan to build kudos through your Personal Charisma, your Personal Team and your Personal Network.

My personal call to action: I _____

If not, go back and do the exercises now. You don't have to find the perfect answers. The secret is in the doing and the redoing. As soon as you've found the answer, it's probably time for a new one anyway. The important thing is that you learn how to drill down, not what you hit. Every day your reality will shift. New crises will need to be defused. New causes will need to be pursued. New people will need your help. Armed with your takeaways, you can now play the role of Keeper of The Flame.

I'm also curious to find out about your one main "aha!" or breakthrough. After all the hours you've invested in hanging with me, what epiphany did you experience? This is a question I always ask my delegates at the end of a session. It's the thing that guarantees the value of my program, if they apply it. Send yours to me at mike.lipkin@environics.ca.

And here's a final cluster of Lipkinisms that epitomizes the ethos of the whole book:

1. **Everyone is lighting the way for everyone else.**

2. **To be fully alive means to find the inspiration in every experience and transfer it to others.**

3. **Everything pleasurable must be celebrated and savored. Everything painful must be celebrated and honored for what it has taught us.**

4. **We justify our presence by consciously pursuing personal greatness – whatever that means for each of us. Every day must be played like a contest for Olympic gold – with no hesitation and no regrets.**

5. **We must be hard when we need to be hard and gentle when we need to be gentle, and have the wisdom to know when to be what.**

6. **Forgiveness is our safety net, both for ourselves and for others.**

7. **Tomorrow is a dazzling opportunity to begin all over again.**

That's it. I now pronounce you Keeper of The Flame. Go and light some fires.

My personal call to action: I _____

Join The Keepers of The Flame Circle: We need you.

I want to build a community of Keepers of The Flame. I want to share my learning with you. I want to learn from you. I also want to connect you to other like-minded souls who are making a difference every day.

If you've liked what you've read, if you're ready to inspire others on the Cusp of change, if you want to experience the thrill of connecting with other change-makers, visit my site, www.mikelipkin.com, and register as a Keeper of The Flame.

Every month we'll send you a newsletter with the latest insights and inspiration from Keepers of The Flame around the world. You'll also be invited to live physical and online events so you can communicate with the kind of people who will make sure that you stay on fire without burning out. I need you. Your fellow Keepers of The Flame need you. Heed the need—register now.

As always, I invite you to communicate with me directly. My coordinates are

Mike Lipkin
President
Environics/Lipkin
33 Bloor Street East, Suite 1020
Toronto, Ontario
Canada M4W 3H1

www.mikelipkin.com
mike.lipkin@environics.ca
416-969-2811
416-920-3299 fax

My personal call to action: I _____

Acknowledgements

Every time I finish a book, I forget how hard it was to start it. When I cross the finish line, the only thing that matters is the end result. But every time I begin a book, I'm reintroduced to the terror of the blank page followed by the blank page followed by the blank page.

Contrary to conventional belief, writing is not a solo activity. Without the help of great people, the blank pages would have defeated me. The final word is always the responsibility of the author. But it's the culmination of a process populated by many partners. My partners in this process have been:

My wife, Hilary, who has always believed in me so much I had to believe in myself.

My assistant and digital navigator, Erica Cerny, who made the contacts, did much of the research, and coordinated the entire production process.

My editor, Gillian Watts, who made so many subtle changes that made such a big difference.

My designer, Sarah Battersby, who enhanced the content so much with her exquisite optics.

My business partner, Michael Adams, who so generously shared his data and insights with me.

The thousands of people who share their thoughts and insights with me every year. They thrill, delight and inspire me to keep doing what I'm doing.

You, the reader—for being the reason why I do all of this.

Thank you.

Personal Notes

Personal Notes

Personal Notes

Personal Notes

Personal Notes

Personal Notes

Personal Notes